YOUNG ROMANCE

Fantagraphics Books
7563 Lake City Way NE
Seattle, Washington 98115

Editor: Michel Gagné
Editorial Staff: Gary Groth, Jason T. Miles and Kristy Valenti
Designer: Tony Ong
Associate Publisher: Eric Reynolds
Publishers: Gary Groth and Kim Thompson

Distributed in the U.S. by W.W. Norton and Company, Inc. (800-233-4830)
Distributed in Canada by Canadian Manda Group (800-452-6642 x862)
Distributed in the U.K. by Turnaround Distribution (44 020 8829-3002)
Distributed to comic book specialty stores by Diamond Comics Distributors (800-452-6642 x215)

First Fantagraphics Books Edition: February 2012
ISBN: 978-160699-502-0
Printed in Singapore

Young Romance

The Best of
SIMON
&
KIRBY'S
Romance Comics

TABLE OF CONTENTS

INTRODUCTION

by Michelle Nolan

Hearts and flowers, most of Joe Simon and Jack Kirby's output most assuredly was not; the pair was unquestionably the best, most versatile, and prolific creative team of cartoonists during the first 25 years of the American comic book. Despite their reputation for, and financial success with, action and adventure, strange tales and superheroes, one of their most commercially successful ventures was actually their line of romance comics of the 1947-1959 period for tiny Crestwood Publications (1947-1959). Just as their Captain America had made his debut shortly before the U.S. entered World War II, Simon and Kirby were once again at the right place at the right time with the right genre. Their realistic post-war romances would prove to be some of the most compelling and captivating narratives in the cheap world of pulp fiction — true confession magazines, pulp magazines, paperbacks, and, of course, comic books.

Hokey true confession magazines and their equally melodramatic movie counterparts had been available to the reading public well before the modern comic book appeared in the mid-1930s. Most of the romance magazines were on the way out by the time Simon and Kirby created the first genuine romance comic book, *Young Romance* (1947). The best and most enduring of these periodicals, Street & Smith's *Love Story Magazine*, died the same year *Young Romance* was born. Meanwhile, paperback romances were seldom published in the 1940s; their marketplace dominance was yet to come. Simon and Kirby's creations were nothing if not emotionally raw and vibrant, at least in the days before the industry's self-censorship (the Comics Code Authority) toned down the content of all comics. As demonstrated in this long-overdue, essential and lovingly shaped book, edited by cartoonist Michel Gagné, readers can now discover or re-discover Simon and Kirby's romantic tales, some of the most dramatic and emotionally powerful comics of their time.

Most of Simon and Kirby's epic romances had cheerful endings. While a few were fittingly grim, most ended happily (not sappily), after one of the protagonists had learned his or her life lesson. The same could hardly be said of most of Simon and Kirby's many competitors and imitators, although another second-tier publishing house, St. John, consistently published progressive and artistically polished tales by writer Dana Dutch and artist Matt Baker, as detailed by author and historian John Benson in *Romance Without Tears* (2003) and *Confessions, Romances, Secrets and Temptations* (2007), both published by Fantagraphics Books. Baker, however, was guilty of glamorizing women, and the sound psychology of Dutch's characters meant that he largely eschewed comic-book-style melodrama. Simon and Kirby could, and sometimes did, utilize these tactics, but wisely, they seldom went so far over the top as to cause the reader to exclaim, "That could never happen!"

Take the first story in this volume, "Boy Crazy," from the second issue of *Young Romance* (1947); it contains many of the elements that distinguish a Simon and Kirby romance. Obviously intended for teen girls, its protagonist Suzi Burnette ("Suzi" was not a common spelling in 1947) exclaimed, "... I lived with Aunt Martha who looked even younger than her thirty-five years. I sometimes think I was jealous of her!!!" In true melodramatic fashion, this jealousy leads to her ruin; at the end of the story Suzi's alone, musing, "Well, that's the story of my foolish campaign against my aunt. I never thought my victory would turn info a life-long defeat."

In the late 1940s and early 1950s, when comic book publishers replaced superheroic and patriotic themes with an anything-goes search for profits, pretty much anything went in many of the earliest romance comics. Thus Simon and Kirby's ability to transition among or blend genres figures largely into "Her Tragic Love," a story that would have fit well in any crime comic of the day. Such noir did not last long in romance comics, but Simon and Kirby made more effective use of it than most, with story titles such as "The Savage in Her!" and "Gang Girl!" But the Comics Code Authority began to censor comics in early 1955, eliminating themes such as crime and suicide, etc. as can be seen in the final seven tales of this book.

"Fraulein Sweetheart," the third story in this book, in which Simon and Kirby inject a realistic form of prejudice, is a vivid period piece, published three years after the end of World War II and dealing with the ethics of love and nationalism. What also makes this tale so different is that, though the reader knows the female protagonist's attitude is changing, it's downbeat: a happy ending is only hinted at, and the reader is left with something to think about.

Issues of social class, religious conflicts and the like are dealt with nicely in "Shame" and "The Town and Toni Benson." These are typical of the many times Simon and Kirby covered these concerns, usually in a way not often seen in most other comics. To this writer's best knowledge, Simon and Kirby dealt with virtually every type of social issue except the still-forbidden interracial romance — which was still against the law in most states — since in the 1950s such stories would have resulted in serious sanctions from parents, headline-seeking politicians and profit-hungry news dealers. The idea that a black person and a white person could fall in love and marry happily was simply commercial suicide. Of course, any publisher of romance comics could only hint at gay and lesbian issues in vague terms. Such content was left to under-the-table pornographic comics and later the underground comics of the 1960s and 1970s.

Look at the art in "Shame," a tale of a girl's self-sacrificing mother, and see if it doesn't reflect real life. This may well be the best and most fully realized story found here; it packs a real punch in only seven pages. It's a good example of how well Simon and Kirby and other top-line storytellers could handle a complex theme in relatively few pages. The 14-page "I Want Your Man" is about

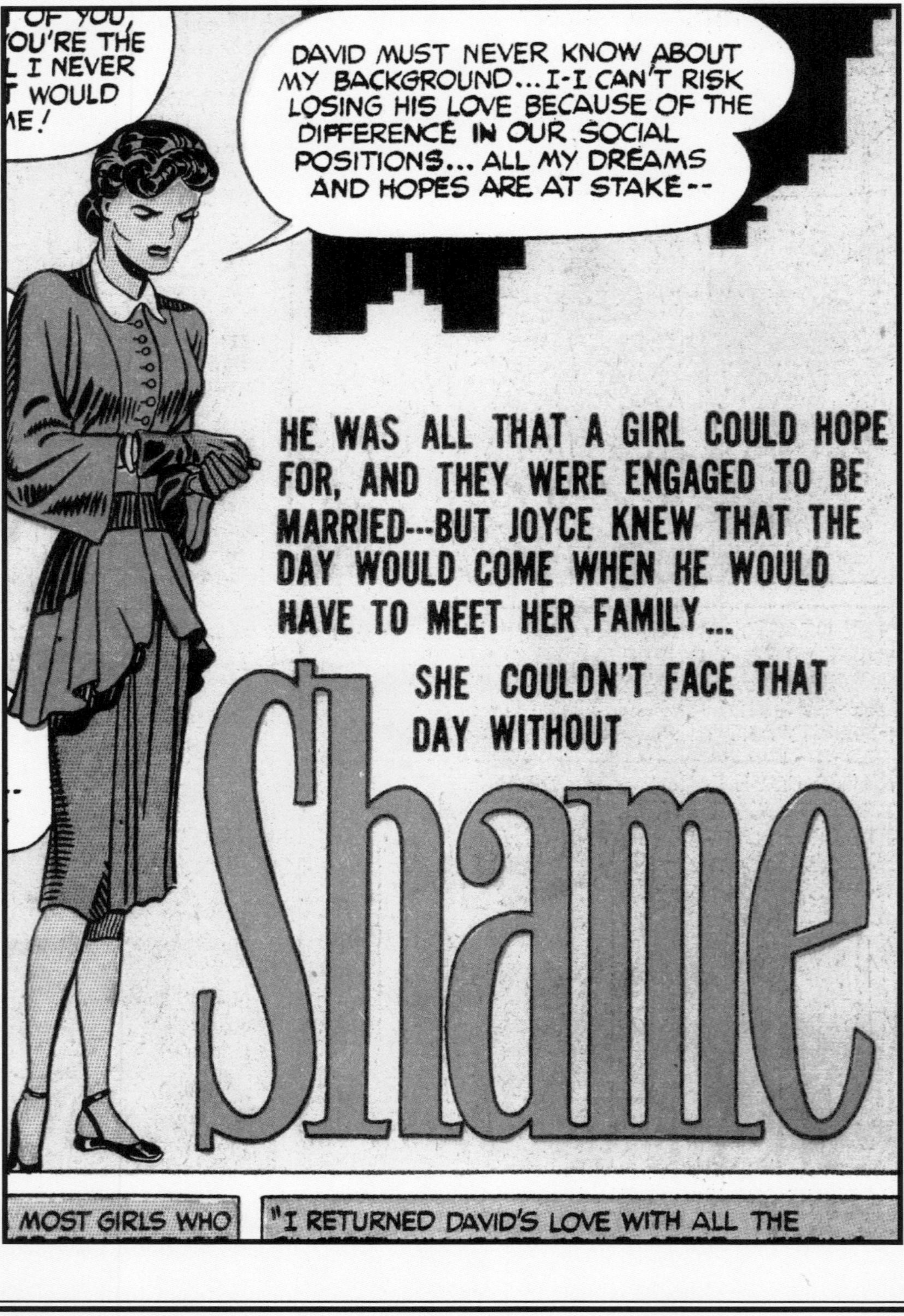

OU'RE THE
I NEVER
WOULD
DAVID MUST NEVER KNOW ABOUT MY BACKGROUND...I-I CAN'T RISK LOSING HIS LOVE BECAUSE OF THE DIFFERENCE IN OUR SOCIAL POSITIONS... ALL MY DREAMS AND HOPES ARE AT STAKE--
HE WAS ALL THAT A GIRL COULD HOPE FOR, AND THEY WERE ENGAGED TO BE MARRIED---BUT JOYCE KNEW THAT THE DAY WOULD COME WHEN HE WOULD HAVE TO MEET HER FAMILY...
SHE COULDN'T FACE THAT DAY WITHOUT
Shame
MOST GIRLS WHO
"I RETURNED DAVID'S LOVE WITH ALL THE

female jealousy stemming from childhood — a much more common plot device in the hearts-and-flowers offerings from DC Comics, it was unusual for Simon and Kirby: still, the pair throw a melodramatic-but-not-implausible twist into the familiar narrative.

"Sailor's Girl" is typical of the somewhat-sexist but nonetheless reasonable and realistic, lesson-learned, romance story. This type of tale was common, as was the "teach me how to live" request from the female in the happy ending of "I Want Your Man." In romance comics, it's almost always the woman who is taught by the man, most likely because middle-aged men wrote and drew the majority of comics, even though in this case the intended audience was female. What makes this story stand out is Simon and Kirby's portrayal of the girl's fantasy, which takes the form of a hunky, pillaging Viking warrior.

"Mr. Know-It-All Falls in Love" is typical of the scheming-woman story, or the "man falls in love with woman until she catches him" variety, though fortunately there are fewer of these than might be expected. "Wedding Presents" exemplifies the many Korean War stories found in the early 1950s romance comics. Except for a short-lived flirtation with Western romance comics (1949-1950), Simon and Kirby used their regular titles to explore themes of wartime romance, while several other publishers devoted whole titles to this subgenre.

The seven post-Code stories demonstrate how radically the Comics Code Authority affected romance comics: the occasional downbeat ending, post-Code, has been mended with a lovers' embrace. It's no coincidence that the art is cleaner and less gritty; the censors employed by the Comics Code Authority frowned upon ugliness of any type. Despite the Comics Code Authority's influence, the last seven stories reveal a lot in their own right — this book truly is a window into post-war America through the end of the 1950s, when the Simon and Kirby team ended their partnership. What makes all these stories seem so evocative of their era is their ever-so-earnest innocence; there will never be the likes of these romance comics again.

Michelle Nolan, a journalist and comics historian for more than 40 years, is the author of Love on the Racks: A History of American Romance Comics *(2008) from McFarland.*

THE STORY OF A GIRL WHO LEARNED HER LESSON THROUGH HEARTBREAK

I GUESS I WAS JEALOUS OF MY OWN AUNT!--- THAT'S WHY I SWORE I'D GET EVEN WITH HER WHEN SHE CALLED ME---

BOY CRAZY

I *LOVE* CLINT, SUZI -- IT'S MY LAST CHANCE FOR HAPPINESS!--I WANT YOU TO STAY AWAY FROM HIM!

YOU'RE TOO LATE, *AUNT MARTHA!* CLINT LOVES *ME!*

"TO THOSE WHO ONCE PROFESSED TO BE MY FRIENDS, AND WHO NOW CONDEMN ME AS A WICKED, SELFISH ADVENTURESS, I AM WRITING THIS TRUE STORY OF MY TERRIBLE MISTAKE---

THIS IS NOT WRITTEN AS AN APOLOGY---IN FACT, I AM NOT CERTAIN BUT THAT I WOULD DO IT ALL OVER AGAIN HAD HE ABOVE GIVEN ME ANOTHER CHANCE---

THAT IS WHY I ASK NO FORGIVENESS ---NO SOLACE FOR THE ACHE IN MY LONELY HEART!"

SIGNED
SUZI BURNETTE

"HAD MY PARENTS BEEN ALIVE, MY LIFE MIGHT HAVE RUN A TRUER COURSE...I LIVED WITH *AUNT MARTHA*, WHO LOOKED EVEN *YOUNGER* THAN HER THIRTY FIVE YEARS...I SOMETIMES THINK I WAS *JEALOUS* OF HER!!!"

ANOTHER DATE TONIGHT, SUZI? WHO IS IT THIS TIME! THAT PIMPLE-FACED JENSEN BOY?

PLEASE, AUNT MARTHA!

IS HE COMING HERE TO CALL FOR YOU?

WELL, NO...I'M MEETING HIM DOWNTOWN...IT'S MUCH MORE CONVENIENT FOR HIM!

YOU'LL COME TO NO GOOD THE WAY YOU'RE CARRYING ON, WITH A NEW BOY FRIEND EVERY NIGHT, SUZI!

I'M ONLY SEVENTEEN, MARTHA...I *LIKE* TO MEET NEW BOYS! DON'T MAKE AN OLD WOMAN OUT OF ME!

THAT'S JUST THE POINT, SUZI! YOU'RE A LITTLE GIRL PLAYING 'HOUSE'! SOME DAY YOU'LL FLIRT WITH THE WRONG MAN! YOU'RE PLAYING WITH FIRE, MY DEAR!

THANKS FOR THE ADVICE, MARTHA, BUT TRY USING IT *YOURSELF!* GOODBYE, DARLING!

"THAT'S THE WAY IT WAS WITH MARTHA AND ME! I COULD NEVER CONFIDE IN HER LIKE OTHER GIRLS DID IN THEIR MOTHERS! SHE WAS ALWAYS SO SARCASTIC--SHE CUT ME DEEPLY!"

GOLLY--I'M LATE FOR THIS DATE...OH, WELL, TED WILL WAIT FOREVER IF I WANT HIM TO!

"I DON'T KNOW WHAT ATTRACTED ME TO *TED JENSEN*...I MET HIM ON A DOUBLE DATE AND HE SEEMED TO PREFER ME TO THAT WASHED-OUT BLONDE HE WAS WITH...IT GAVE ME A SENSE OF CONQUEST!"

I-I THOUGHT YOU'D *NEVER* GET HERE--BUT I'M GLAD YOU MADE IT!

YOU MEAN YOU THOUGHT I'D STAND YOU UP? *WHY* SHOULD I DO A THING LIKE THAT?

2

"WE TOOK A TROLLEY TO THE CARNIVAL — AND I THOUGHT OF STANLEY JORDAN WITH HIS NEW, RED CONVERTIBLE... I KNEW STANLEY WAS A GOOD FRIEND OF TED'S...

TED WASN'T VERY FAST... WHEN HE LOOKED DOWN AT THE INSTRUMENT PANEL TO SEE HOW THE CAR OPERATED, I WAS OFF!!! THEN ---

OOF! DON'T YOU KNOW YOU HAVE TO STICK OUT YOUR HAND TO MAKE A TURN, HONEY?

OUCH!

YOU'RE MUCH TOO INEXPERIENCED TO DRIVE BY YOURSELF, SUGAR! WHY NOT LET ME DRIVE YOU TO YOUR HOME?

YOU WOULDN'T GET FAR IN THIS GADGET!

I'VE GOT A BETTER ONE THAN THIS OUTSIDE!-- HOW ABOUT IT?

A REAL CAR? MMM — I'M TEMPTED...

"SURE-- IT WAS A DIRTY TRICK ... BUT IT WAS SO HOT AND STICKY FOR A TROLLEY -- WELL, A GIRL IS YOUNG ONLY ONCE!!

SO YOUR NAME IS RODNEY MIDDLETON -- SO WHAT, AS LONG AS YOU HAVE THIS BEAUTIFUL CAR

YOU'LL LEARN TO LOVE ME IN TIME, BABY!

"I DIDN'T LEARN TO LOVE ROD THAT EVENING, ALTHOUGH WE HAD A SWELL TIME ...IT WAS LATE WHEN ROD TOOK ME HOME ...

THANKS FOR THE RIDE, ROD! I'D BETTER GO IN, NOW!

WAIT, SUZI! YOU'RE NOT GOING TO DROP ME LIKE THIS, ARE YOU?

I-I MEANT THOSE THINGS I SAID TO YOU!--WHEN CAN WE GO OUT AGAIN?

REALLY, ROD! I'M DATED UP FOR WEEKS-- CALL ME --

"ROD WAS GETTING SO SERIOUS, HE SCARED ME! I DASHED INSIDE ...MARTHA WAS IN THE LIVING ROOM ...SHE HAD A CALLER ...

OH, HELLO MARTHA! I DIDN'T KNOW--

SUZI! IT'S TWO A.M.!

4

SO IT IS! YOU'RE UP *LATE*, MARTHA!

SUZI! TED JENSEN WAS HERE! HE WAS WORRIED ABOUT YOU!

I'M WORRIED ABOUT YOU TOO, SUZI CHILD!

I'M SURE YOUR NIECE WILL BE ALL RIGHT, MARTHA!

"I HAD COMPLETELY FORGOTTEN ABOUT MARTHA'S CALLER... NOW, I LOOKED AT THIS BRAVE KNIGHT WHO THOUGHT HE WAS RESCUING ME FROM A TYRANT AUNT! HE SEEMED YOUNGER THAN MARTHA---OUR EYES MET-- MINE WAVERED FIRST!

YOUTH IS SO WONDERFUL! --LET THE GIRL HAVE HER FLING!

WHO'S YOUR FRIEND, MARTHA?

YES, MARTHA-- WHERE ARE YOUR MANNERS? INTRODUCE US!

OH-ER-SUZI-- THIS IS A-- FRIEND, MISTER ROBERTS--CLINT ROBERTS--

NOW, GO TO BED!

I HOPE WE'LL BE SEEING MORE OF YOU--CLINT-- GOOD NIGHT--

HIS NAME IS *MISTER* ROBERTS, SUZI!

"CLINT ROBERTS! THE NAME STUCK IN MY MIND AND ROLLED ON MY TONGUE. HE COULDN'T BE MORE THAN THIRTY, I THOUGHT TO MYSELF-- MUCH TOO YOUNG FOR MARTHA!

HE'S SHORTER THAN TED-- NOT AS RUGGED LOOKING AS ROD-- AND I'LL BET HE DOESN'T DANCE HALF AS WELL AS GIL-- BUT WHAT IS THERE ABOUT HIM THAT MAKES ME FEEL THIS WAY?

"WE DIDN'T SEE CLINT ROBERTS FOR A WEEK-- AND THEN, I NOTICED MARTHA MAKING WITH THE "GLAMOUR" --USING HER MOST EXPENSIVE PERFUME--

HAVING COMPANY, TONIGHT, MARTHA? --NOT *MISTER ROBERTS?*

YES, SUZI-- AREN'T YOU GOING OUT THIS EVENING?

5

14

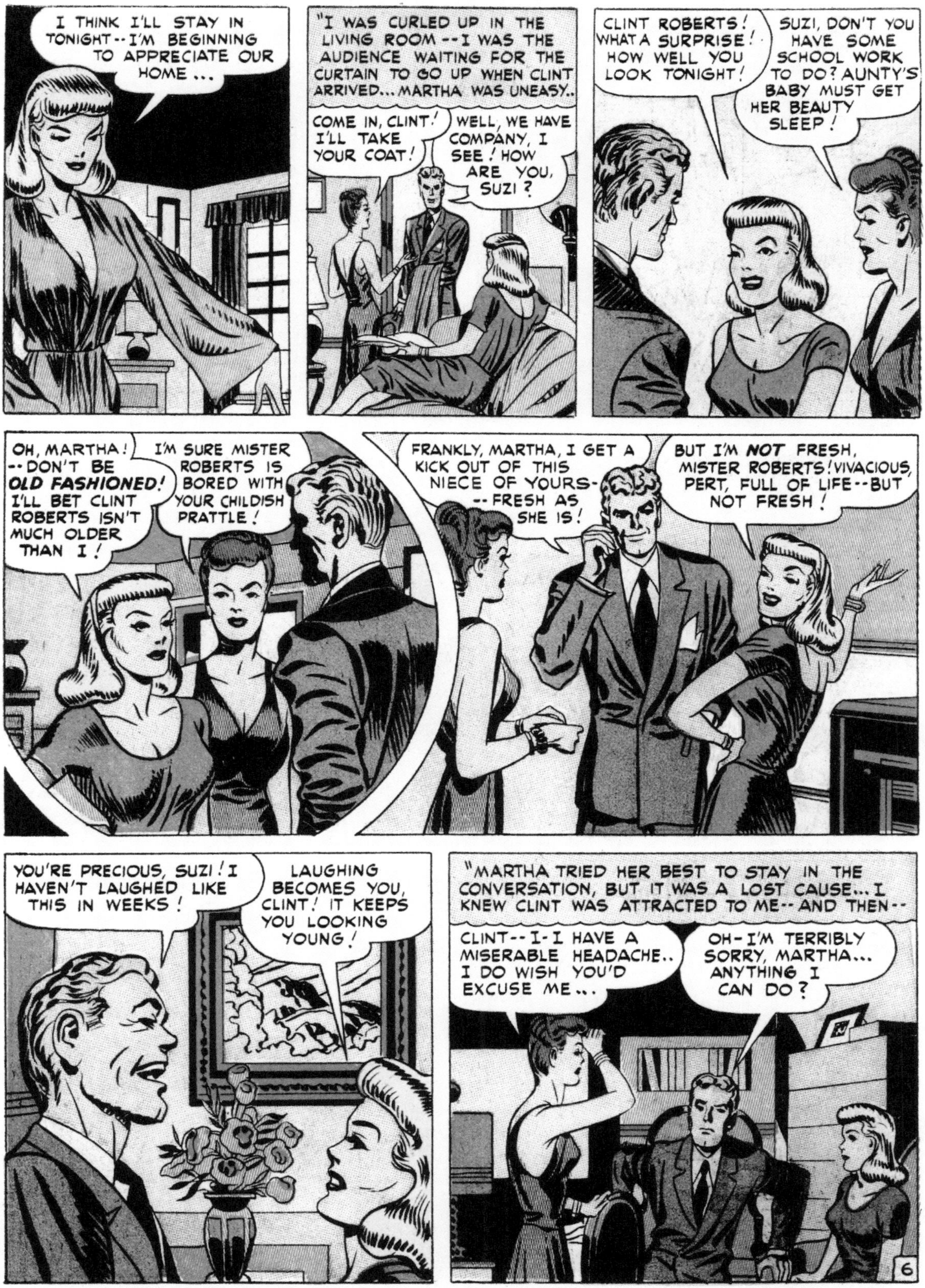
I THINK I'LL STAY IN TONIGHT--I'M BEGINNING TO APPRECIATE OUR HOME ...
"I WAS CURLED UP IN THE LIVING ROOM --I WAS THE AUDIENCE WAITING FOR THE CURTAIN TO GO UP WHEN CLINT ARRIVED... MARTHA WAS UNEASY..
COME IN, CLINT! I'LL TAKE YOUR COAT!
WELL, WE HAVE COMPANY, I SEE! HOW ARE YOU, SUZI?
CLINT ROBERTS! WHAT A SURPRISE! HOW WELL YOU LOOK TONIGHT!
SUZI, DON'T YOU HAVE SOME SCHOOL WORK TO DO? AUNTY'S BABY MUST GET HER BEAUTY SLEEP!
OH, MARTHA! --DON'T BE OLD FASHIONED! I'LL BET CLINT ROBERTS ISN'T MUCH OLDER THAN I!
I'M SURE MISTER ROBERTS IS BORED WITH YOUR CHILDISH PRATTLE!
FRANKLY, MARTHA, I GET A KICK OUT OF THIS NIECE OF YOURS- --FRESH AS SHE IS!
BUT I'M NOT FRESH, MISTER ROBERTS! VIVACIOUS, PERT, FULL OF LIFE--BUT NOT FRESH!
YOU'RE PRECIOUS, SUZI! I HAVEN'T LAUGHED LIKE THIS IN WEEKS!
LAUGHING BECOMES YOU, CLINT! IT KEEPS YOU LOOKING YOUNG!
"MARTHA TRIED HER BEST TO STAY IN THE CONVERSATION, BUT IT WAS A LOST CAUSE... I KNEW CLINT WAS ATTRACTED TO ME-- AND THEN--
CLINT-- I-I HAVE A MISERABLE HEADACHE.. I DO WISH YOU'D EXCUSE ME...
OH-I'M TERRIBLY SORRY, MARTHA... ANYTHING I CAN DO?
6

THANK YOU, NO... I-I'M SURE SUZI WILL ENTERTAIN YOU...

GOOD NIGHT, ♪ ♪ AUNTY, DEAR... ♪ ♪

"THAT WAS MY VICTORY... I'D BEEN JEALOUS OF MARTHA, OF HER BEAUTY, HER GLAMOUR... HUMILIATED AT THE WAY SHE KEPT REMINDING ME THAT I WAS A BABY!! AND, NOW, I'D TAKEN HER MAN FROM HER! ---AS I LOOK BACK NOW, I SEE THE HOLLOW VICTORY IT WAS!!

LOOK, SUZI! WHY DON'T WE TAKE A RIDE, STOP FOR A COCKTAIL -- OR IS IT SODA THAT YOU DRINK? THE NIGHT IS YOUNG --

NO, THANKS, CLINT.. I'LL SEE YOU AGAIN... CALL ME, WILL YOU?

"I HAD SUDDENLY LOST INTEREST IN CLINT-- I WANTED TO GLOAT... WHEN I WENT UPSTAIRS, MARTHA WAS STILL UP...

FEELING BETTER, MARTHA?

STOP SMIRKING, SUZI! I WANT TO TALK TO YOU!

ABOUT CLINT, MARTHA? HE ASKED ME OUT...

SUZI... I KNOW YOU DON'T CARE ANY-THING ABOUT CLINT! THAT'S WHY I WANT YOU TO LISTEN... IT-IT'S DIFFERENT WITH CLINT AND ME ---

YOU KNOW, SUZI, I'M NOT AT THE AGE ANYMORE IN WHICH I CAN INDULGE IN TEEN AGE CRUSHES... THIS IS MY LAST CHANCE FOR REAL HAPPINESS! THIS IS SERIOUS, SUZI! I LOVE CLINT ROBERTS!

REALLY, MARTHA-- AT YOUR AGE?

"IN THE REFLECTION OF HER MIRROR, I COULD SEE THE HURT IN HER EYES, AND FOR A MOMENT I WAS SORRY... THEN --

YOU'RE A MEAN, CONTEMPTUOUS LITTLE FOOL, SUZI! EVERY YOUNG MAN IN TOWN KNOWS WHAT YOU ARE -- BOY-CRAZY!

MARTHA!

I WON'T GIVE UP, SUZI! I'LL FIGHT FOR CLINT! --AND DON'T THINK I'LL MISS A TRICK! -- CLINT WANTS A WOMAN, NOT A CHILD!

7

"MY PITY FOR HER VANISHED -- AND WAS IMMEDIATELY REPLACED BY A SOUL-SEARING HATRED! WE DIDN'T SPEAK FOR DAYS! LATER, ONE EVENING, SHE ANSWERED THE PHONE...

OH, CLINT! HELLO--HOW NICE OF YOU TO CALL!

I'M FINE, DARLING... I WAS WONDERING WHAT HAPPENED TO---OH--SUZI? YES, SHE'S HERE --

IT-IT'S FOR YOU, SUZI--

THANK YOU--

"CLINT ASKED ME FOR A DATE, AND I SAID I'D LOVE IT... WHEN HE CALLED FOR ME, MARTHA WAS IN BED...

I HAVE SOMETHING TO ASK YOU, SUZI----HOW ABOUT THE YACHT CLUB ...WE CAN TALK ON THE PIER...

SOUNDS EXCITING!

"CLINT WAS STRANGELY SILENT AS WE WALKED OUT TO THE END OF THE PIER, LINED WITH ITS SPRAWLING CRUISERS AND ROMANTIC LITTLE SLOOPS... THEN HE SPOKE!!

SUZI, YOU KNOW MY BACKGROUND, DON'T YOU?

LET ME SEE -- YOU'RE A SUCCESSFUL AUTHOR, A FASCINATING BACHELOR, YOU WERE A WAR HERO-YOU'RE TERRIFIC CLINT!

WHAT I MEANT, SUZI, WAS THAT I'M -- WELL, NOT A BAD CATCH... I CAN SUPPORT A WIFE IN GOOD STYLE ...I'M STEADY, AND I'LL BE DEVOTED--

"MY HEART STOPPED AS I WAITED FOR HIM TO ASK ME... THIS WAS INDEED A MOMENT OF TRIUMPH! I TURNED TO HIM--

YES, -- CLINT?

WELL, YOU SEE, SUZI, I WANTED YOUR CONSENT BEFORE I ASK YOUR AUNT TO BE MY WIFE!

8

"HIS WORDS HIT ME LIKE A THUNDER BOLT! I LOOKED UP AT THE MOON AND THEN DOWN AT ITS REFLECTION, RIPPLING IN THE BAY...THE TEARS IN MY EYES MADE A GROTESQUE DISTORTION OF HIS FACE AS I LOOKED UP AT CLINT....

YOU--WANT-TO--MARRY--*MY AUNT?*

SUZI--DON'T--

I DIDN'T MEAN IT, SUZI--IT'S *YOU* I LOVE-- CAN'T YOU SEE? I WAS AFRAID YOU'D THINK ME TOO OLD FOR YOU!

CLINT, I *LOVE YOU--* I LOVE YOU-- I LOVE YOU!

"FACED WITH THE THOUGHT OF LOSING CLINT, I SUDDENLY REALIZED I LOVED HIM!

OH, CLINT-- CLINT--

DON'T CRY, SUZI--PLEASE DON'T CRY!

"IT WAS ALMOST DAYLIGHT WHEN WE LEFT THE PIER...WE'D BEEN TALKING OF HOUSES, GARDENS, FURNITURE AND KIDS... HOW STUPID I'D BEEN BEFORE THIS, I THOUGHT, WHEN I SAID I WAS ALIVE....

CLINT--IT'S DAWN-- MUCH AS I HATE THE THOUGHT, DARLING ... WE'D BETTER LEAVE!

"WE FLOATED HOME ON A CLOUD--AND HE KISSED ME GOOD MORNING ...

YOU'RE MY OWN, SUZI -- MY VERY OWN--

SUZI!!

"IT WAS TED JENSEN! I NEVER SAW HIM SO ANGRY!!!

OUT WITH *ANOTHER* GUY, SUZI? WHERE DID YOU FIND THIS ONE?

SEE HERE, YOU YOUNG HOODLUM, I'LL ...

9

18

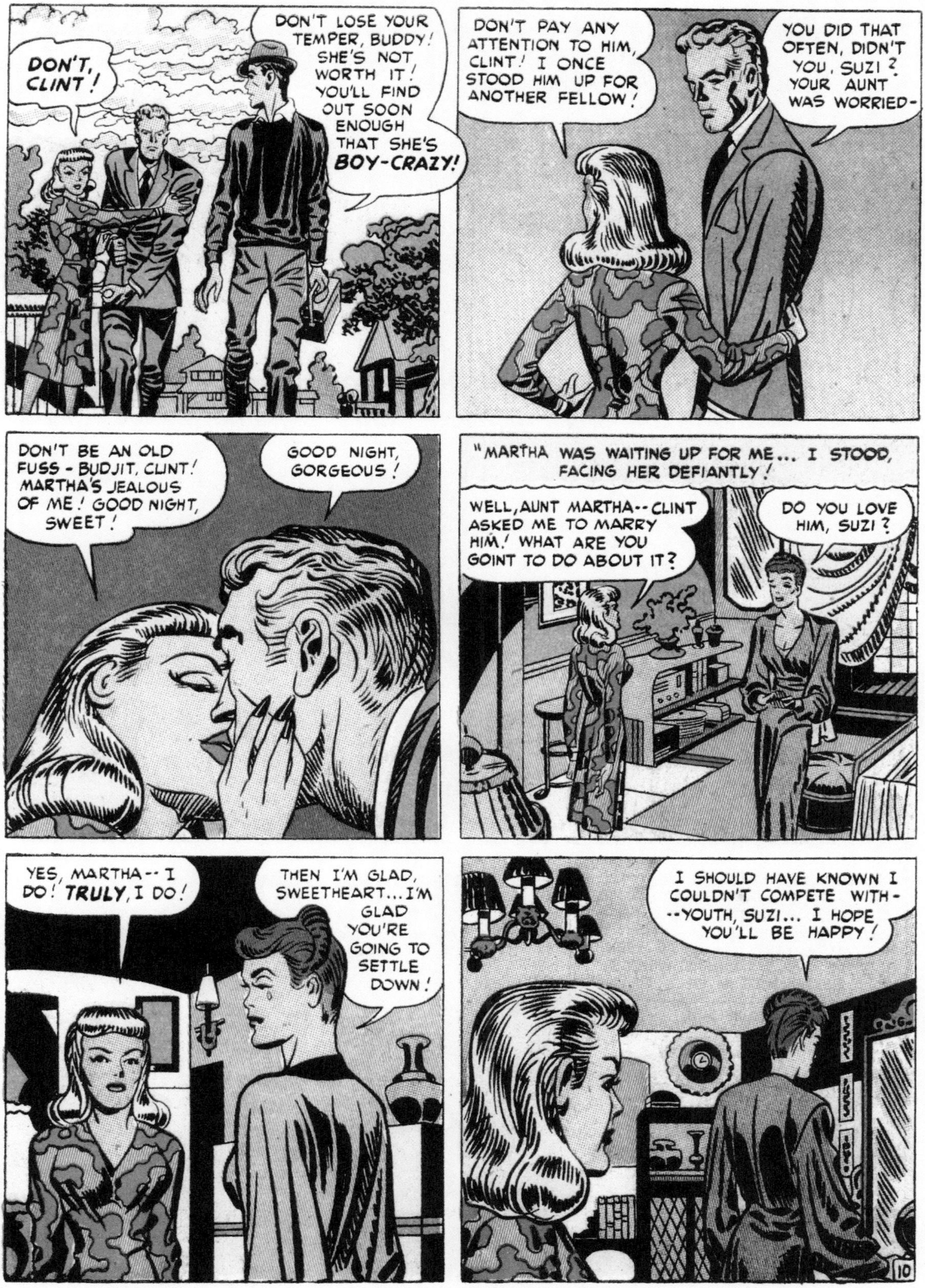
DON'T, CLINT!
DON'T LOSE YOUR TEMPER, BUDDY! SHE'S NOT WORTH IT! YOU'LL FIND OUT SOON ENOUGH THAT SHE'S BOY-CRAZY!
DON'T PAY ANY ATTENTION TO HIM, CLINT! I ONCE STOOD HIM UP FOR ANOTHER FELLOW!
YOU DID THAT OFTEN, DIDN'T YOU, SUZI? YOUR AUNT WAS WORRIED-
DON'T BE AN OLD FUSS - BUDJIT, CLINT! MARTHA'S JEALOUS OF ME! GOOD NIGHT, SWEET!
GOOD NIGHT, GORGEOUS!
"MARTHA WAS WAITING UP FOR ME... I STOOD, FACING HER DEFIANTLY!
WELL, AUNT MARTHA--CLINT ASKED ME TO MARRY HIM! WHAT ARE YOU GOINT TO DO ABOUT IT?
DO YOU LOVE HIM, SUZI?
YES, MARTHA--I DO! TRULY, I DO!
THEN I'M GLAD, SWEETHEART...I'M GLAD YOU'RE GOING TO SETTLE DOWN!
I SHOULD HAVE KNOWN I COULDN'T COMPETE WITH--YOUTH, SUZI... I HOPE YOU'LL BE HAPPY!
10

"MARTHA MEANT WHAT SHE SAID...PERHAPS I MISJUDGED HER...SHE WAS SO BRAVE WHEN CLINT CALLED ON ME...

YOU'RE GOING TO BE MY NEPHEW SOON, CLINT--- IMAGINE?

YOU'LL BE A WONDERFUL AUNT--IN-LAW, MARTHA!

SUZI, I'VE RENTED A SHACK IN THE MOUNTAINS TO WORK ON A NEW NOVEL--IT'S ABOUT *YOU*, DARLING...I'M REALLY INSPIRED...BUT YOU WON'T BE SEEING MUCH OF ME FOR A FEW WEEKS!

BUT, CLINT--

YOU'VE GOT TO LEARN *PATIENCE*, SUZI! AN INSPIRATION CAN'T WAIT! THIS NOVEL WILL GIVE US A GREAT START! WE'LL BUILD A DREAM HOUSE AND YOU'LL HAVE ALL THE THINGS YOU'VE EVER WANTED!

"I THOUGHT I *KNEW* WHAT I WANTED, BUT WHEN THE DAYS STRETCHED INTO WEEKS, THE LONELINESS ENGULFED ME UNTIL I COULD STAND IT NO LONGER!!!

IT WON'T DO ANY HARM TO SEE AN OLD FRIEND NOW AND THEN! LET'S SEE--*ROD* HAS A NICE CAR--

HELLO, ROD? YOU HAVEN'T CALLED ME IN WEEKS! WHY DON'T YOU TAKE ME RIDING TONIGHT?

"ROD WAS EASY! IN LESS THAN HALF AN HOUR, HIS BIG CAR PULLED UP TO THE HOUSE, AND THEN MARTHA WAS STANDING BETWEEN ME AND THE DOOR!

YOU'RE *NOT* GOING OUT WITH ROD, SUZI!

PLEASE STEP ASIDE, MARTHA!

I WON'T *LET* YOU, CHILD! YOU'RE RUINING YOUR LIFE!

I'M NOT A CHILD, MARTHA! I'M WARNING YOU! --DON'T DELAY ME ANY LONGER!

NOW, WILL YOU MOVE ASIDE?

SUZI!!

SLAP!

"I WAS SORRY, SO WHAT? WHY WAS SHE ALWAYS INTERFERING WITH MY LIFE, I FUMED! OH, IF I'D ONLY LISTENED TO HER!

WHAT TOOK YOU SO LONG, BABY?

ROD! TAKE FOR A LONG RIDE-- TAKE ME WHERE I CAN SEE PEOPLE!

SOME OF THE GANG ARE THROWING A PARTY TONIGHT, SUZI! THEY'VE GOT A COTTAGE ON THE BEACH... HOW'D YOU LIKE THAT?

THAT SOUNDS KEEN, ROD! LET'S HURRY OUT OF THIS DEAD TOWN!

"ONCE MORE I WAS DRINKING IN THE RAPTURES OF YOUTH! AND, WHEN I ARRIVED AT THE PARTY, I KNEW THIS WAS MY LIFE!

HERE WE ARE, SUZI! LIKE?

HEY! IT'S ROD! AND, WHOO! WHOO! WHAT A DISH! COME ON IN! JOIN THE CATS!

"THE MUSIC WAS BLARING, THE LIGHTS WERE DIM, THE LAUGHTER WAS GAY... I WAS IN HEAVEN!... THEN--

HEY, KIDS! LOOK AT ME! WHO WANTS TO JOIN ME IN A SWIM?

COUNT ME IN, ANGEL! HOW ABOUT IT, SUZI?

I BORROWED A SWIM SUIT AND WE WERE OFF!

SUZI! YOU'RE MY DREAM GIRL! DON'T EVER TAKE THAT SUIT OFF!

YOU JUST WAIT THERE, BABY! OLD ROD IS GOING TO SHOW YOU WHAT A MAN YOU'RE OUT WITH!

ROD! YOU'RE NOT GOING TO DIVE OFF THAT LEDGE? YOU MIGHT HIT A ROCK IN THE WATER!

BAH! I'VE DONE THIS DOZENS OF TIMES! HERE GOES NOTHING!

ROD!

"WE WERE ALONE, NOW... AND I WAS FRIGHTENED FOR ROD... I CLIMBED DOWN TO THE WATER'S EDGE···

ROD! I DON'T HEAR YOU! ROD! ARE YOU ALL RIGHT?

"I SEARCHED THROUGH THE SPRAY OF THE POUNDING SURF! THEN, I SAW HIM! HE WAS IN TROUBLE!

SUZI--I-I'M HURT--

ROD! HANG ON! I'M COMING OUT TO GET YOU!

"I FOUND HIS LIMP FORM AND CLUTCHED AT IT! I VAGUELY REMEMBER TRYING TO FIGHT THE SURF!

YOU- WERE - RIGHT, SUZI--HIT A- ROCK—

"THEN, THE WAVES CLOSED IN ON ME AND I LOST ALL SENSE OF BEING... WHEN I AWOKE, I WAS ON THE BEACH!

SHE'S COMING TO, THANK GOODNESS!

YOU'RE LUCKY WE FOUND YOU, SUZI! YOU WERE ALMOST A GONER!

ROD! WHAT ABOUT ROD?

SUZI, YOU DID THE BEST YOU COULD...YOU'VE GOT TO REST--

"ROD HAD DROWNED! IT WAS MY FIRST CONTACT WITH DEATH AND I TOOK IT HARD! AS FOR ME, MY PICTURES WERE IN ALL THE PAPERS...

I BROUGHT YOU THE MORNING PAPERS, DEAR! THEY SAY YOU'RE A HEROINE!

MARTHA! HAS CLINT BEEN HERE?

HERE I AM, SUZI-- I READ ABOUT IT IN THE NEWSPAPERS --AND RUSHED DOWN TO SEE YOU! HOW DO YOU FEEL?

OH, CLINT, DEAR! I'M FINE! WAIT A MOMENT- I'LL DRESS AND BE RIGHT WITH YOU!

13

WHY, CLINT, DARLING--WHAT'S WRONG? YOU--LOOK SO PECULIAR--
SUZI,--I DON'T BLAME YOU FOR WHAT YOU DO--IT'S JUST THAT YOU DON'T KNOW RIGHT FROM WRONG--
SINCE I SAW THOSE PICTURES IN THE PAPERS, AND READ THE STORY, I'VE BEEN DOING A LOT OF THINKING... YOU'D NEVER BE HAPPY WITH A DULL PERSON LIKE ME, SUZI---
"HE TURNED AND SLOWLY WALKED OUT OF THE ROOM AND OUT OF MY LIFE! THOUGH I KNEW THAT I WOULD NEVER LOVE ANYONE AS I LOVED CLINT ROBERTS, I DIDN'T CALL TO HIM!"
SUZI! ASK HIM BACK! HE LOVES YOU! --BEG HIS FORGIVENESS--
NO, MARTHA!
"I HAVEN'T SEEN CLINT SINCE, AND SOMETIMES, WHEN I'M ALONE IN MY ROOM, I THINK OF HIM AND WONDER IF HE'LL EVER RETURN..."
WELL, THAT'S THE STORY OF MY FOOLISH CAMPAIGN AGAINST MY AUNT--I NEVER THOUGHT MY VICTORY WOULD TURN INTO A LIFE-LONG DEFEAT--I'LL ALWAYS MISS CLINT--ALWAYS--

The Pitiful Story of a Girl Who Could Find but One Solution to... HER TRAGIC LOVE

"ALTHOUGH, I WAS ALMOST FIVE YEARS OLDER THAN MY SISTER MARJORIE, I NEVER HAD TO PLAY BIG SISTER! WE SHARED THE SAME HAPPY OUTLOOK, INTERESTS AND SECRETS-- THAT IS, UNTIL **SAM FORD** CAME ALONG...

GOING OUT WITH SAM FORD AGAIN TONIGHT, AREN'T YOU, MARJORIE---

YES, I AM! I *LIKE* SAM! I LOVE TO BE WITH HIM! I'LL CONTINUE TO SEE HIM AS OFTEN AS I LIKE!

BUT, MARGE, SAM IS *ENGAGED!* NO GOOD CAN COME OF THAT KIND OF A FRIENDSHIP! PLEASE LISTEN TO ME--

GOOD-BYE, KATE! DON'T WAIT UP FOR ME!

"POOR, LOVE-STRICKEN LITTLE MARJORIE--- EMERGING ON THE THRESHOLD OF YOUNG WOMANHOOD--AND ACCEPTING THIS HOPELESS SITUATION WITH THE UNTRIED OPTIMISM OF YOUTH--

MARJORIE! MARJORIE! WHY WON'T YOU LISTEN?

"AND HANDSOME, MILD-MANNERED SAM FORD--- FOOLISH BUT SINCERE--DISOWNING HIS PROMISED FOR THE LIGHT-HEARTED CHARM OF YOUTHFUL MARJORIE--AS I WATCHED THEM LEAVE TOGETHER, I FELT IT AGAIN---*THE CHILL OF IMPENDING TRAGEDY!*

SOMETIMES I WONDER WHERE ALL THIS WILL LEAD TO, MARGE! BREAKING OFF WON'T BE EASY! MEANWHILE, WE—

MEANWHILE WE'VE GOT EACH OTHER, SAM! I KNOW IT'S DIFFICULT-- AND I'LL WAIT--FOREVER, IF I HAVE TO—

THIS IS MAD, MARGE, BUT YOU MEAN SO MUCH TO ME-- I-I CAN'T TURN BACK--

WE'LL SEE IT THROUGH, SAM-- MY DARLING SAM --

2

"IT HAD TAKEN TIME FOR SAM TO DECIDE BETWEEN HIS BETROTHAL AND NEW-FOUND LOVE-- IN THAT INTERVAL, HIS FIANCÉE HAD GUESSED! IT MUST HAVE BEEN SHEER TORMENT TO LOSE A MAN LIKE SAM FORD!

I'M GOING TO TELL ELLA TONIGHT! SHE'S ALL HEART! SHE'LL UNDERSTAND!

OH, SAM--I-I'D GIVE ANYTHING NOT TO HURT HER THIS WAY... PLEASE BE GENTLE WITH HER!

"YES, MY PREMONITION OF IMPENDING TRAGEDY WAS WELL-FOUNDED! FOR, WHEN SAM VISITED HIS FIANCÉE THAT EVENING---

ELLA! ELLA, ARE YOU HOME?

SHE CAN'T BE ANYWHERE ELSE, MAC!--NOT IN THE CONDITION SHE'S IN NOW! SHE'S DEAD!

WE'RE FROM HOMICIDE! ARE YOU SAM FORD?

NO! NO! SHE CAN'T BE-- ELLA! ELLA!

OH, GOOD HEAVENS--

DON'T TOUCH ANYTHING, FORD!

YOUR GIRL DIED OF CYANIDE POISONING, FORD! KNOW ANYTHING ABOUT CYANIDE?

THERE ARE A FEW THINGS THAT NEED EXPLAINING, FORD! WE'RE BOOKING YOU ON SUSPICION OF MURDER!

"THE DREAD MISGIVINGS THAT PLAGUED ME EXPLODED INTO SHOCKING REALITY AND SNOWBALLED INTO A FEARSOME NIGHTMARE THAT ENMESHED US ALL IN ITS HIDEOUS CONSEQUENCES!!!

OH, KATE! I'M FRIGHTENED! (SOB), WHAT WILL THEY DO TO HIM? (SOB) OH - SAM--!

WE KNOW SAM COULDN'T HAVE DONE IT! HE WAS WITH *YOU* THAT EVENING!

SUSPECT HELD IN GIRL'S DEATH!

"POOR SAM---IT MUST HAVE BEEN MADDENING TO ENDURE POLICE QUESTIONING WHILE BURDENED WITH GRIEF!

WHY NOT SPILL IT, FORD! WE KNOW THE FACTS! WHAT WAS THE MOTIVE?

WAS THERE ANOTHER WOMAN?

COME ON! COME ON! WE KNOW YOU BOUGHT THE CYANIDE! WHY? WE KNOW YOU POISONED YOUR GIRL! WHY?

ONLY YOUR FINGER PRINTS WERE ON THE BOTTLE! YOU MURDERED HER! *WHY? WHY DID YOU DO IT, FORD?*

WE'RE NOT OUT TO GET YOU, FORD! WE'D LET YOU OUT RIGHT NOW, IF YOU'D CLEAR UP THE MOTIVE BEHIND YOUR FIANCÉE'S DEATH!

WE CHECKED YOUR GIRL'S ACTIVITIES! SHE WAS PLAYING SQUARE! IF SHE COMMITTED SUICIDE, IT WAS BECAUSE OF YOU-- *WHY?* WHO ARE YOU SHIELDING, FORD?

"THE DAYS THAT PASSED WERE AGONIZING FOR MARJORIE---AND FOR ME! THE NEWSPAPERS TORE HUNGRILY INTO THE MYSTERY THAT WAS SAM FORD... MARJORIE AND I READ THEM DAILY--- SICK WITH FEAR!!!

DAILY BULLETIN
FORD MAINTAINS STOIC SILENCE!
PROSECUTION RUSHES PLANS FOR INDICTMENT!

FORD INDICTED!

DATE SET FOR FORD TRIAL!

NEWS
CHERCHEZ LA FEMME!
POLICE SEEK OTHER WOMAN IN FORD'S LIFE!

"THE CIRCUMSTANTIAL EVIDENCE CLOSED IN ON SAM AND THROTTLED HIS EVERY CHANCE!!! THEN ONE DAY--

KATE! KATE! SAM IS GOING TO DIE! NO THEY CAN'T---

MARJORIE! WHAT'S WRONG?

CHRONICLE
FORD CONVICTED! TO DIE IN CHAIR!

4

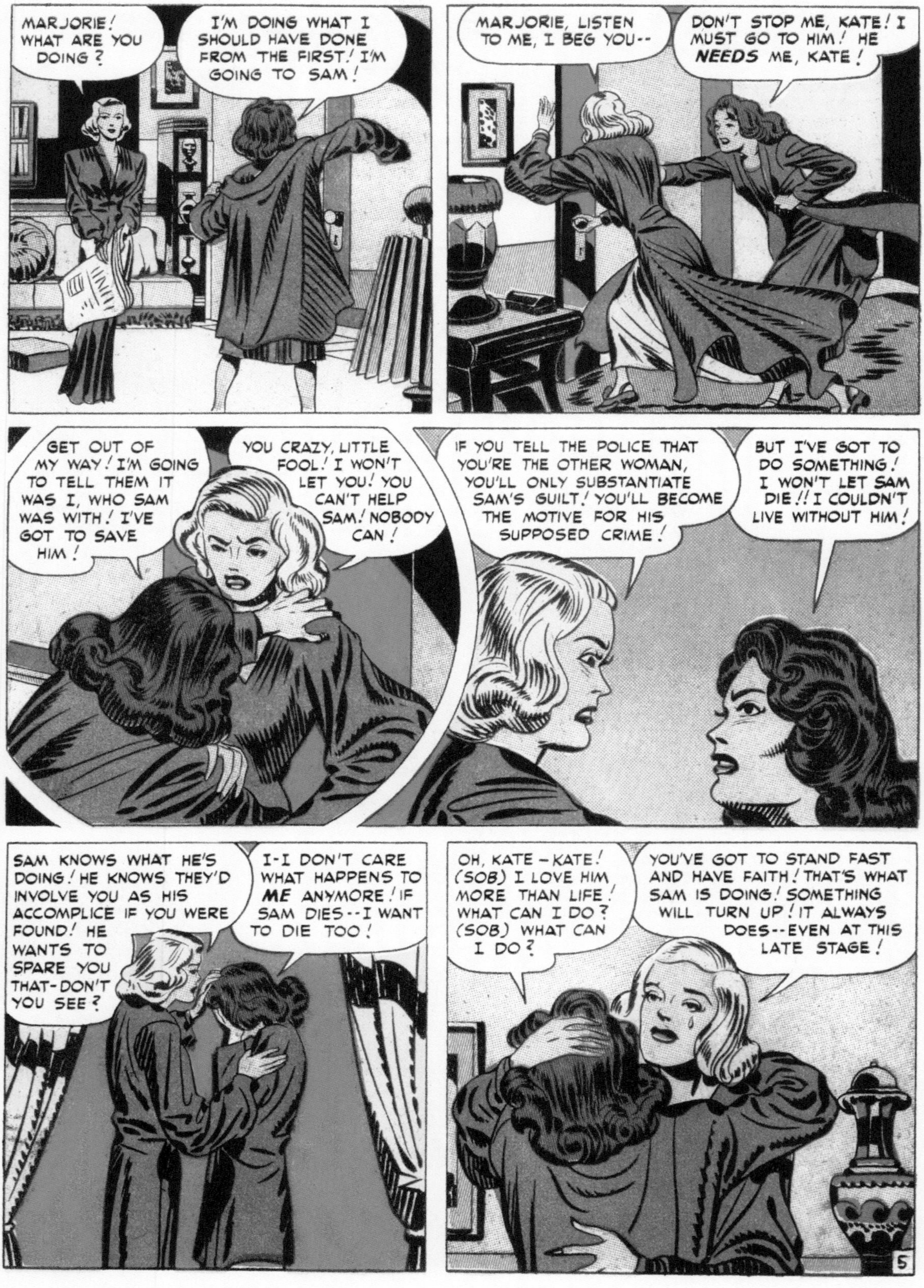
MARJORIE! WHAT ARE YOU DOING?
I'M DOING WHAT I SHOULD HAVE DONE FROM THE FIRST! I'M GOING TO SAM!
MARJORIE, LISTEN TO ME, I BEG YOU--
DON'T STOP ME, KATE! I MUST GO TO HIM! HE NEEDS ME, KATE!
GET OUT OF MY WAY! I'M GOING TO TELL THEM IT WAS I, WHO SAM WAS WITH! I'VE GOT TO SAVE HIM!
YOU CRAZY, LITTLE FOOL! I WON'T LET YOU! YOU CAN'T HELP SAM! NOBODY CAN!
IF YOU TELL THE POLICE THAT YOU'RE THE OTHER WOMAN, YOU'LL ONLY SUBSTANTIATE SAM'S GUILT! YOU'LL BECOME THE MOTIVE FOR HIS SUPPOSED CRIME!
BUT I'VE GOT TO DO SOMETHING! I WON'T LET SAM DIE!! I COULDN'T LIVE WITHOUT HIM!
SAM KNOWS WHAT HE'S DOING! HE KNOWS THEY'D INVOLVE YOU AS HIS ACCOMPLICE IF YOU WERE FOUND! HE WANTS TO SPARE YOU THAT-DON'T YOU SEE?
I-I DON'T CARE WHAT HAPPENS TO ME ANYMORE! IF SAM DIES--I WANT TO DIE TOO!
OH, KATE-KATE! (SOB) I LOVE HIM MORE THAN LIFE! WHAT CAN I DO? (SOB) WHAT CAN I DO?
YOU'VE GOT TO STAND FAST AND HAVE FAITH! THAT'S WHAT SAM IS DOING! SOMETHING WILL TURN UP! IT ALWAYS DOES--EVEN AT THIS LATE STAGE!
5

"AS THE DAY FOR SAM'S EXECUTION DREW CLOSER, I KEPT A SHARP WATCH OVER MARJORIE...SHE HAD BECOME LISTLESS--SELDOM SPOKE AND GAZED SILENTLY OUT THE WINDOW FOR HOURS...I WAS WORRIED--

"AND SAM, WHAT THOUGHTS WERE RACING THROUGH HIS MIND--WITH THE GRIM SHADOW OF THE ELECTRIC CHAIR ALMOST UPON HIM?

NO USE HOPING FOR ANY MIRACLES! IN A FEW HOURS I'M GOING TO FRY! I'D GIVE ANYTHING FOR A LAST GLIMPSE OF MARJORIE! POOR KID! SHE'LL TAKE THIS HARD!

YOU'VE GOT A VISITOR, FORD! --YOUR LAST!! IN HERE MISS!

I DON'T WANT TO SEE ANYONE! LEAVE ME ALONE!

SAM! SAM! I. HAD TO SEE YOU! I JUST HAD TO!

MARJORIE! YOU SHOULDN'T HAVE--

YOU'VE GOT TWO MINUTES-- THAT'S THE RULE!

I HAD TO RISK IT, SAM! I COULDN'T STAND IT ANY LONGER--SAM- SAM--WHAT HAVE THEY DONE TO YOU?

LISTEN TO ME, HONEY! YOU'VE GOT TO FORGET ABOUT ME! I-I AM GUILTY! THEY'VE PROVEN THAT! NOW---

I DON'T BELIEVE YOU! SAM, I'VE MADE UP MY MIND! WHEN YOU DIE AT MIDNIGHT, I'M GOING TO KILL MYSELF! NOTHING CAN SEPARATE US! --NOT EVEN ETERNITY!

"I COULD HEAR SAM'S OUTCRY OF PROTEST AT MARJORIE'S HYSTERICAL WORDS! THEN THE GUARD EMERGED WITH MY SISTER, WHO SHOOK WITH SOBS! SAM'S CRIES OF ANGUISH STILL REACHED MY EARS WHEN WE LEFT...

MARJORIE— DON'T— YOU MUSN'T—

"BUT, UNKNOWN TO MARJORIE AND MYSELF, SAM WAS RELEASED FROM HIS CELL A HALF HOUR BEFORE HIS EXECUTION WAS TO TAKE PLACE AND TAKEN TO THE OFFICE OF THE WARDEN!

FORD—IT SEEMS THE OBSERVANT EYE OF A NEW TENANT HAS PROBABLY PREVENTED A MISCARRIAGE OF JUSTICE AND MOST LIKELY, HAS SAVED YOUR LIFE!

SAVED MY LIFE? YOU MEAN I'M NOT—?

ONE OF THE PEOPLE WHO OCCUPIED YOUR OLD APARTMENT, FOUND THIS IN AN OBSCURE PART OF THE ROOM IN WHICH YOUR GIRL DIED! IT CLEARS YOU OF POISONING HER!

WHY, IT'S A *SUICIDE NOTE* WRITTEN BY ELLA—

YES, YOUR FIANCÉE DIED BY HER OWN HAND! WE'LL MAKE PREPARATIONS FOR YOUR RELEASE!

IT'S ALMOST TWELVE O'CLOCK! MARJORIE WILL THINK I'M—

WARDEN! IT'S A MATTER OF LIFE AND DEATH THAT I BE RELEASED RIGHT NOW! I'VE ONLY GOT SECONDS TO SPARE!

WELL, THERE ARE A FEW ROUTINE MATTERS TO BE TAKEN CARE OF FIRST BUT—

"I CAN WELL IMAGINE THE NEW HORROR THAT GRIPPED SAM AS MARJORIE'S WORDS CAME BACK TO HIM!! HIS PLEAS MUST HAVE TOUCHED THE WARDEN, BECAUSE HE LEFT THE PRISON IN A POLICE CAR THAT TORE THROUGH THE CITY TO OUR APARTMENT HOUSE....

7

"OH, IF WE HAD ONLY KNOWN -- WHAT I WOULDN'T HAVE GIVEN TO KNOW ABOUT SAM'S RELEASE! MARJORIE HAD WITHDRAWN WITHIN HERSELF AGAIN... I REMAINED CLOSE TO HER — AND WATCHED THE MINUTES TICK SLOWLY AWAY---

TICK TOCK
TICK TOCK

"THE STROKE OF TWELVE WAS LIKE A GHASTLY SIGNAL! A WILD, MOURNFUL CRY ESCAPED MARJORIE'S LIPS! I FOUND MYSELF SPRAWLING AS SHE DASHED BY ME LIKE A THING POSSESSED!

SAM! SAM! I'M GOING WITH YOU!

MARJORIE ---NO--

"I DON'T KNOW HOW LONG I SCREAMED! PERHAPS I NEVER STOPPED! I'LL HEAR THOSE ECHOES UNTIL MY DYING DAY! DOWN BELOW, A CROWD QUICKLY GATHERED AROUND POOR MARJORIE'S BROKEN BODY -- AND WHEN I SAW THE POLICE CAR PULL UP AND SAM GET OUT--- I FAINTED !!!

IT'S BEEN A YEAR SINCE MARJORIE'S DEATH!...AS FOR SAM, --- I SEEM TO THINK HE DIED THAT NIGHT, TOO! WHATEVER LIT THE GENTLE LIGHT IN HIS EYES AND TRANSMITTED HIS WONDERFUL PERSONALITY --IS GONE--POSSIBLY FOREVER ---

A LOVE THAT GREW IN THE SHADOW OF SAM'S TRAGEDY HAS DESTROYED HIS SPIRIT!! HE'S IN THE NEXT ROOM NOW, WHERE I VISIT AND ATTEND HIM EACH DAY - HOPING AGAINST HOPE THAT IN TIME, PERHAPS A FRESH SPARK -- A BRIGHTER SPARK WILL MAKE HIM LIVE AGAIN... YOU SEE --- I LOVE HIM TOO !

8

31

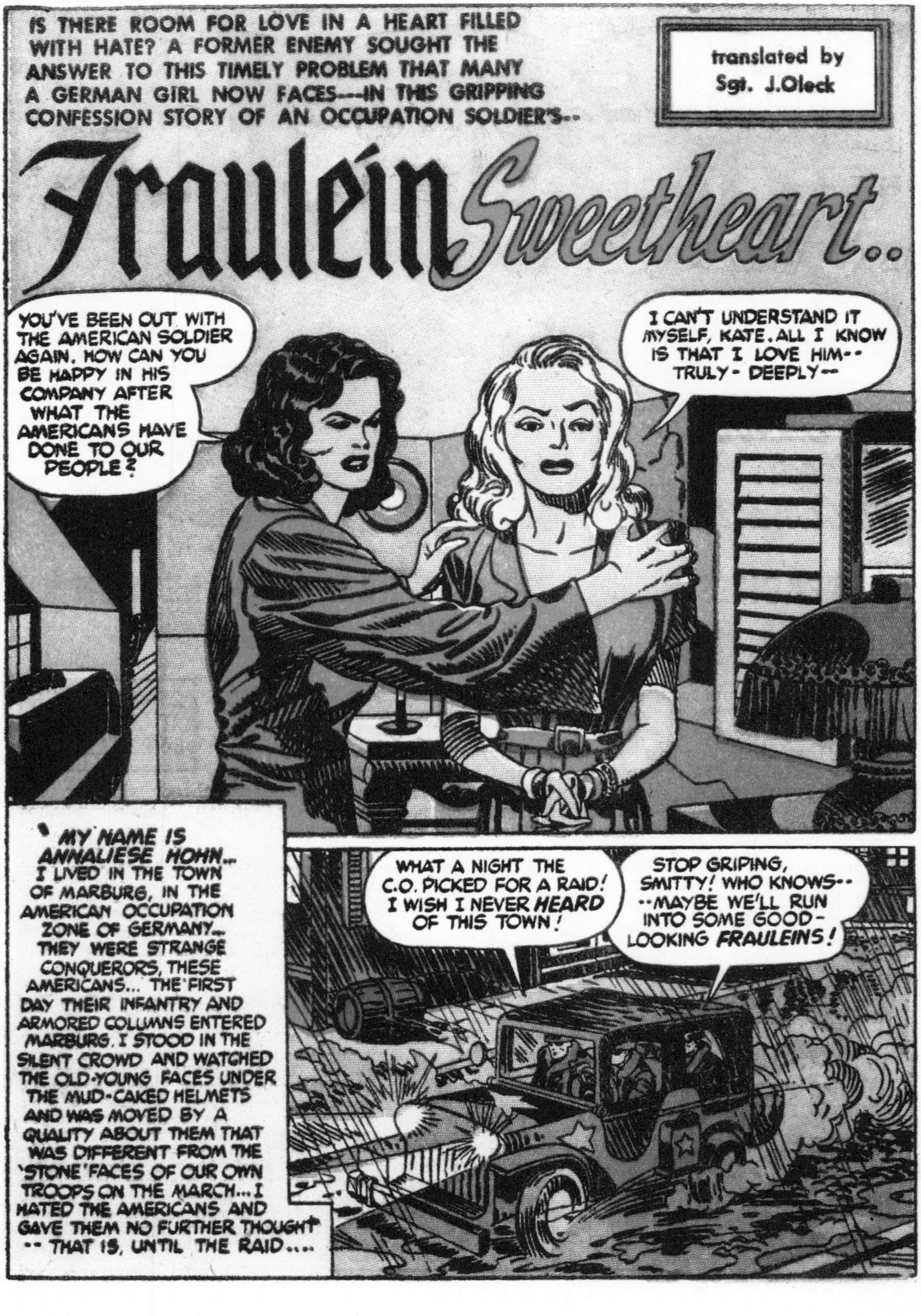

IS THERE ROOM FOR LOVE IN A HEART FILLED WITH HATE? A FORMER ENEMY SOUGHT THE ANSWER TO THIS TIMELY PROBLEM THAT MANY A GERMAN GIRL NOW FACES---IN THIS GRIPPING CONFESSION STORY OF AN OCCUPATION SOLDIER'S--
translated by Sgt. J.Oleck
Fraulein Sweetheart..
YOU'VE BEEN OUT WITH THE AMERICAN SOLDIER AGAIN. HOW CAN YOU BE HAPPY IN HIS COMPANY AFTER WHAT THE AMERICANS HAVE DONE TO OUR PEOPLE?
I CAN'T UNDERSTAND IT MYSELF, KATE. ALL I KNOW IS THAT I LOVE HIM-- TRULY - DEEPLY--
"MY NAME IS ANNALIESE HOHN... I LIVED IN THE TOWN OF MARBURG, IN THE AMERICAN OCCUPATION ZONE OF GERMANY... THEY WERE STRANGE CONQUERORS, THESE AMERICANS... THE FIRST DAY THEIR INFANTRY AND ARMORED COLUMNS ENTERED MARBURG, I STOOD IN THE SILENT CROWD AND WATCHED THE OLD-YOUNG FACES UNDER THE MUD-CAKED HELMETS AND WAS MOVED BY A QUALITY ABOUT THEM THAT WAS DIFFERENT FROM THE 'STONE' FACES OF OUR OWN TROOPS ON THE MARCH... I HATED THE AMERICANS AND GAVE THEM NO FURTHER THOUGHT -- THAT IS, UNTIL THE RAID....
WHAT A NIGHT THE C.O. PICKED FOR A RAID! I WISH I NEVER HEARD OF THIS TOWN!
STOP GRIPING, SMITTY! WHO KNOWS-- --MAYBE WE'LL RUN INTO SOME GOOD-LOOKING FRAULEINS!

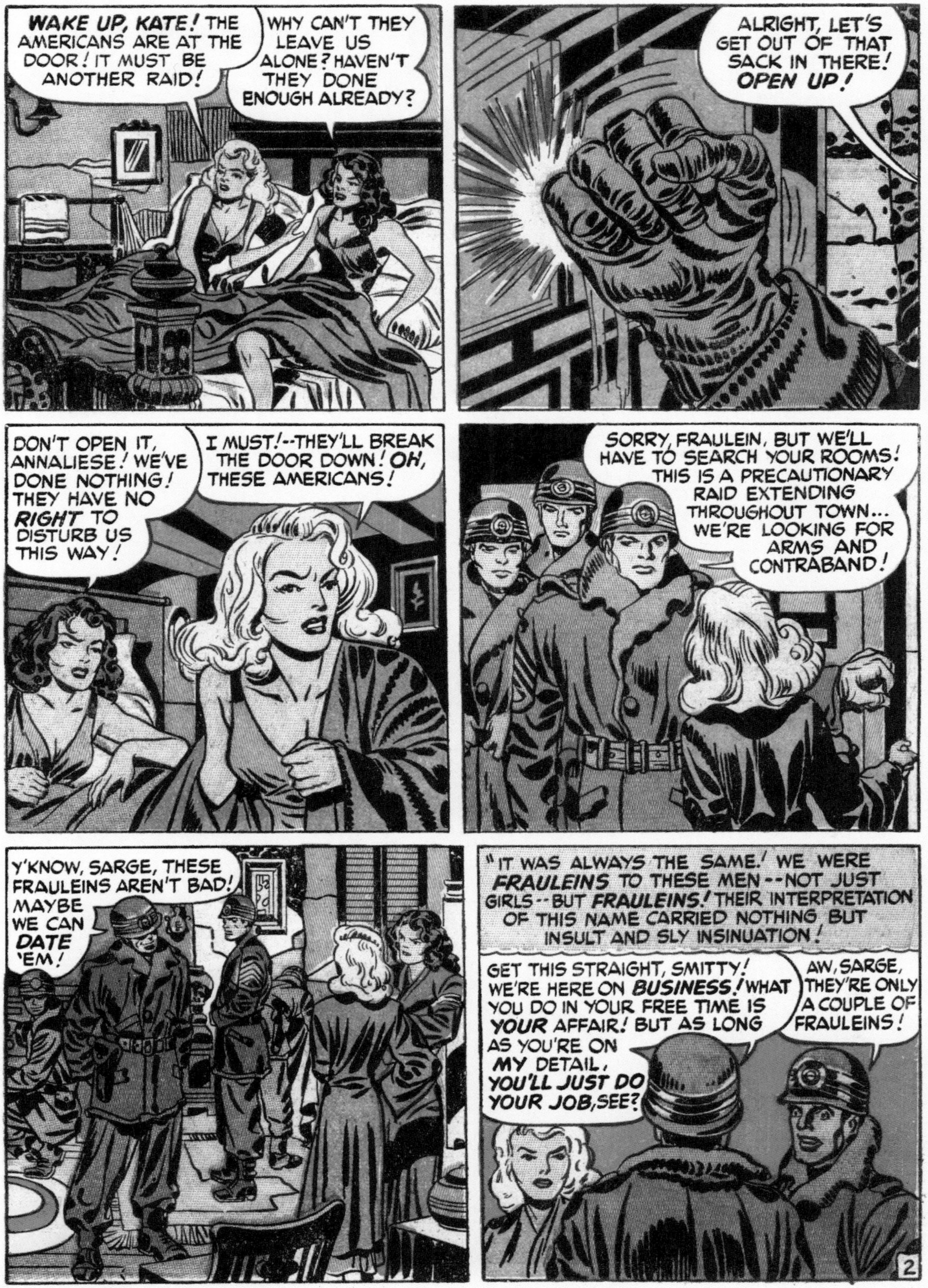

WAKE UP, KATE! THE AMERICANS ARE AT THE DOOR! IT MUST BE ANOTHER RAID!
WHY CAN'T THEY LEAVE US ALONE? HAVEN'T THEY DONE ENOUGH ALREADY?
ALRIGHT, LET'S GET OUT OF THAT SACK IN THERE! OPEN UP!
DON'T OPEN IT, ANNALIESE! WE'VE DONE NOTHING! THEY HAVE NO RIGHT TO DISTURB US THIS WAY!
I MUST!--THEY'LL BREAK THE DOOR DOWN! OH, THESE AMERICANS!
SORRY, FRAULEIN, BUT WE'LL HAVE TO SEARCH YOUR ROOMS! THIS IS A PRECAUTIONARY RAID EXTENDING THROUGHOUT TOWN... WE'RE LOOKING FOR ARMS AND CONTRABAND!
Y'KNOW, SARGE, THESE FRAULEINS AREN'T BAD! MAYBE WE CAN DATE 'EM!
"IT WAS ALWAYS THE SAME! WE WERE FRAULEINS TO THESE MEN--NOT JUST GIRLS--BUT FRAULEINS! THEIR INTERPRETATION OF THIS NAME CARRIED NOTHING BUT INSULT AND SLY INSINUATION!
GET THIS STRAIGHT, SMITTY! WE'RE HERE ON BUSINESS! WHAT YOU DO IN YOUR FREE TIME IS YOUR AFFAIR! BUT AS LONG AS YOU'RE ON MY DETAIL, YOU'LL JUST DO YOUR JOB, SEE?
AW, SARGE, THEY'RE ONLY A COUPLE OF FRAULEINS!
2

"I SHOULD HAVE BEEN FURIOUS...WE HID NO ARMS NOR CONTRABAND! BUT SOMEHOW, THE SOLDIER'S INSULT HAD LOST ITS STING..IT WAS THE *SERGEANT* WHO HELD MY INTEREST.. HE WAS THE YANKEE CONQUEROR, ALOOF--IMPERSONAL -- YET, WHEN OUR EYES MET IN BRIEF GLANCES--I TURNED SOFT INSIDE... THE SEARCH LASTED A FEW MINUTES...THEN--

THANKS, FRAULEINS! YOU'VE BEEN MORE COOPERATIVE THAN *MOST!*

COOPERATIVE? WE HAVE *NO CHOICE* BUT TO BE COOPERATIVE! THESE STUPID RAIDS ONLY ADD TO OUR MISERY!

"KATE'S OUTBURST ANGERED HIM --- I COULD SEE HIS HATRED FOR US LEAP LIKE FLAMES IN HIS EYES... TO HIM, WE WERE *NAZIS*--THE ENEMIES OF HIS DEMOCRACY!

DON'T *KID* ME, SISTER! YOU PEOPLE ARE HARDLY ELIGIBLE TO COMPLAIN ABOUT MISERY--WHEN YOU'VE INFLICTED IT ON THE WHOLE WORLD! GOOD NIGHT!

"WHEN THE DOOR SHUT BEHIND HIM, I YIELDED TO THE TEARS WHICH I COULD NO LONGER CONTROL --YES, I WEPT--WEPT FOR THE PEACE I COULD NOT FIND--FOR THE ONLY MAN I COULD EVER GIVE MY LOVE TO --- THE MAN WHO COULD ONLY RETURN IT WITH LOATHING AND SCORN!

WHY DO YOU *CRY*, YOU LITTLE FOOL? SOME DAY WE WILL *FIGHT* AGAIN-- AND THE AMERICAN WILL *PAY* FOR HIS INSULTS!

"HOW COULD KATE, BLINDED BY PARTY FANATICISM, KNOW THE REASON FOR MY UNHAPPINESS... I WANTED LOVE! I YEARNED FOR A TOUCH, A CARESS, A KISS, FROM THIS MAN WHO HAD SUDDENLY KINDLED A FIRE WHERE THERE HAD ONCE BEEN NOTHING BUT A COLD EMPTINESS ....

"JUST OUTSIDE THE CITY THERE IS A LITTLE FOOT BRIDGE THAT CROSSES A RIVER... ONCE THE YOUNG MEN OF *MARBURG* WALKED THERE WITH THEIR SWEETHEARTS, BUT NOW IT IS LONELY AND DESERTED...I WENT THERE THE NEXT DAY-- TO BE ALONE ---

YOU!

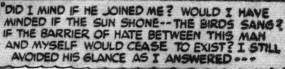

MIND IF I JOIN YOU?

"DID I MIND IF HE JOINED ME? WOULD I HAVE MINDED IF THE SUN SHONE--THE BIRDS SANG? IF THE BARRIER OF HATE BETWEEN THIS MAN AND MYSELF WOULD CEASE TO EXIST? I STILL AVOIDED HIS GLANCE AS I ANSWERED···

IF YOU WISH, SERGEANT--

THE NAME IS HAMILTON---JACK HAMILTON!

"THE AFTERNOON FLOWED ALONG LIKE A TRANQUIL STREAM... JACK WAS GENTLE, KIND AND SOFT-SPOKEN..WE MUST HAVE TALKED FOR HOURS....

GOLLY, IT'S LATE! WE'VE PUT AWAY A LOT OF CONVERSATION! WE'D BETTER GET BACK TO TOWN!

OH, JACK...IT FRIGHTENS ME TO THINK WE MIGHT HAVE NEVER MET AGAIN!

WE'D HAVE MET, ANNALIESE! IF NOT TODAY, THEN SOME OTHER DAY, BUT WE'D HAVE MET--

YOU SEE, ANNALIESE--OUR MEETING TODAY WAS NOT AN ACCIDENT.. I-I WAITED UNTIL I SAW YOU LEAVE THE HOUSE-- AND FOLLOWED YOU!--ARE YOU ANGRY?

ANGRY?--WITH YOU, LIEBSCHEN? OH, NO, JACK! I AM HAPPY! SO HAPPY--

ANNALIESE! ANNALIESE! HEAVEN HELP US BOTH!

"THE WEEKS THAT FOLLOWED WERE GLORIOUS! JACK AND I WERE IN LOVE-- *MADLY* IN LOVE!

"I BEGAN TO THINK THAT NOTHING WOULD EVER COME BETWEEN JACK AND MYSELF-- BUT I WAS WRONG...THE PAST GRIMLY WAITED FOR ME AT HOME..KATE SAW TO THAT!!

YOU'RE HOME LATE AGAIN, ANNALIESE! I SUPPOSE YOU'VE BEEN WITH YOUR AMERICAN AGAIN?

WELL, WHAT IF I HAVE?

YOU CAN TOLERATE THE UNIFORM YOUR AMERICAN WEARS BECAUSE HE IS HANDSOME --BUT CAN YOU FORGET THIS--?

--THIS: YOUR EMBLEM OF LOYALTY TO THE THIRD REICH! REMEMBER THE INSCRIPTION? IT SAYS; -- *TO ANNALIESE HOHN - FOR SERVICES RENDERED TO THE FEUHRER- 1943!*

HAVE YOU FORGOTTEN THAT YOU WERE A HITLER YOUTH LEADER? HAVE YOU FORGOTTEN YOUR *FATHERLAND* THESE AMERICANS ARE TRYING TO DESTROY? HOW CAN YOU FEEL ANYTHING BUT *HATE* FOR THEM?

YES! YES! *I HAVE FORGOTTEN!* I *WANT* TO FORGET! LOVE DOES NOT CHOOSE BETWEEN UNIFORMS! LOVE OWES ALLEGIANCE TO *NO* PARTY OR FATHERLAND! I CAN ONLY BE HAPPY WITH JACK! I WANT NO MORE OF THE PAST!

HAH! DO YOU EXPECT ME TO BELIEVE THIS GREAT LOVE HAS REPLACED YOUR DEVOTION TO THE FEUHRER? *WE ARE NAZIS AND ALWAYS WILL BE!*

NO! NO! I *RENOUNCE* MY PARTY RANK! I-I LOVE JACK!

"ALTHOUGH, I SHOUTED MY LOVE FOR JACK, I KNEW KATE WAS RIGHT! I COULD NOT DENY MY UNFALTERING BELIEF IN THE GLORY AND POWER THAT WAS THE REICH AND ADOLF HITLER! I HAD BEEN A NAZI SINCE THE DAY I WAS BORN.. THE PARTY WAS MY VERY LIFE! TO BE ANYTHING BUT A NAZI WAS UNTHINKABLE ....

I MUST BE SINCERE WITH JACK-- HE MUST KNOW--- IT WILL HURT HIM -- BUT IT WILL BE A HURT THAT WILL MEND -- IN TIME --

"WHEN I SAW HIM THE NEXT DAY, IT WAS JACK WHO LED THE CONVERSATION TO THE SUBJECT I FEARED MOST TO DISCUSS WITH HIM ....

ANNALIESE, YOU JUST TOLD ME YOU LOVED ME -- I WANT TO HEAR YOU SAY IT *AGAIN* BEFORE--

BEFORE *WHAT,* JACK?

ANNALIESE-- WHEN HITLER WAS IN POWER-- WHAT DID YOU THINK?-I MEAN -WHAT DID YOU *BELIEVE?* DID YOU BELIEVE IN WHAT YOUR COUNTRY WAS DOING?

WHAT DOES IT MATTER NOW, JACK? *WE* LOST THE WAR --

IT MATTERS TO ME! *ANSWER ME, ANNALIESE!*

"BUT JACK DID **NOT** KISS ME.. INSTEAD HIS FEATURES HARDENED INTO THE RIGID MASK HE WORE THE NIGHT OF THE RAID... JACK HAMILTON WAS LOST TO ME FOREVER...I RELEASED HIM AS HE TURNED AND WALKED SILENTLY ACROSS THE FIELD...

SO YOU'VE FINALLY COME TO YOUR SENSES! WHAT DID YOU TELL HIM?

NOTHING--EXCEPT THAT I WAS A NAZI-- THAT WAS ENOUGH!

THAT WAS UNWISE! HOWEVER, THE LOVESICK FOOL WILL PROBABLY KEEP THE INFORMATION TO HIMSELF! PERHAPS NOW YOU CAN CONCENTRATE ON MORE IMPORTANT MATTERS! *WILLY AND HANS* WILL BE HERE SOON ... THEY HAVE *PLANS* TO DISCUSS!

PLANS? PLANS TO DO *WHAT*?

---TO BLOW UP THE MILITARY HEADQUARTERS IN TOWN-- AND A FEW AMERICAN SWINE WITH IT!

"AS A FAITHFUL NAZI I SHOULD HAVE RECEIVED THIS NEWS WITH MORE ENTHUSIASM THAN I DID...WILLY AND HANS WERE FORMER S.S. MEN AND KNEW THEIR DEADLY WORK TO GRIM PERFECTION ...

THE BOMB IS PLANTED! IT WILL EXPLODE AT SIX, TOMORROW! IT IS TIME TO FIGHT BACK!

BUT, WILLY! THAT'S *MURDER*!

DO YOU CALL CARRYING OUT THE DESTINY OF THE THIRD REICH *MURDER*? THE FEUHRER HAS GIVEN ALL GERMANS A MISSION...ONLY *WE* ARE FIT TO RULE THE WORLD-- AND THOSE WHO STAND IN OUR WAY DESERVE TO DIE!

"THE THOUGHT THAT JACK WOULD BE ENDANGERED BY THIS MAD SCHEME DROVE ME TO RISK THE SUSPICION I HAD ALREADY DRAWN FROM MY SO-CALLED FRIENDS... THAT NIGHT I PASSED A NOTE UNDER THE DOOR OF CONSTABULARY HEADQUARTERS... HOWEVER, I HAD FORGOTTEN THAT JACK WAS FAMILIAR WITH MY HANDWRITING...

8

"TO KATE, WILLY AND HANS, THE DISCOVERY OF THE BOMB WAS AN UNFORSEEN ACCIDENT! THEY WERE DISCOVERED AND IMPRISONED BY THE DENAZIFICATION COURT---JACK STOPPED ME IN THE STREET THE NEXT DAY...

ANNALIESE! I WANT TO TALK TO YOU!

ANNALIESE, I WON'T ASK YOU HOW YOU KNEW OF THE BOMB... I WANT TO THANK YOU FOR SAVING MANY LIVES IN MY OUTFIT!--I ALSO WANT TO SAY GOODBYE--

G-GOODBYE? YOU - ARE-- LEAVING--?

YES, ANNALIESE -- I'M GOING HOME... WE'LL PROBABLY NEVER SEE EACH OTHER AGAIN .. I'LL *ALWAYS* LOVE YOU, ANNALIESE, BUT---

YES, I KNOW, JACK. OUR WORLDS ARE TOO FAR APART! YOUR WORLD IS BRIGHT WITH PROMISE--MINE STILL SMOULDERS FROM DARK HATREDS!

YOU'RE *LEARNING*, ANNALIESE ...THERE'S GOOD IN YOU. YOU'VE PROVEN THAT YOU'RE CAPABLE OF LOVING SINCERELY-- THAT'S A GOOD BEGINNING...KEEP THAT LOVE ALIVE IN YOUR HEART--IT WILL BE YOUR BRIGHT PROMISE! -AUFWEIDERSEHN--

"I WANTED TO PLEAD--TO BEG- TO THROW MYSELF IN HIS ARMS AND TELL HIM HOW DEEP MY LOVE REALLY WAS...BUT HE WAS HURRYING DOWN THE STREET BEFORE I COULD CRY OUT TO HIM...FOR ONE BRIEF INSTANT HE TURNED AND WAVED TO ME---AND THEN HE WAS GONE...

AUFWEIDERSEHN- --LIEBSCHEN--

"MY AMERICAN WAS BUT A TENDER MEMORY NOW.. ...HE HAD OPENED THE DOOR OF MY HEART SO I COULD SEE A LITTLE MORE OF THE TRUTH ... I KNEW, NOW, WHAT JACK HAD BEEN TRYING TO TELL ME: THAT ONE CANNOT HARBOR LOVE AND HATE IN THE SAME HEART...THAT ONE MUST LOVE *EVERYBODY* IN ORDER TO LOVE AT ALL...THE SUN SUDDENLY SPLASHED THE SHADOWED STREETS WITH WARM LIGHT...WAS IT AN OMEN?

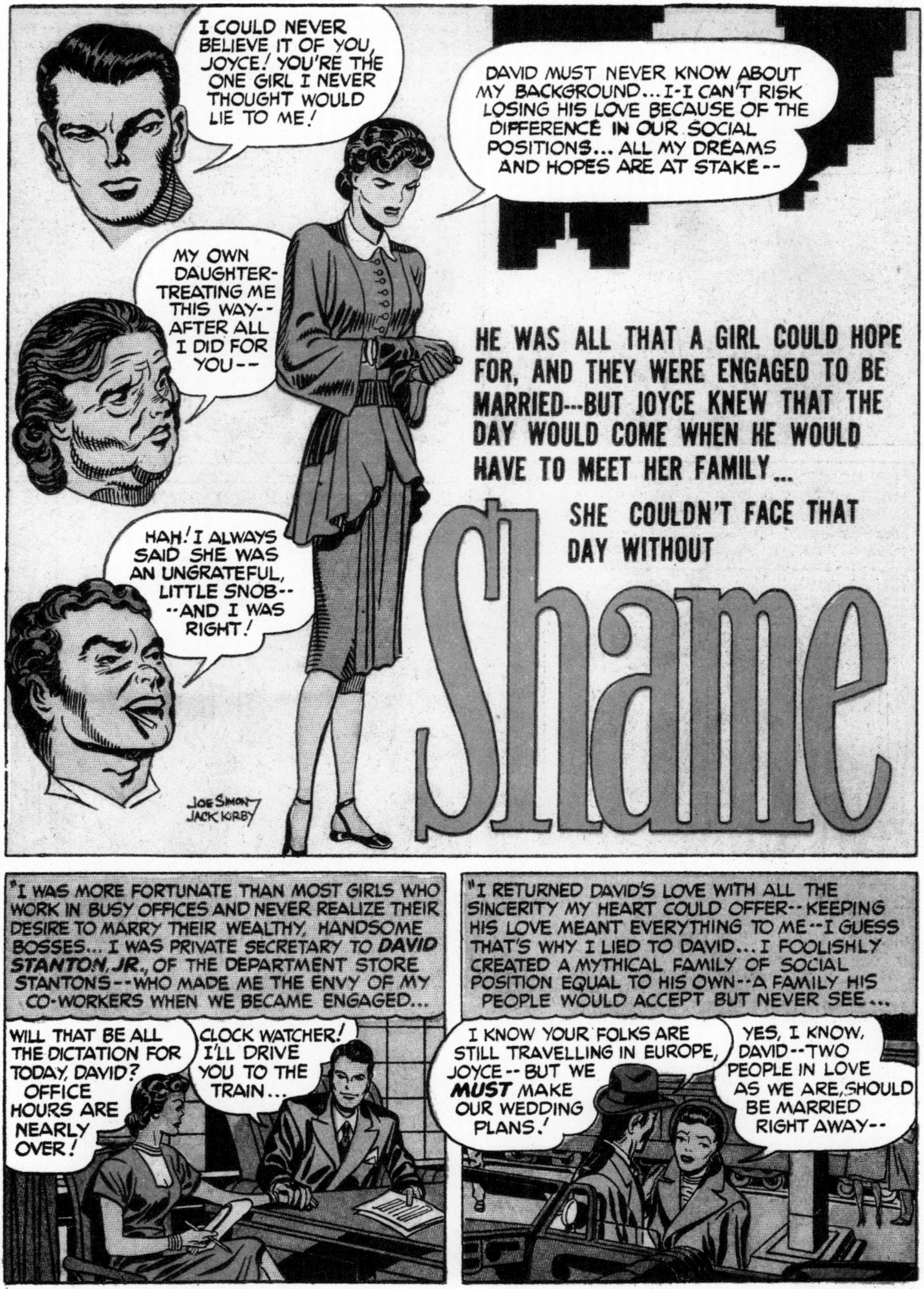
I COULD NEVER BELIEVE IT OF YOU, JOYCE! YOU'RE THE ONE GIRL I NEVER THOUGHT WOULD LIE TO ME!
DAVID MUST NEVER KNOW ABOUT MY BACKGROUND... I-I CAN'T RISK LOSING HIS LOVE BECAUSE OF THE DIFFERENCE IN OUR SOCIAL POSITIONS... ALL MY DREAMS AND HOPES ARE AT STAKE--
MY OWN DAUGHTER-TREATING ME THIS WAY--AFTER ALL I DID FOR YOU--
HAH! I ALWAYS SAID SHE WAS AN UNGRATEFUL, LITTLE SNOB----AND I WAS RIGHT!
HE WAS ALL THAT A GIRL COULD HOPE FOR, AND THEY WERE ENGAGED TO BE MARRIED---BUT JOYCE KNEW THAT THE DAY WOULD COME WHEN HE WOULD HAVE TO MEET HER FAMILY...
SHE COULDN'T FACE THAT DAY WITHOUT
Shame
JOE SIMON
JACK KIRBY
"I WAS MORE FORTUNATE THAN MOST GIRLS WHO WORK IN BUSY OFFICES AND NEVER REALIZE THEIR DESIRE TO MARRY THEIR WEALTHY, HANDSOME BOSSES... I WAS PRIVATE SECRETARY TO DAVID STANTON, JR., OF THE DEPARTMENT STORE STANTONS--WHO MADE ME THE ENVY OF MY CO-WORKERS WHEN WE BECAME ENGAGED...
WILL THAT BE ALL THE DICTATION FOR TODAY, DAVID? OFFICE HOURS ARE NEARLY OVER!
CLOCK WATCHER! I'LL DRIVE YOU TO THE TRAIN...
"I RETURNED DAVID'S LOVE WITH ALL THE SINCERITY MY HEART COULD OFFER--KEEPING HIS LOVE MEANT EVERYTHING TO ME--I GUESS THAT'S WHY I LIED TO DAVID... I FOOLISHLY CREATED A MYTHICAL FAMILY OF SOCIAL POSITION EQUAL TO HIS OWN--A FAMILY HIS PEOPLE WOULD ACCEPT BUT NEVER SEE...
I KNOW YOUR FOLKS ARE STILL TRAVELLING IN EUROPE, JOYCE--BUT WE MUST MAKE OUR WEDDING PLANS!
YES, I KNOW, DAVID--TWO PEOPLE IN LOVE AS WE ARE, SHOULD BE MARRIED RIGHT AWAY--

WE WON'T WAIT ANY LONGER, DARLING! I'LL WRITE DADDY TODAY, THAT HIS PAMPERED DAUGHTER IS *SIMPLY MAD* ABOUT HER HANDSOME BOSS!

--WHO INTENDS TO FIRE HER--AND MAKE HER *MRS. DAVID STANTON JR.*! YOU CAN WRITE *THAT* TO THE OLD BOY!

"A HALF HOUR LATER, I REACHED MY STATION--THE SHANTY DISTRICT--A PART OF TOWN IN WHICH DAVID STANTON'S KIND MOVED ONLY AS DETACHED SIGHTSEERS.. IT WAS A DIFFERENT WORLD--A GLOOMY, SHABBY WORLD--A RAGGED SPECTRE HAUNTING MY EVERY STEP TOWARD HAPPINESS!!

HELLO, JOYCE! HOW'S YOUR MA?

S-SHE'S FINE, MISTER SMITH!

"THE DRAFTY, WEATHER-BEATEN HOUSE ON WEST STREET, WHERE I WAS BORN AND RAISED, WAS STILL MY HOME... I LONGED DESPERATELY TO FLEE FROM IT--FOR COMFORT, SECURITY AND THE WARMTH OF DAVID'S ARMS!

YOU'RE HOME EARLY TONIGHT, JOYCE! WE'LL EAT AS SOON AS *HAL* COMES HOME.

I-I'M NOT TOO HUNGRY, MOM--

I'LL JUST HAVE SOME COFFEE AND TOAST.. I DON'T FEEL UP TO A BIG MEAL RIGHT NOW!

ALL RIGHT, JOYCE.. I UNDERSTAND, CHILD...

"MOM *DID* UNDERSTAND!! HANDICAPPED BY POVERTY AND POOR EDUCATION, SHE HAD ALWAYS USED EVERY OPPORTUNITY WITHIN HER REACH TO GIVE ME THE THINGS A CRUEL DESTINY HAD DENIED HER...

I-I'VE GOT A *SURPRISE* FOR YOU, JOYCE. IT'LL LOOK WONDERFUL ON YOU, HONEY.

WHY, MOM! IT LOOKS LIKE A FORMAL GOWN-- H-HOW ON EARTH DID YOU MANAGE TO BUY IT!

OH, MOM--*IT'S BEAUTIFUL!* YOU SHOULDN'T HAVE BOUGHT IT! YOU MUST HAVE SPENT YOUR ENTIRE SAVINGS!

WELL, I *HAVE* BEEN SAVING A LITTLE HERE AND THERE--AND I SAW THIS GOWN IN AN EXCLUSIVE SHOP---I DECIDED THAT I JUST *HAD* TO BUY IT FOR YOU!

YOU'RE SO GOOD TO ME, MOM! HOW AM I EVER GOING TO **REPAY** YOU FOR THE WAY YOU'VE STRUGGLED TO MAKE THIS MISERABLE EXISTENCE A LITTLE EASIER FOR ME TO BEAR?

NEVER MIND, BABY... YOU AREN'T LIKE YOUR BROTHER AND ME! --YOU'RE MEANT FOR BETTER THINGS ..DO YOU THINK YOUR YOUNG MAN WILL LIKE YOU IN THIS DRESS?

W-WHY HOW DID **YOU** KNOW ABOUT--?

A WOMAN CAN KEEP A SECRET FROM A MAN, HONEY -- BUT NEVER FROM ANOTHER WOMAN! I WAS NEVER A PRETTY GIRL, BUT I WAS YOUNG ONCE-- AND VERY GAY. WHEN I WOULD DRESS FOR A DATE WITH YOUR PA I'D LOOK IN THE MIRROR-AND SEE THE SAME LIGHT IN **MY** EYES AS THAT I'VE NOTICED IN **YOURS.**

BRAVO! BRAVO! NOW RING DOWN THE CURTAIN AND RUSTLE ME SOME CHOW, MOM--THIS SOAP OPERA STUFF MAKES ME CRY IN MY BEER!

HAL! IF YOU MUST LISTEN, I DO WISH YOU'D SPARE MOM YOUR VULGAR SARCASM!

"MY BROTHER, HAROLD, HAD DISLIKED ME EVER SINCE, AS A THREE YEAR OLD, HE HAD WITNESSED THE AFFECTION LAVISHED ON ME AT BIRTH... ALTHOUGH HAL POSSESSED SOME ADMIRABLE QUALITIES, HE WAS A TYPICAL WEST STREET TOUGH-- DARING THE WORLD TO STRIKE THE CHIP OFF HIS SHOULDER!

WELL, PARDON ME FOR NOT BOWIN' AT THE WAIST, DUCHESS.. WHERE'D YOU GET THE NEW DRESS? --NEW BOY FRIEND?

HAL!

YOU LOW-MINDED HOODLUM!

I'LL SHOW YOU WHO'S LOW-MINDED! YOU AND YOUR SMART-SET IDEAS! I'LL BEAT 'EM OUT OF YOU FAST ENOUGH!

YOU STOP THAT, HAL! **I** BOUGHT THIS GOWN FOR JOYCE! YOU'VE GOT NO RIGHT SAYING SUCH THINGS TO HER!

WHO SAYS I HAVEN'T! I'M PART OF THE FAMILY TOO, YOU KNOW! GO AHEAD, MOM- WORK YOURSELF SICK AND SAVE YOUR PENNIES TO PUT SIS IN THE BLUE BOOK! MAYBE ONE OF THESE DAYS SHE'LL DROP A DIME IN YOUR CUP WHEN SHE GOES SLUMMING THROUGH WEST STREET! AAAA-- PFFT!

"THE WIDE GULF EXISTING BETWEEN DAVID'S FAMILY AND MY OWN WAS REVEALED TO ME WITH TERRIFYING CLARITY IN HAL'S CRUDE DISPLAY... THE DAY THE STANTONS MET THE OWENS WOULD BE THE END OF ALL MY DREAMS. I WAS FRANTIC WITH WORRY!

I GUESS THAT TAKES CARE OF BUSINESS FOR TODAY. NOW, FOR SOME *PLEASURE*, MISS OWENS.. SHALL WE SAY COCKTAILS AT FIVE?

IF MY MASTER COMMANDS, HIS SLAVE OBEYS! OF COURSE, DAVID!

"ONLY WHEN I WAS WITH DAVID AT THE OFFICE WERE THE SOCIAL BARRIERS LOWERED TO ADMIT ME TO MY LOVE... EVERY LOGICAL THOUGHT TOLD ME I WAS AN IMPUDENT TRESSPASSER, YET MY HEART IGNORED ALL REASON... BUT AS DAVID AND I LEFT THE OFFICE BUILDING, MY BLOOD FROZE IN MY VEINS ---"

"COMING TOWARD US ACROSS THE LOBBY WAS *MY MOTHER!* I STOPPED--TRANSFIXED BY FEAR AND INDECISION... IN MOM'S EYES, RECOGNITION FLARED BUT WAS INSTANTLY HIDDEN BY LOWERED LIDS...SHE RUSTLED SOFTLY BY ME. WE MIGHT HAVE BEEN PERFECT STRANGERS..

ANYTHING WRONG, JOYCE?

WHY NO, DAVID -- I-I--

"MOM WAS STILL UP WHEN I CAME HOME THAT NIGHT. I DIDN'T RELISH FACING HER AFTER THE SHAMEFUL WAY I HAD TREATED HER....

OH--MOM-MOM--I-I MUST HAVE BEEN SO CRUEL--

DON'T FEEL THAT WAY, HONEY...I UNDERSTAND. NOW LET'S JUST FORGET WHAT HAPPENED ..LET'S GO TO YOUR ROOM... I'VE GOT SOMETHING TO SHOW YOU!

MOM! WHAT AN ADORABLE FUR JACKET! HOW DID YOU EVER *MANAGE* IT?

THAT'S *MY* SECRET, JOYCE. I JUST WANT TO HELP YOU IMPRESS YOUR YOUNG MAN! HE LOOKS *VERY* NICE!

"THAT WAS MOM.. ALWAYS UNDERSTANDING AND FORGIVING..I WASN'T WORTHY OF THE DEVOTION, LOYALTY AND GENEROSITY SHE SHOWED ME! I BEGAN TO TAKE THIS PRECIOUS WOMAN FOR GRANTED.. IN A FEW DAYS I WAS MY OLD SELF AGAIN AS I FACED DAVID ACROSS HIS DESK...

GET YOUR COAT, DARLING... AS SOON AS I'M THROUGH WITH THIS CALL, I'M GOING ON A BUYING TRIP IN THE TEXTILE DISTRICT. I'LL NEED YOU ALONG.

OH, SWELL! I LOVE TO LOOK OVER THOSE STUNNING NEW STYLES!

"I HAD A WONDERFUL TIME ACCOMPANYING DAVID ON HIS BUYING TRIP.. I WAS INTRODUCED EVERYWHERE AS DAVID'S FIANCE -- MY HEART KEPT JOYOUS PACE WITH OUR TOUR THROUGH THE CITY..

THIS IS THE LAST STOP, HONEY-- EVANS AND CASE! THIS OUTFIT HANDLES BROOMS AND MOPS AND STUFF *YOU* WON'T NEED WHEN YOU'RE MRS. DAVID STANTON JR.!

SILLY! I'D WORK MY FINGERS TO THE BONE FOR *YOU*, DARLING!

"AS WE ENTERED THE EXECUTIVE OFFICE OF EVANS AND CASE, I RECEIVED A SHOCK THAT DRAINED MY ENTIRE BEING OF ITS GAYETY AND FILLED ME WITH DREAD!

THAT SCRUB-WOMAN! IT'S MOM! *THAT'S* WHERE THE MONEY FOR THE DRESS AND JACKET CAME FROM!

I'LL FINISH IN HERE. YOU CAN SCRUB THE CORRIDOR OUTSIDE...

SHE HASN'T SEEN US.. AND SHE'S LEAVING! IF I TURN MY BACK, SHE'LL NEVER KNOW I WAS HERE!

DAVID! BE CAREFUL!

SAY, YOU PEOPLE MAKE SOME FINE MOPS, CASE!

OH! *HELP* -- I-I'M HURT!

CRASH!

IT'S THE SCRUB-WOMAN! SHE'S BEEN CUT!

MOM!

EASY, NOW- EASY! WE'VE GOT TO GET HER TO A HOSPITAL! THIS IS TERRIBLE!

MOM--OH MOM-- -WHY DID THIS HAVE TO HAPPEN?

5

JOYCE, I'M TAKING THIS WOMAN TO THE HOSPITAL.. RETURN TO THE OFFICE AND TELL THEM I WON'T BE BACK TODAY!

Y-YES, DAVID..OF COURSE!

"I CALLED THE OFFICE, BUT DIDN'T RETURN THERE... INSTEAD, I WALKED THE STREETS, MY MIND A WHIRLING CHAOS OF FOREBODING THOUGHTS!... SELFISHLY ENOUGH, DAVID'S DISCOVERY OF MY IDENTITY TROUBLED ME MORE THAN MOM'S CONDITION ...

IT LOOKS LIKE IT'S ALL OVER NOW... MY HOPES--MY PLANS-- ALL OVER ...

"SUDDENLY, THE ENORMITY OF THE LIE I WAS LIVING FILLED ME WITH SHAME!... MY BEHAVIOR TOWARD MY OWN MOTHER WAS ABOMINAL! THIS HUNGER FOR COMFORT AND SECURITY... WHAT HAD IT DONE TO ME? WHAT KIND OF CREATURE HAD I BECOME?

-AND MOM-- WHAT A MISERABLE DISAPPOINTMENT I'VE BEEN AS A DAUGHTER!

"SOMETHING WITHIN ME SEEMED TO RIGHTEN ITSELF AT THAT MOMENT... I BEGAN TO SEE THINGS IN A NEW PERSPECTIVE AND FOUND HOW LITTLE I AND MY SELF-CENTERED PLANS MATTERED NEXT TO GRAND PEOPLE LIKE MOM AND DAVID... I WAS OVERCOME WITH UNBEARABLE REMORSE...

I GUESS I DON'T DESERVE EITHER MOM OR DAVID'S LOVE NOW! THINGS WILL BE BETTER THIS WAY FOR US ALL!

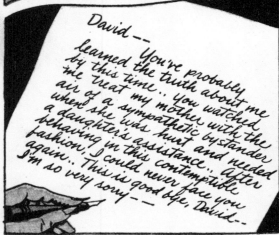

David --
You've probably learned the truth about me by this time.. You watched me treat my own mother with the air of a sympathetic bystander when she was hurt and needed a daughter's assistance.. After behaving in this contemptible fashion, I could never face you again.. This is good bye, David--
I'm so very sorry -- --

"AND SO I LEFT TOWN... WENT TO ANOTHER CITY WHERE I COULD START FROM SCRATCH... TO MAKE OF MYSELF THE KIND OF WOMAN WHO COULD FACE LIFE WITH THE COURAGE THE OLD JOYCE OWENS SORELY NEEDED...

THAT HAPPY PAIR MIGHT BE DAVID AND ME--IF I HADN'T BEEN THE SILLY *FOOL* I WAS--

6

"TWO MONTHS WENT BY.. I OBTAINED A JOB, GOOD LODGINGS AND FOR THE FIRST TIME, I FOUND A SERENITY I HAD NEVER KNOWN BEFORE...THEN, ONE EVENING, I HAD A VISITOR..."

HELLO, SIS!

W-WHY *HAL!* HOW DID YOU--?

HOW I FOUND YOU ISN'T IMPORTANT.. WHAT *DOES* MATTER IS THAT MOM IS KINDA WORRIED ABOUT YOU.. WHY DON'T YOU WRITE, SIS?

I-I DIDN'T THINK SHE'D EVER WANT TO HEAR FROM ME AGAIN AFTER HOW I ACTED.

THAT'S RIGHT! YOU CERTAINLY GAVE MOM A BUM DEAL.. I WAS ANGRY ENOUGH TO BLOW A FUSE--*BUT NOT MOM*--SHE'S SOFT ON YOU, I GUESS---ALWAYS HAS BEEN...SHE'S THE BEST, JOYCE--AND, NOW, SHE'S WORRIED SICK OVER YOU--

OH, HAL--WHY DID YOU COME? I-I'D ALMOST *FORGOTTEN* HOW ROTTEN I'D BEEN--

AW, SIS--IT WASN'T FAIR OF ME TO HIT LOW LIKE THAT.. I KNOW IT'S BEEN TOUGH FOR YOU--HAVING TO LIVE WITH YOUR MISTAKES ..I-I'M SORRY!

HAL, I'VE TRIED SO HARD TO BE SELF-RELIANT--TO MAKE MYSELF *WORTHY* OF MOM'S KINDNESS... I-I'VE WORKED SO HARD...

I KNOW, KID. I'VE BEEN KEEPING TABS ON YOU... SO HAS A *CERTAIN OTHER PARTY!* HE WAS THE ANGRIEST OF US ALL-- THE *SOFTEST* TOO, I GUESS--BUT THAT'S EASILY UNDERSTOOD--HE'S IN LOVE-- THE SAP! IT WON'T TAKE MUCH TO MAKE *HIM* COME AROUND...

HAL--YOU MEAN DAVID STILL--

--LOVES YOU? WHY, HE'S CRAZY ABOUT YOU--*FACT* IS-- WE *ALL* LOVE YOU, SIS! --MOM, MISTER BLUE BOOK --AND ME... WHY DON'T YOU COME HOME?

OH, YES, HAL, *YES!* I WANT SO MUCH TO GO HOME-- THE PEOPLE THERE ARE THE MOST WONDERFUL ON EARTH!

Just one year ago, this magazine published the story of Toni Benson, the girl they called "**Pick Up**." Our readers recognized Toni to be a living, heart-warming personality... For since the publication of her story, Young Romance has been flooded with numerous requests--asking one question---**Did Toni and her ex-gambler husband eventually find happiness in the town that didn't want them?** We decided to get the answer from Toni herself...

FOR WE KNEW THAT, UNLIKE FICTIONAL CHARACTERS, TONI'S PROBLEMS DID NOT END WITH HER MARRIAGE TO THE MAN SHE LOVED--THERE WAS STILL-

The TOWN and TONI BENSON!

SIMON·KIRBY

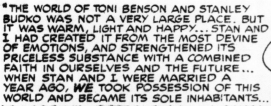

"THE WORLD OF TONI BENSON AND STANLEY BUDKO WAS NOT A VERY LARGE PLACE. BUT IT WAS WARM, LIGHT AND HAPPY... STAN AND I HAD CREATED IT FROM THE MOST DEVINE OF EMOTIONS, AND STRENGTHENED ITS PRICELESS SUBSTANCE WITH A COMBINED FAITH IN OURSELVES AND THE FUTURE... WHEN STAN AND I WERE MARRIED A YEAR AGO, **WE** TOOK POSSESSION OF THIS WORLD AND BECAME ITS SOLE INHABITANTS...

WE'VE BEEN MAN AND WIFE THREE DAYS, FIVE HOURS AND TEN MINUTES! ANY REGRETS, HONEY?

REGRET MARRYING THE HANDSOMEST, MOST CHARMING AND CONSIDERATE MAN IN THE WORLD? SURELY YOU'RE JOSHING, MISTER "B"!

THAT DOESN'T SEEM TO BE THE OPINION OF THE SO-CALLED **RESPECTABLE** CITIZENS OF BRADLEY, PENNSYLVANIA!

STRANGE-- I CAN'T RECALL EVER HEARING OF SUCH A TOWN... I DON'T BELIEVE IT **EXISTS**! NOTHING IS REAL OUTSIDE THIS ROOM!

STAN! I-I DON'T UNDERSTAND YOUR SUDDEN CHANGE OF MOOD. IT'S NOT LIKE YOU TO TAKE SUCH AN ISSUE SERIOUSLY... THE TOWN HAS NEVER TAKEN EITHER OF US TO ITS BOSOM.. BUT WE'VE NEVER LET IT DISTURB US!

IT DOES NOW, TONI! THINGS HAVE CHANGED, YOU KNOW...

YES, THINGS HAVE CHANGED... WE'RE **MARRIED**, TONI... OUR HAPPINESS NOW DEPENDS ON SOUND SECURITY... SECURITY WHICH WE MUST FIND IN BRADLEY!

BUT, DARLING, IF YOU FEEL OUR PROSPECTS ARE UNCERTAIN IN BRADLEY, WHY CAN'T WE TRY OUR FORTUNE IN SOME **OTHER** TOWN?

BECAUSE BRADLEY HAS JUST AS MUCH TO OFFER US AS ANY OTHER TOWN IN AMERICA!.. BECAUSE IT'S **OUR** TOWN... ...BECAUSE WE'RE NOT THE RUNNING KIND!

YOU'RE RIGHT, OF COURSE... OH, STAN, WE WERE SO HAPPY A MOMENT AGO-- UNTIL THIS SUBJECT AROSE...

I'M SORRY, PIGEON! BACK GOES BRADLEY INTO THE UNFINISHED BUSINESS FILE! **NOW**, MRS. BUDKO, HOW ABOUT SOME MORE LAUGHS!

YOU CAN'T WORM YOUR WAY OUT OF THIS UNFORGIVABLE BREACH OF MARRIED BLISS, STANLEY BUDKO! PUT ME DOWN, YOU, YOU HEEL!

"STAN AND I DID THE BEST WE COULD TO MAKE A HOME OF THE ROOM ADJOINING HIS SMALL GAS STATION REPAIR SHOP...STAN WAS STRIVING TO DEVELOP HIS TRADE, AND THE WEEKLY PROFITS WERE BARELY ENOUGH TO ENABLE US TO GET BY...HOWEVER, WE MANAGED TO PUT ASIDE ENOUGH EACH WEEK TO PAY FOR LITTLE IMPROVEMENTS IN OUR TINY LIVING QUARTERS...

IT'S AMAZING WHAT NEW WALLPAPER WILL DO FOR A PLACE!

AT A BUCK A ROLL, THIS PAPER *SHOULD* DO MIRACLES!

THAT SOUNDS LIKE THE PHONE, STAN! A MOTORIST IN DISTRESS, NO DOUBT! *I'LL* ANSWER IT!

R-R-RINNNGG!

OKAY, WHO IS IT? -- AND WHERE IS HIS CAR STRANDED?

TONI! DIDN'T YOU HEAR ME? HEY-- WHAT'S WRONG?

YES, DOCTOR JENKINS, AS SOON AS I CAN -- ER-- GOODBYE, SIR--

WELL, FOR PETE'S SAKE, TONI! *ANSWER ME!* WHAT'S HAPPENED?

THAT WAS DOCTOR JENKINS, GRAND-MOTHER'S HAD A BAD ATTACK... WE'VE GOT TO GO TO HER -- RIGHT AWAY -- STAN.. I'M AFRAID SHE'S --

"POOR GRANDMOTHER...LIFE HADN'T GIVEN HER MANY HAPPY MOMENTS -- ONLY A STOIC COURAGE TO WITHSTAND HER TRAGIC BURDENS...I HAD BEEN ONE OF THEM -- LEFT IN HER CARE BY A SCANDAL WHICH HOUNDED MY MOTHER FROM TOWN AND CAUSED THE DEATH OF MY FATHER... YEARS LATER, GRANDMOTHER WAS TO WITNESS ANOTHER SCANDAL EVOLVE FROM AN INNOCENT ESCAPADE WITH MYSELF AS THE SUBJECT OF GOSSIP... MY MARRIAGE TO STAN LEFT GRAND-MOTHER EMPTY AND BITTER -- FOR STAN WAS NEVER AMONG THE TOWN'S MORE DESIRABLE CATCHES...

I DON'T THINK THERE'S ANY CAUSE FOR ALARM, TONI.. YOUR GRANNY'S PULLED OUT OF THESE ATTACKS BEFORE.

HURRY, STAN.. PLEASE HURRY--

BUDKO'S TOWING SERVICE

3

"THE BENSON HOUSE, BUILT BY MY FATHER'S FAMILY, ROSE TALL AND WHITE ABOVE THE STATELY OLD ELM TREE... LIKE ALL THE OTHER HOUSES ON AIKEN STREET... ITS LINES BORE THE STRAIGHT-LACED PROPRIETY OF BRADLEY'S GOD-FEARING ELDERS...

MAYBE IT'S BEST THAT I WAIT OUT HERE, TONI. YOU KNOW HOW YOUR GRANDMOTHER FEELS TOWARDS ME!

NO, STAN! WE GO TOGETHER! YOU'RE MY HUSBAND! A MAN WHO CAN HOLD HIS HEAD HIGH IN FRONT OF ANYBODY!

ALL RIGHT, CHICKEN, I'VE NOTHING TO BE ASHAMED OF...

"GRANDMOTHER LAY MOTIONLESS IN THE SNOWY WHITENESS OF HER GREAT BED... THERE WAS LITTLE LEFT OF LIFE IN THE ASHEN, WAX-LIKE FEATURES. I DIDN'T STIFLE THE INCOHERENT SOUND THAT ESCAPED MY LIPS IN MY UNHEEDING DASH TO GRAND-MOTHER'S BEDSIDE... THE YEARS THAT BOUND US WERE SNAPPING CORDS OF LIVING TISSUES THAT INFLICTED HORRIBLE PAIN UPON US BOTH AS THE HAND OF DEATH REACHED TO SEVER THE LAST REMAINING STRAND...

TONI - CHILD-- MY-- POOR SWEET, CHILD--

"A BRIGHT LIGHT FLARED MOMENTARILY IN THE CAVERNOUS SHADOWS OF GRANDMOTHER'S EYES WHEN HER GAZE FELL UPON STAN... HE READ THE SUMMONS AND CAME QUIETLY FORWARD.. I FELT HIS PRESENCE BESIDE ME-- TENSE AND WAITING --UNAFRAID OF WHATEVER MIGHT COME FROM THOSE BLOODLESS LIPS...

STANLEY BUDKO-- I-- I'VE CALLED YOU BY MANY NAMES --ALL OF THEM BAD-- IT IS A SINFUL THING I-- I MUST TAKE WITH ME ...

WE SOMETIMES FORGET UNTIL THE LAST MOMENT THAT WE'RE NOTHING BUT CLAY.. THAT JUDGING OTHERS IS THE PRIVILEGE OF A HIGHER POWER.. YOU CAME TO US FROM THE DREGS OF TOWN WITH A STRANGE NAME AND THE STIGMA OF THAT DISTRICT.. YET I WILL CALL YOU SON, FOR WHEN I LEAVE, YOU WILL BE A BENSON...

"STANLEY'S SHADOW STIRRED ON THE DELICATE PATTERN'S OF GRANDMOTHER'S BLANKET... IT WAS OBVIOUS THAT THE FADING VOICE HAD DRAWN A REACTION EQUAL TO THE UNEXPECTED WORDS...

I GO WITH-- FAITH IN BOTH OF YOU-- MY CHILDREN-- --MY-- EH...

4

"EXCEPT FOR MY SMOTHERED SOBS, THE ROOM WAS HEAVY WITH THE STILLNESS OF ETERNITY.. THEN THERE WAS THE SOFT TREAD OF DOCTOR JENKINS AND THE STRONG ARMS OF STAN LIFTING ME TO THE SMOOTH FOLDS OF HIS LEATHER JACKET... GRANDMOTHER WAS GONE-- LEAVING IN HER PASSING A MEMORY FOREVER STAMPED IN OUR HEARTS..."

GOODBYE, SARAH..YOU WERE A GOOD WOMAN----A GOOD WOMAN--

STANLEY BUDKO-- WHAT I KNOW ABOUT YOU IS STRICTLY TOWN GOSSIP... BUT I'VE BEEN SARAH BENSON'S GOOD FRIEND FOR MANY YEARS... BELIEVE ME WHEN I TELL YOU THAT HERS WERE NOT MERELY THE WORDS OF A DYING WOMAN ... YOU ARE A BENSON!-- AT LEAST YOU CAN BE ONE! YOU'LL KNOW WHAT I MEAN IN A FEW DAYS...

"GRANDMOTHER HAD EVIDENTLY CONFIDED IN DOCTOR JENKINS.. WHAT HE MEANT TO CONVEY STOOD OUT IN BOLD RELIEF IN GRANDMOTHER'S LEGACY...ALBERT RHEINBECK, THE FAMILY ATTORNEY, UNDERSCORED THE MEANING OF IT WHEN HE CALLED STAN AND MYSELF TO HIS OFFICE LATER THAT WEEK..."

THE BENSON HOUSE AND PROPERTY NOW BELONG TO BOTH OF YOU...THAT'S ABOUT ALL THERE IS!

YOU MEAN THE HOUSE IS OURS?

BOTH OF US?

YES, YOU'RE CO-OWNER OF THE BENSON HOUSE, BUDKO.. IT'S A GREAT STROKE OF FORTUNE FOR AN EX-GAMBLER WHO CAN USE THE PROPERTY FOR READY CASH-- BUT IT CAN BE AN EVEN GREATER GIFT TO A MAN WHO'S BUILDING A SOUND FUTURE!

SEE HERE, RHEINBECK--

I KNOW YOU OPERATE A SMALL GAS STATION. BUT I'M ALSO AWARE OF YOUR EARLIER AFFILIATIONS! THAT'S WHY, AS A BENSON FRIEND AS WELL AS LEGAL ADVISOR, I CAUTIONED SARAH AGAINST THIS MOVE... BUT SHE ACTED ACCORDING TO HER OWN PLAN... A PLAN I STILL CONSIDER TO BE A FINE WOMAN'S VAIN HOPE!

I BELIEVE YOU'VE SAID QUITE ENOUGH, MISTER RHEINBECK!

THERE WAS NO INTENT ON MY PART TO OFFEND EITHER OF YOU, TONI! BETWEEN LAWYER AND CLIENT, A SPADE BY ANY OTHER NAME IS STILL A SPADE... I SINCERELY HOPE YOU PROVE ME A CYNICAL AND SUSPICIOUS OLD MAN!

YOU'VE PROVEN THAT YOURSELF, RHEINBECK! I'D ADVISE YOU TO LOOK TO *YOUR OWN* LINEN! IT'S NOT AS WHITE AS IT APPEARS!

INDIGNANT AS YOU'VE MADE US FEEL, MISTER RHEINBECK, WE REALIZE YOUR INTENTIONS WERE NOT ENTIRELY TAINTED BY PREJUDICE... BUT I ASSURE YOU THAT IT AFFORDS US LITTLE COMFORT! GOOD DAY, SIR!

"WE WERE TOO PRE-OCCUPIED BY THOUGHT TO SAY MUCH DURING THE DRIVE BACK TO THE GAS STATION... EXCEPT FOR OCCASIONAL GLANCES AT THE SURROUNDING TRAFFIC, STAN'S EYES STARED WITH SMOLDERING INTENSITY AT SOME FIXED OBJECT AHEAD-- VISIBLE ONLY TO HIMSELF... HOW WOULD HIS CONFUSED AND TORTURED MIND RATIONALIZE THESE UNFORSEEN DEVELOP- MENTS? I PUT AN END TO THE CONFLICT IN MY OWN BRAIN-- AND TABLED ALL DECISIONS FOR THE NEAR FUTURE...

WE'RE ALMOST HOME, STAN.. IS THERE ANYTHING YOU'D PARTICULARLY LIKE FOR DINNER?

WHAT? OH! WHY, WHATEVER YOU SERVE TONIGHT WILL DO, HONEY!

"THAT EVENING, WE RECEIVED TWO VISITORS WHO, TO ME, WERE AS UNEXPECTED AS SNOW IN JULY... STRANGELY ENOUGH, STAN DIDN'T REGISTER ANY SURPRISE AT THEIR SUDDEN APPEARANCE. WHATEVER THE PURPOSE OF THE VISIT, I THOUGHT, THERE WOULD BE MANY A RAISED EYE- BROW AMONG THE TOWN'S INFLUENTIAL FAMILIES WHEN IT WAS LEARNED THAT AMON CLEVELAND AND HIS SON MARSHALL, PAID A PERSONAL CALL ON THOSE QUESTION- ABLE BUDKO'S!

GOOD EVENING, BUDKO. I HOPE YOU DON'T MIND OUR DROPPING IN LIKE THIS!

I DON'T-- IF *YOU* DON'T, MISTER CLEVELAND. HELLO, MARSH!

HELLO, STAN-- SEEMS LIKE YEARS SINCE WE PLAYED BALL TOGETHER AT HUDSON HIGH!

AND YOU, TONI-- A GROWN, MARRIED WOMAN! MY-- MY.. I'M SORRY TO HEAR ABOUT YOUR GRAND- MOTHER, MY DEAR!

WON'T YOU SIT DOWN?

YOU KNOW, BUDKO, UNLIKE OTHERS IN THIS TOWN, I'VE ALWAYS MAINTAINED THAT A MAN IS ENTITLED TO LIVE IN ANY MANNER IN WHICH HE CHOOSES.. HIS VICES AND VIRTUES SHOULD BE HIS *OWN* AFFAIR...

THAT'S A VERY LIBERAL ATTITUDE, MISTER CLEVELAND. UNFORTUNATELY, IN BRADLEY, SUCH PHILOSOPHIES ARE A RARITY!

HA-HA-HEH-HEH-- HOW WELL I KNOW, MY BOY! DON'T THINK OLD AMON CLEVELAND HAS *ALWAYS* ESCAPED THE TOWN'S WAGGING TONGUES! LIKE MARSHALL, HERE, I SOWED MANY A WILD OAT UNTIL THE OLD MAN TOOK A HAND AND PUSHED ME, NOSE FIRST, INTO THE *REAL ESTATE BUSINESS!* FACT IS, I STILL TAKE AN OCCASIONAL NIP, AND PLACE A WAGER NOW AND THEN!

YES.. I REMEMBER SEEING YOU QUITE OFTEN WHEN I WORKED FOR MCCREEDY AT THE GAMBLING CASINO.. YOU USUALLY DID OKAY, TOO!

AHEM--ER- OF COURSE - WELL, A MAN HAS TO RELAX FROM THE PRESSURE OF RESPONSIBILITIES! BUT SPEAKING OF GOOD FORTUNE, BUDKO, I UNDERSTAND THAT YOU TWO FOUND A LARGE SHARE OF IT IN SARAH BENSON'S LEGACY!

WE DON'T CONSIDER GRANDMOTHER'S PASSING "GOOD FORTUNE", MISTER CLEVELAND..

THAT'S NOT WHAT I MEANT, CHILD.. SARAH BENSON'S DEATH WAS A GREAT SHOCK TO US ALL! BUT NEVERTHELESS SHE IS GONE--AND YOU TWO ARE IN POSSESSION OF THE BENSON HOUSE AND PROPERTY-- VERY VALUABLE ASSETS -- VERY, VERY VALUABLE...

COULD MEAN A LOT OF "READY CASH" FOR US, EH?

TWELVE THOUSAND GOOD AMERICAN DOLLARS -- ANY TIME YOU WANT IT-- BUDKO! THAT'S WHAT THE REAL ESTATE FIRM OF CLEVELAND AND SON THINKS OF THAT PROPERTY! ANY TIME YOU WANT IT ---

THAT'S VERY INTERESTING, MISTER CLEVELAND.. BUT IT'S A LITTLE TOO SOON FOR EITHER TONI OR MYSELF TO BE THINKING ABOUT ANY OFFERS...

OH, NOW, WE'RE NOT SO CALLOUS AS TO PROPOSE ANY DEAL AT THIS TIME!

IT'S SOMETHING TO THINK ABOUT, THOUGH .. THAT KIND OF CAPITAL COULD GO A LONG WAY TOWARDS EASING THE BURDEN FOR A YOUNG, MARRIED COUPLE LIKE YOURSELVES

I SEE...

WELL MARSHALL AND I CERTAINLY ENJOYED CALLING ON YOU YOUNGSTERS! YOU'RE MAKING A FINE BEGINNING HERE.. YOU DESERVE MUCH MORE ENCOURAGEMENT THAN THE COMMUNITY HAS GIVEN YOU. GOOD NIGHT...

SHREWD YOUNG PEOPLE, THOSE TWO.. SO PROPERLY INDIGNANT AT DISCUSSING BUSINESS IN TIME OF MOURNING...AND AS EAGER FOR THE MONEY AS **WE** ARE FOR THE PROPERTY!

I DON'T KNOW... THEY SEEMED RATHER SINCERE! STAN WAS NEVER A GERANIUM -- BUT HE WAS A LIKEABLE SORT WHEN I KNEW HIM AT SCHOOL!

DON'T BE A COMPLETE IDIOT, MARSHALL. BUDKO HAS TRAVELLED WITH THE WORST ELEMENT IN TOWN SINCE HE FIRST BEGAN TO EARN HIS DOLLAR. TONI AND HE ARE TWO OF A KIND.. THEY'LL TURN POOR SARAH'S LEGACY INTO AS MUCH MONEY AS IT WILL BRING... WE'LL HEAR FROM THEM SOON ENOUGH. MARK MY WORDS!

"UNTIL THE COMING OF THE LEGACY, THE TOWN'S PREJUDICE AGAINST BOTH STAN AND MYSELF HAD CLOAKED ITS EXISTENCE IN THE UNPLEASANT SILENCE OF A GLARE AND THE EVIL HISS OF DISTORTED RUMOR... BUT, NOW, IT STOOD ON OUR DOORSTEP -- MOCKING AND UNASHAMED -- A CHALLENGE TO OUR SELF-RESPECT... A DEAD WOMAN HAD PLANNED THIS SITUATION -- AND, SOMEHOW I FELT SHE WAS WATCHING THE OUTCOME...

TONI -- I-- I WISH TO HEAVEN YOUR GRANNY HADN'T DONE THIS THING!

I KNOW ALL THIS HAS DISTURBED YOU DREADFULLY, STAN... BUT LETS NOT BE GOADED INTO ANY EMOTIONAL DECISIONS WHICH ONLY THESE NASTY SNOBS WOULD PROFIT BY!

HAH! THAT'S NO LIE! THOSE REAL ESTATE JACKALS STAND TO MAKE A PRETTY PENNY ONCE THEY BUY THE BENSON HOUSE! BUT THAT'S NOT THE ISSUE!

YOU MEAN **WE'RE** THE ISSUE! STAN WE MUSTN'T ALLOW THE TOWN TO INVADE OUR LIVES THIS WAY! IT'S BOUND TO CAUSE US GREAT UNHAPPINESS!

ON THE CONTRARY, CHICKEN.. OUR ONLY CHANCE FOR HAPPINESS AMONG THESE PEOPLE IS TO WADE INTO THEIR OWN MIDST AND ESTABLISH A RESPECTED HOUSE-HOLD TO MATCH ANY IN TOWN! THAT'S OUR **GOAL!** THAT'S OUR ONLY WAY TO PEACE OF MIND AND A GOOD LIFE!

WE'LL **KEEP** THE BENSON HOUSE, TONI! THAT'S OUR BEACH-HEAD! IT'LL TAKE STAMINA AND COURAGE TO SECURE IT TILL WE'VE WON.. ANY VOLUNTEERS FOR THE MISSION?

HERE'S ONE, MISTER! SINK OR SWIM, I'M WITH YOU! I'VE NEVER BEEN MORE PROUD OF ANYONE IN MY LIFE!

"INCORPORATING THE BENSON HOUSE INTO OUR BUDGET PROVED TO BE A MATHEMATICAL IMPOSSIBILITY... STAN AND I WORKED DILIGENTLY FOR HOURS ON END UNTIL OUR FINGERS COULD NO LONGER HOLD A PENCIL-- UNTIL EVERY CHANNEL OF THOUGHT HAD BEEN DRAINED OF ITS CONTENTS...I GAZED WEARILY ACROSS THE TABLE AT STAN. HE CRUSHED ANOTHER CIGARETTE STUB INTO THE CRUMPLED MASS OF ITS HALF SMOKED PREDESSESORS AND FACED ME WITH A FOOLISH GRIN...

WELL, BABY, THESE FIGURES *STILL* ADD UP TO THE SAME TOTAL-- NO CAN DO!

NO--OUR PRESENT INCOME WILL NEVER MEET THE ADDED EXPENSE OF MAINTAINING THE BENSON HOUSE!

OF COURSE, BUSINESS IS GOOD--AND GETTING BETTER..BUT PROPERTY TAXES AND NEEDED REPAIRS WON'T WAIT FOR *FUTURE* PROFIT INCREASE...

WE COULD SECURE A LOAN FROM THE BANK, STAN... PAY IT BACK IN SMALL INSTALLMENTS WHILE THE BUSINESS GROWS.

YEAAP-- MIGHT BE THE ANSWER--FOR A SMITH OR JONES.. BUT NOT FOR A *BUDKO*...OLD MAN SCOTT DOESN'T GIVE LOANS TO UNSAVORY CHARACTERS.. REMEMBER? I'M TIRED-- BABY...WE'LL HIT ON AN ANGLE TOMORROW!

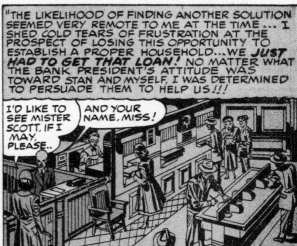

"THE LIKELIHOOD OF FINDING ANOTHER SOLUTION SEEMED VERY REMOTE TO ME AT THE TIME ... I SHED COLD TEARS OF FRUSTRATION AT THE PROSPECT OF LOSING THIS OPPORTUNITY TO ESTABLISH A PROPER HOUSEHOLD...WE *JUST HAD TO GET THAT LOAN!* NO MATTER WHAT THE BANK PRESIDENT'S ATTITUDE WAS TOWARD STAN AND MYSELF, I WAS DETERMINED TO PERSUADE THEM TO HELP US!!!

I'D LIKE TO SEE MISTER SCOTT, IF I MAY, PLEASE..

AND YOUR NAME, MISS!

THAT'S ALL RIGHT, JENNINGS. I KNOW THE YOUNG LADY... HELLO, TONI!

WHY, BOB! BOB SCOTT! MY GOODNESS-- IT SEEMS AGES SINCE I'VE SEEN YOU... I-I CAME TO SEE YOUR FATHER...

DAD'S BUSY RIGHT NOW..MAYBE I CAN BE OF SOME SERVICE.. WON'T YOU COME INTO THE OFFICE!

THANK YOU, BOB! I CAN *USE* SOME ASSISTANCE!

"A FEW MOMENTS LATER, I SAT OPPOSITE THIS FORMAL, WELL GROOMED, YOUNG EXECUTIVE IN HIS PATRICIAN SURROUNDINGS OF RICH LEATHER AND PANELLED OAK.. IT STRUCK ME AS INCONCEIVABLE THAT ONLY TWO YEARS BEFORE THIS SAME BOB SCOTT HAD LED ME ON A MADCAP TOUR OF NIGHT CLUBS AND INVOLVED ME IN A SCANDALOUS GAMBLING RAID--THAT THIS INGRATIATING VOICE ADDRESSING ME SO PATRONIZINGLY HAD ONCE SO WRONGFULLY CALLED ME 'PICK UP!'...

IT'S BEEN TWO YEARS HASN'T IT, TONI? I UNDERSTAND YOU MARRIED THAT CHAP.. WHAT'S HIS NAME-- OH, YES! BUDKO-- STAN BUDKO-- FUNNY MY FORGETTING THE NAME OF A MAN WHO GAVE ME A "SHINER!"

YOU'VE MADE GREAT STRIDES SINCE THOSE DAYS, BOB... SURELY YOU'VE BECOME TOO BIG A MAN TO HARBOR GRUDGES!

OH, PLEASE DON'T MISUNDER-STAND, TONI! I DESERVED THAT WALLOP FOR TRYING TO RUN OUT ON YOU DURING THE GAMBLING RAID! I CERTAINLY WAS A WILD UNPRINCIPLED STINKER WASN'T I?--AND YET IT'S NOSTALGIA I FEEL RATHER THAN REGRET-- WHY SHOULD THAT BE, TONI?

WHO CAN SAY, BOB? LIFE WAS MADE FOR LAUGHS IN THOSE DAYS...THERE WAS LITTLE TIME FOR CARES OR RESPONSIBILITIES!

YES, LIFE, THEN, WAS GREAT FUN. GUESS I WAS QUITE THE CUT-UP. THE PACE HAS SLOWED DOWN TO A MORE DIGNIFIED WALK THESE PAST TWO YEARS.. I'VE MARRIED TOO, YOU KNOW... SOPHIE MORRISON-- PROMINENT FAMILY BACKGROUND-- YOU MUST HAVE READ THE PAPERS. I'VE LIVED A MOST EXEMPLARY EXISTENCE... IT'S A "MUST" FOR MEN IN FINANCE!

"POOR BOB... IT WASN'T DIFFICULT TO SEE THAT HIS RESTLESS SPIRIT HAD NOT COMPLETELY ADJUSTED ITSELF TO THE RIGID MORES OF HIS SOCIAL GROUP... HOWEVER, THIS MUTUAL REMINISCING WAS CONSUMING PRECIOUS TIME NEEDED FOR THE EFFECTIVE PRESENTA-TION OF MY PROBLEM ... I DISCREETLY SHUT THE DOOR TO THE PAST AND BROUGHT BOB'S ATTENTION TO THE ORIGINAL PURPOSE OF MY CALL ...

--AND THAT ABOUT SUMS UP OUR SITUATION, BOB..A LOAN AT THIS TIME WILL HELP US HOLD THE BENSON HOUSE!

UH-HUH--I SEE! OF COURSE YOU REALIZE YOU MAY HAVE TO MORTGAGE THIS HERITAGE-- UNLESS STAN HAS OTHER COLLAT-ERAL!

BUT THAT'S PUTTING THE CART BEFORE THE HORSE! THERE'S DAD TO RECKON WITH FIRST.. HIS IS THE FINAL WORD IN THESE MATTERS.. I'LL DO EVERY-THING I CAN FOR YOU, TONI ...FOR OLD TIME'S SAKE, EH?

DEAR ME! HOW PROGRESSIVE THIS STODGY OLD BANKING BUSINESS HAS BECOME. HOW UTTERLY REVOLUTION-ARY! BUT, THEN IT IS SO LIKE BOB TO BLAZE NEW TRAILS!

10

"MY MEETING WITH SOPHIE MORRISON SCOTT RECALLED TO MY MIND THE JUNGLE SEQUENCE OF AN OLD MOVIE IN WHICH THE UNARMED NATIVE HAVING BEEN FROZEN INTO IMMOBILITY BY THE OMINOUS LOW RUMBLE OF SOUND BEHIND HIM, TURNS SLOWLY ABOUT—AND WATCHES WITH TERRIBLE FASCINATION THE STEALTHY MOVEMENTS OF THE TIGRESS AS HER SLEEK, CAT-LIKE SHAPE EMERGES INTO FULL VIEW... PEERING OUT OF SOPHIE'S BLASÉ MASK WAS A PREDATORY ANIMAL POISED TO SPRING...

YOU HAVE A TALENT FOR DISTORTING WHAT YOU SEE, MY DEAR... THIS IS TONI BENSON... WE WERE CLASSMATES IN SCHOOL.

SCHOOL MUST HAVE BEEN FUN! I SUPPOSE YOU BOTH WERE HOLDING HANDS IN THOSE DAYS TOO.

I—I MUST BE GOING, BOB! STAN AND I WOULD BE VERY GRATEFUL IF THE BANK WOULD EXTEND US THE LOAN... GOODBYE, MRS. SCOTT...

I'LL DO MY BEST WITH DAD, TONI. YOU CAN BE SURE OF THAT! WE'LL GET IN TOUCH WITH YOU!

"THE QUARREL I KNEW WAS BREWING BROKE IN FULL FURY BEFORE I HAD CLOSED THE DOOR TO BOB'S OFFICE... THE BANK EMPLOYEES NEARBY MADE NO EFFORT TO DISGUISE THEIR INTEREST IN WHAT WAS TRANSPIRING... EACH SCRUTINIZING GLANCE HELD ITS OWN NASTY CONCLUSION.

"I DID MY SHOPPING THAT AFTERNOON UNDER A LINGERING CLOUD OF APPREHENSION — HOPING THAT THE UNFORTUNATE INCIDENT WOULDN'T JEOPARDIZE MY CHANCES FOR A LOAN... BUT SOPHIE SCOTT'S JEALOUS WRATH WAS DESTINED TO PROVOKE A SITUATION WITH MUCH GRAVER CONSEQUENCES... WHEN I RETURNED HOME AT FOUR... ITS DARK SHADOW HAD ALREADY FALLEN...

WHY, DARLING! I DIDN'T EXPECT TO FIND YOU IN BEFORE SUPPER TIME!

TONI... WHERE ON EARTH HAVE YOU BEEN?

LOTS OF PLACES, STAN... ..THE MARKET— THE DEPARTMENT STORES— THE BANK— WHY DO YOU ASK?

THE BANK—JUST LIKE THAT, YOU SAY IT— THE BANK!

STAN! WHAT ARE YOU DRIVING AT? WHAT'S HAPPENED?

YOU TELL ME, BABY! THERE ARE 59 DIFFERENT VERSIONS FLOATING ABOUT TOWN! EACH ONE MORE SORDID THAN THE OTHER!

OH, NO, STAN! IT **COULDN'T** HAVE GONE THAT FAR! WHY, THE WHOLE THING IS SO RIDICULOUS! I NEVER DREAMED IT WOULD HAVE SUCH REPERCUSSIONS! STAN THIS IS TERRIBLE!

YES, IT DIDN'T TAKE THE TOWN LONG TO MAKE YOUR LITTLE TRIP TO THE BANK THE DAY'S NUMBER ONE TOPIC!

I ALMOST **BEAT** THE STORY OUT OF HARVEY GRIFFIN WHEN HE STOPPED FOR GAS AND STARTED DROPPING SIX CRACKS!.. MY TEMPER GOT OUT OF HAND THEN...I TOOK OFF TO CONFRONT BOB SCOTT FOR THE TRUTH! HE BECAME IMPATIENT AND ABUSIVE! I--I THINK HE'LL NEED A NEW UPPER PLATE!

YOU-- **FOUGHT**-- WITH--BOB ---OVER SUCH A SILLY--- OVER **NOTHING AT ALL!**

STAN--STAN-- HOW COULD YOU BE TAKEN IN BY SUCH AN UNFOUNDED TALE? IF THERE WAS ANY POSSIBILITY OF A LOAN AT ALL-- IT'S GONE NOW... STAN-- I FEEL **SO** TIRED -- SO INEFFECTIVE--

BELIEVE ME, TONI, I NEVER DOUBTED YOU FOR A SECOND! BUT IT ALL HAPPENED SO SUDDENLY-- LIKE BEING HIT BY A ROTTEN TOMATO-- I--I JUST LOST MY HEAD!

I KNOW THIS WON'T BOOST OUR MORALE, DARLING -- BUT I'M GOING TO CRY... FORGIVE ME, STAN..I-I JUST CAN'T HELP MYSELF...

CUT LOOSE, HONEY, I'VE STILL GOT ANOTHER SHIRT. BLAST IT, TONI. IT ISN'T FAIR! THIS TOWN JUST **WON'T** GIVE US A CHANCE!

WELL, I'M THROUGH PLAYING WHIPPING BOY FOR THE "**HOLIER THAN THOU**" CROWD IN TOWN... I KNOW SOMEONE WHO **ISN'T** SQUEAMISH ABOUT DEALING WITH STAN BUDKO! HELLO, OPERATOR! I WANT LANE 4-7301!

STAN! WHOM ARE YOU CALLING?

WHO IS THIS -- CHIPS? YEAH, HOW'S TRICKS? LISTEN, IS McCREEDY IN? I'VE GOT TO TALK TO HIM!

McCREEDY-- **THE GAMBLER!** STAN! I WON'T LET YOU DO THIS!

STOP IT, TONI! THERE'S NO OTHER ALTERNATIVE! YOUR GRANNY DIDN'T LEAVE THAT HOUSE TO ANYONE BUT US! NOW I'M FIGHTING FOR IT IN THE ONLY WAY LEFT TO ME!

NOT *THAT* WAY, STAN! THAT'S NOT WHAT GRANDMOTHER WANTED!

DON'T YOU SEE THAT IT WASN'T THE HOUSE ITSELF THAT GRANDMOTHER MEANT US TO HAVE!-- BUT THE HONEST, DECENT LIFE IT REPRESENTED! SHE WOULD HAVE RATHER SEEN US LOSE THE *HOUSE* THAN OUR *SELF RESPECT!*

I'LL LEAVE THE NOBLE IDEALS FOR SUCH PEOPLE AS THE SCOTTS, TONI.. THEY'VE MONEY ENOUGH TO *AFFORD* RIGHTEOUSNESS! HELLO, THIS YOU, McCREEDY?

LISTEN, McCREEDY, I'D LIKE TO SEE YOU TONIGHT. SURE IT CONCERNS *DOUGH!* YES, IT'S IMPORTANT! I'M IN A SPOT.. AND YOU'RE THE GUY TO HELP ME! OKAY, I'LL BE DOWN IN ABOUT A HALF HOUR OR SO...

I'M GOING TO SEE McCREEDY, TONI. WHEN I COME BACK -- WE'LL HAVE THAT HOUSE!

BUT LITTLE ELSE, STAN.. USING McCREEDY'S MONEY TO BUILD A GOOD LIFE WOULD MAKE A HOLLOW MOCKERY OF EVERYTHING WE'RE STRIVING FOR! WE'D NEVER KNOW HAPPINESS AGAIN!

I COULD NEVER HAVE BOUGHT THIS GAS STATION WITHOUT THE MONEY I EARNED AT McCREEDY'S CASINO! WE HAVEN'T FELT TAINTED BY IT SO FAR!

YOU CAN'T SELL ME ON THAT, STAN.. IF YOU GO THROUGH WITH THIS MADNESS.. I WON'T BE HERE WHEN YOU GET BACK...

SLAM!

"I SAT ROOTED TO THE CHAIR--HORRIBLY SHAKEN BY THE VIOLENCE OF STAN'S DEPARTURE... TIME ITSELF HAD DISINTEGRATED IN ONE CLAP OF THUNDER--LEAVING NO PAST-- NO PRESENT--NOTHING VISIBLE AHEAD. NOTHING REMAINED--BUT THE FIRMNESS OF CONVICTION--A POOR REPLACEMENT FOR A SHATTERED HEART... BUT EMBODIED WITH SUFFICIENT STRENGTH TO GENERATE MOVEMENT IN MY LIFELESS LIMBS..."

IT'S ALL OVER-- IT DOESN'T SEEM POSSIBLE... YET HERE--I AM--PACKING--LEAVING STAN-- OUR LOVE-- OUR PLANS--

I CAN'T DO IT! HEAVEN HELP ME--I CAN'T DO IT! I KNOW WHAT STAN IS DOING IS WRONG--BUT I *CAN'T* WALK OUT ON HIM THIS WAY... OH, WHY HAS THIS HAPPENED TO US? WHY HAVE WE BEEN DRIVEN TO THIS INSANE BEHAVIOR? WE'VE TRIED SO HARD TO LIVE LIKE DECENT HUMAN BEINGS...

OH--SORRY!--ER-- YOU MUST BE MRS. BUDKO...

FORGIVE US IF WE'VE INTRUDED, MRS. BUDKO. BUT WE JUST HAD TO SEE YOU FOLKS... I'M DON SAVOLDI AND THE BIG DROP OF WATER WITH ME IS JACK FONTAINE.

PLEASE FEEL AT EASE, GENTLEMEN. CAN I BE OF ANY HELP?

OUT OF MY WAY, FELLAS! *TONI!* THANK HEAVEN, YOU DIDN'T LEAVE!

STAN! STAN!

I COULDN'T GO THROUGH WITH IT, TONI! I-I NEVER GOT TO MCCREEDY'S! IT SUDDENLY STRUCK ME THAT I MIGHT REALLY *LOSE* YOU--I KNEW THAT NOTHING IN THIS WORLD WAS WORTH THAT KIND OF SACRIFICE--TONI, TONI--HOW I *LOVE* YOU!

OH, DARLING! I DON'T CARE WHAT HAPPENS NOW-- AS LONG AS WE HAVE EACH OTHER! STAN, I-- I WAS SO TERRIBLY FRIGHTENED!

ER-AHEM-- WE HATE TO INTERRUPT. BUT WE'RE HERE ON AN URGENT MATTER--AND WE'D LIKE TO GET IT SETTLED!

SAY, WHO *ARE* YOU GUYS? WHAT DO YOU WANT?

A PLACE TO LIVE FOR OUR WIVES AND KIDS, MISTER BUDKO! WE UNDERSTAND YOU FOLKS OWN THE BENSON HOUSE.. WE'VE SEEN THE PLACE..IT'S GOT TEN ROOMS...WONDER IF YOU'D CONSIDER RENTING SOME OF THOSE ROOMS?

JACK AND I ARE NEW IN TOWN, BUT WE'VE GOT WELL PAYING JOBS AT THE STEEL-MILL ... FOR A COUPLE OF EX-GI'S, I'D SAY WE'RE DOING FINE-- EXCEPT THAT THE *HOUSING SHORTAGE* IN TOWN HAS US STYMIED!

OUTSIDE OF PITCHING TENTS IN THE PARK-- THE BENSON HOUSE SEEMS TO BE OUR ONLY HOPE OF FINDING SHELTER!

STAN! WE COULD MAINTAIN THE HOUSE WITH THEIR RENT MONEY ADDED TO OUR INCOME... AND THE BOYS' FAMILIES DO NEED A PLACE TO LIVE!

THIRTY DOLLARS A MONTH FOR THREE ROOMS FOR EACH OF YOU. ALSO A LITTLE COOPERATION WHEN ANY OF US NEED IT... OKAY?

SOUNDS REASON-ABLE TO ME.. WE CAN MEET THAT.. YOU'VE GOT YOURSELF SOME *TENANTS*, MISTER BUDKO!

GOOD DEAL!

"IT WAS A LOVELY DAY--A GLORIOUS DAY.. THE SAVOLDIS AND FOUNTAINES BEAMED HAPPILY WHEN WE MET THEM AT THE GATE OF THE BENSON HOUSE.. STAN AND I WERE IMMEDIATELY AWARE OF THE AFFINITY WE SHARED WITH PLEASANT YOUNG PEOPLE... ALL OF US WERE YOUNG, HARDY AND EAGER TO BECOME A PART OF THE TOWN'S VITALITY! STAN SUDDENLY SWEPT ME UP IN HIS ARMS--AS THE WARM LAUGHTER OF OUR NEW FOUND FRIENDS FOLLOWED US ACROSS THE FLAGSTONE WALK WHICH LED TO THE HOUSE... HAPPINESS HAD RETURNED...

Young city-bred Dan Adams could sell anything...but his hardest job was selling himself to pretty Kathy Remington! ..How did he finally swing the sale?..Well, that's the story of—

KATHY and the MERCHANT of SUNSET CANYON!

DAN! THIS IS NO TIME TO RESUME PETTY DIFFERENCES! LET ME HELP YOU!

DON'T LET EMOTION RULE YOUR OPINION, KATHY! I'M STILL DAN ADAMS THE MERCHANT.. THE MOST DISLIKED MAN IN TOWN!

"I GUESS WE WERE ALL STANDING AROUND GAWKING THE DAY DAN ADAMS CAME TO TOWN! WE WANTED TO GET A LOOK AT THE MAN WHO WOULD TAKE ADVANTAGE OF OLD FRED ADAMS' MISFORTUNE, AND BUY THE STORE FROM HIM BECAUSE HE NEEDED MONEY BADLY! FRED TOLD US THAT HIS NEPHEW WAS A NICE ENOUGH FELLOW, BUT THERE WERE NONE OF US WHO HAD A GOOD WORD FOR HIM THAT DAY...

THAT MUST BE YOUR NEPHEW NOW, FRED!

DON'T TAKE IT SO HARD, KATHY! THE MONEY FROM THE STORE WILL GIVE ME A CHANCE TO SETTLE DOWN ON A PLACE OF MY OWN!

GENERAL STORE

"I DON'T KNOW WHAT I HAD EXPECTED HIM TO LOOK LIKE-- WE'RE RIGHT PREJUDICED AGAINST CITY FOLKS, BUT I REMEMBERED BEING SURPRISED THAT *THEY* COULD GROW ANYONE THAT *BIG!* HE WAS TERRIBLY LARGE-- THERE WAS SOMETHING ALMOST MASSIVE ABOUT HIM, AND HE HAD A SLIGHT SNEER ON HIS FACE! IN THE ONE MOMENT THAT OUR EYES MET, I FELT SELF CONSCIOUS ABOUT MY COUNTRY CLOTHES!

FRED, IS THIS A RECEPTION COMMITTEE FOR ME, OR A FAREWELL FOR YOU!

WELL, UNCLE DAN, THEY'RE ALL MY FRIENDS, AND I'M SURE THEY'LL BE YOURS TOO!

"FRED HAD OWNED THE GENERAL STORE FOR AS LONG AS MOST OF US COULD REMEMBER! WE COULDN'T FORGET, EITHER, THAT HE WAS HAVING TO GIVE IT UP BECAUSE OF HIS OWN SOFT-HEARTEDNESS! FRED HAD NEVER BEEN THE TYPE OF PERSON TO TURN AWAY CUSTOMERS--WITH OR *WITHOUT* MONEY!

GOOD-BYE, EVERYBODY! I'LL WRITE AND LET YOU KNOW HOW CITY LIFE AGREES WITH ME!

SO LONG, FRED! COME BACK AND VISIT US ONCE IN A WHILE!

WELL, I'VE HEARD ABOUT GOOD OLD WESTERN SENTIMENTALITY, BUT THIS IS THE FIRST TIME I'VE EVER SEEN IT IN ACTION!

IT'S SOMETHING YOU WOULDN'T EVER UNDERSTAND, YOU... YOU... *YOU STONEHEARTED SHYLOCK!*

"DAN ADAMS LOST NO TIME IN ESTABLISHING A NEW BUSINESS POLICY!-- DESIGNED FOR PROFIT-- NOT FRIENDSHIP...

ABSOLUTELY NO CREDIT CASH ONLY

NO CREDIT? WHO DOES HE THINK HE IS?

"HIS SIGN MADE ME SO BLASTED MAD, I SORT OF LOST MY HEAD FOR A COUPLE OF MINUTES! I TOLD HIM EXACTLY WHAT I THOUGHT OF HIM! ALL THAT TIME, HE JUST STOOD THERE LAUGHING AT ME, AND HIS LAUGHTER MADE ME FEEL A FUNNY KIND OF HELPLESSNESS!

WHAT DO YOU MEAN PUTTING UP THAT SIGN... ACTING AS THOUGH PEOPLE CAN'T BE *TRUSTED* TO PAY THEIR BILLS! THERE WASN'T A PERSON AROUND HERE, WHO DIDN'T GET CREDIT FROM *FRED!*

HEY, NOW! CALM DOWN JUST A LITTLE! YOU'RE MIGHTY SMALL FOR A FULL-FLEDGED TORNADO!

MISS REMINGTON, MY UNCLE WENT *BROKE* EXTENDING CREDIT TO PEOPLE AROUND HERE, AND I DON'T INTEND TO FOLLOW HIS PATTERN! IF YOU'LL LOOK AROUND, YOU'LL SEE THAT I'VE ALSO *RAISED* MOST PRICES!

I THINK YOU'RE MAKING A SMART MOVE, MR. ADAMS! HELLO THERE, KATHY!

"THAT WAS MARY LOU SINCLAIR, WHOSE FATHER OWNED THE BANK AND HELD A LOT OF MORTGAGES AROUND HERE! SHE HAD ALWAYS THOUGHT SHE WAS A LOT BETTER THAN MOST OF US BECAUSE SHE'D GONE TO COLLEGE! I COULD SEE RIGHT AWAY, THAT SHE AND DAN ADAMS OUGHT TO HIT IT OFF FINE!

IT'S REFRESHING, MR. ADAMS, TO MEET A GOOD HARDHEADED *BUSINESSMAN* IN THIS TOWN!

2

OF COURSE, MISS REMINGTON, IF YOU NEGLECTED TO BRING MONEY WITH YOU, I'LL BE GLAD TO TRUST YOU TILL THE NEXT TIME YOU COME TO TOWN!

DON'T DO ME ANY FAVORS!

"THE NEW POLICY OF THE STORE WAS THE TALK OF EVERYONE DURING THE DAYS THAT FOLLOWED! EVERYONE RESENTED IT! WE MIGHT HAVE BEEN A POOR COMMUNITY, BUT NONE OF US TOOK ADVANTAGE OF ANOTHER'S MISFORTUNE... AS DAN ADAMS WAS DOING!

WELL I GUESS I CAN'T REALLY BLAME DAN NONE! VERY FEW OF US EVER PAID FRED THE MONEY WE OWED HIM!

BUT EVERYBODY WOULD HAVE, AS SOON AS WE'D HAD A GOOD YEAR!

"I SHOULD HAVE KNOWN EVEN THEN THAT THERE WAS SOMETHING WRONG ABOUT THE WAY I FELT ABOUT DAN ADAMS! IT WASN'T NATURAL TO HATE SOMEONE ON SUCH SHORT NOTICE, THE WAY I HATED HIM! AS IT WAS, I LAY AWAKE NIGHTS THINKING ABOUT HIM, PICTURING HIM THE WAY HE LOOKED AS HE STOOD THERE LAUGHING AT ME ... SO BIG AND UTTERLY CAPABLE LOOKING!

A MAN LIKE THAT IS DANGEROUS! IF THERE WAS ONLY SOME WAY WE COULD MAKE HIM MOVE OUT OF TOWN!

"I STAYED AWAY FROM THE STORE UNTIL WE WERE COMPLETELY OUT OF SUPPLIES AT THE RANCH! FINALLY, I WENT TO THE BANK AND DREW SOME MONEY FROM THE FAST-DWINDLING SUM DAD HAD LEFT ME AND WENT RELUCTANTLY TO THE STORE!

WELL, MISS REMINGTON, I THOUGHT MAYBE I'D LOST MY FAVORITE CUSTOMER!

IT'S NOT LIKELY SINCE THERE IS NO OTHER STORE I COULD TAKE MY TRADE TO!

"IT WAS THE MOST BEAUTIFUL DRESS I HAD EVER SEEN, AND I WOULD HAVE GIVEN ANYTHING IN THE WORLD TO HAVE OWNED IT! I WAS IMMEDIATELY SELF CONSCIOUS ABOUT THE CLOTHES I WAS WEARING, AND MY GENERAL UNKEMPT APPEARANCE! BUT WHEN A GIRL IS RUNNING A RANCH, SHE DOESN'T HAVE TOO MUCH TIME FOR BEAUTY TREATMENTS!

I'VE JUST GOT SOMETHING IN FROM DENVER! I THOUGHT YOU MIGHT BE INTERESTED IN IT!

YOU OUGHT TO KNOW BY NOW THAT I COULDN'T AFFORD A DRESS LIKE THAT!

I'D BE GLAD TO MAKE YOU A PRESENT OF IT, KATHY, IF YOU'LL GO TO MARY LOU'S PARTY WITH ME!

NO THANK YOU! THE PRICE IS MUCH TOO HIGH! NOW, IF YOU DON'T MIND.. I CAME TO BUY A FEW SUPPLIES!

3

"FOR A SINGLE MOMENT, HE LOOKED AS THOUGH I MIGHT HAVE HURT HIM, BUT IT WAS PROBABLY JUST MY IMAGINATION! RIGHT THEN I KNEW NOTHING WOULD EVER BOTHER HIM! HE WAS A MAN OF STONE-- WITHOUT FEELINGS!

OF COURSE! AND I TRUST YOU BROUGHT CASH!

NATURALLY! I'M USED TO PAYING FOR EVERYTHING I BUY!

"IF I THOUGHT I HATED DAN ADAMS, THEN, IT WAS NOTHING COMPARED TO THE FEELING I WAS TO HAVE FOR HIM LATER! AFTER I HAD PURCHASED MY SUPPLIES, I WAS ABOUT TO HEAD FOR HOME WHEN I CAUGHT THE TAIL-END OF A CONVERSATION!

SO THEN HE SAYS HE'LL GIVE ME WHAT THE BANK OFFERED ON A MORTGAGE, FOR 51% OF THE RANCH-- PROVIDING HE HANDLES THE BUSINESS END OF IT! HE SAYS I CAN BUY IT BACK ANYTIME I GOT THE MONEY PLUS 10%!

I DON'T KNOW WHAT TO THINK OF A DEAL LIKE THAT!

ARE YOU TALKING ABOUT DAN ADAMS?

YEAH! HE'S WILLING TO PAY CASH TOO! HE SAYS HE CAN BORROW THE MONEY FROM A BANK IN DENVER!

"THE MEN WERE MIXED IN THEIR OPINIONS! LIKE ALWAYS THEY WERE WILLING TO GIVE SOMEONE THE BENEFIT OF A DOUBT! BUT IF THEY COULDN'T SEE THROUGH THIS OFFER, I COULD! AS USUAL, DAN ADAMS WAS TAKING ADVANTAGE OF PEOPLE WHEN THEY HAD NO CHANCE TO FIGHT BACK!

I WOULDN'T KNOW WHAT TO SAY IF HE MADE ME AN OFFER LIKE THAT-- AND I SURE COULD USE THE CASH!

WELL, I'LL TELL YOU-- IF HE CAN PUT MY RANCH BACK ON ITS FEET, I'D BE GLAD TO GIVE HIM HALF OF IT!

"THE WORK AT THE RANCH KEPT ME TOO BUSY TO SPEND MUCH TIME IN TOWN, AND I WAS SORT OF GLAD TOO, BECAUSE TOWN REMINDED ME OF DAN NOW! AT HOME IF I WORKED HARD ENOUGH I WAS SOMETIMES ABLE TO FORGET HIM FOR A COUPLE OF HOURS AT A STRETCH!

KATHY-- HELLO! I WASN'T SURE WHETHER YOU GOT AN INVITATION TO MY PARTY OR NOT! YOU ARE COMING, AREN'T YOU?

WELL, YES-- I GUESS I CAN, MARY LOU!

"THERE WAS VERY LITTLE IN THE WAY OF ENTERTAIN-MENT IN TOWN, SO WE JUMPED AT THE CHANCE, EVEN IF IT MEANT GOING TO A PARTY GIVEN BY MARY LOU, WHO NONE OF US CARED MUCH FOR! NEARLY EVERYONE IN TOWN HAD BEEN INVITED, AND AS I ENTERED, EVERYONE SEEMED TO BE HAVING A WONDERFUL TIME DRESSED IN THEIR ONLY GOOD CLOTHES!

KATHY! I'M SO GLAD YOU COULD COME! YOU GO IN NOW AND HAVE A GOOD TIME!

"I DIDN'T SEE DAN ADAMS AROUND, AND I FOUND MYSELF LOOKING FOR HIM! I COULDN'T UNDERSTAND WHY HE SHOULD BE CONSTANTLY ON MY MIND... YET, WHEN HE CAME OVER TO DANCE WITH ME, I TRIED TO IGNORE HIM!"

ARE YOU LOOKING FOR SOMEONE, KATHY?

MAY I CUT IN?

"I WENT INTO HIS ARMS WITHOUT LOOKING AT HIM! DANCING WITH HIM WAS A NEW EXPERIENCE! MOST OF THE BOYS AROUND HERE HAD NEVER LEARNED TO DANCE, AND THEY DID LITTLE MORE THAN WALK YOU AROUND THE FLOOR! BUT WITH DAN IT WAS MORE LIKE EFFORTLESS FLOATING!"

I'M GLAD TO SEE THE DRESS DIDN'T GO TO WASTE! IT WOULDN'T HAVE FITTED ME, ANYWAY, IF IT FITS MARY LOU!

IT WAS YOUR SIZE! MARY LOU HAD IT ALTERED!

"I WAS DISAPPOINTED WHEN THE MUSIC ENDED BECAUSE I EXPECTED HIM TO LEAVE ME AND GO TO MARY LOU.' HE LED ME OUTSIDE, HOWEVER, AND I WENT WITH HIM WILLINGLY! IT WAS THE FIRST TIME, THAT I HAD EVER REALLY BEEN ALONE WITH HIM, AND I WAS STRANGELY AFRAID!"

LET'S GET A LITTLE AIR, KATHY!

I UNDERSTAND YOU'VE GONE INTO THE RANCHING BUSINESS!

PURELY AS AN INVESTMENT! I THINK I CAN MAKE SOME OF THESE RANCHES PAY OFF!

I SUPPOSE IT'S ENTIRELY THE HUMANITARIAN INSTINCT IN YOU THAT MAKES YOU WANT TO HELP THE RANCHERS!

"IF I HADN'T BEEN AFRAID OF HIM RIGHT THEN, I WOULDN'T HAVE GONE ON TALKING SO CRAZILY! BUT MY FEAR MADE ME EXPRESS ALL THE RESENTMENT I HAD BEEN STORING AGAINST HIM FOR SO LONG!"

I'LL IGNORE THE SARCASM! MY ONLY HUMANITARIAN INSTINCT CONCERNS MYSELF! IF MY PLAN WORKS OUT I MAKE 10%! INCIDENTALLY, DON'T YOU EVER STOP TALKING?

"WHEN HE KISSED ME, I KNEW THAT THIS WAS WHAT I HAD BEEN AFRAID OF ALL EVENING. THERE WAS SOMETHING TERRIBLY CONQUERING IN HIS KISS..."

5

"IF HIS KISS HADN'T AFFECTED ME SO, I NEVER WOULD HAVE SLAPPED HIM...BUT I COULDN'T STAND THE IDEA OF SEEING TRIUMPH IN HIS FACE, AFTER HE LET ME GO! SO, WITHOUT LOOKING AT HIM, I HIT HIM AS HARD AS I COULD!"

I WOULDN'T ADVISE YOU TO TRY THAT VERY OFTEN!

"I ONLY REMAINED AT THE PARTY AFTER THAT BECAUSE I WOULDN'T LET DAN ADAMS KNOW FOR THE WORLD HOW HE HAD CONFUSED ME! HE SEEMED TOTALLY UNAFFECTED BY THE WHOLE THING, AS HE DANCED WITH TONY!"

IT'S SUCH A RELIEF DANCING WITH YOU, DAN, AFTER SOME OF THESE LOCAL YOKELS!

ANYBODY SHOULD BE ABLE TO WALTZ YOU AROUND THE FLOOR, TONY!

"IT WAS ABOUT MIDNIGHT THAT NIGHT WHEN SAM HOAX BURST INTO THE DANCE WITH HIS DREADFUL NEWS."

THERE'S A FIRE OUT AT MERIWELL'S! WE NEED EVERYBODY WE CAN GET!

"BY THE TIME I GOT TO THE MERIWELLS, ONE BARN WAS ALMOST GONE, AND THERE WAS NO SAVING IT, ALTHOUGH THE MEN BATTLED HEROICALLY! THEY HAD MANAGED TO SAVE THE ANIMALS THOUGH, AND TO PREVENT THE FIRE FROM SPREADING FURTHER!"

WATCH-OUT -- IT'LL CAVE IN! GET MORE WATER!

"AS I WATCHED, IT SEEMED THAT DAN ADAMS WAS EVERYWHERE AT ONCE, DIRECTING THEM IN THE FIRE-FIGHTING ---RESCUING ANIMALS IN GENERAL, TAKING CHARGE.' THEN, WHEN HE NEARED ME, I SAW THAT HE WAS BADLY BURNED HIMSELF.'

...GOT TO TAKE CARE OF MRS. MERRIWELL!' THE FIRE GOT SETH!

DAN! -- YOUR HAND! LET ME GET YOU SOMETHING!

"SUDDENLY I WANTED TO TAKE CARE OF HIM--TO TEND HIS WOUNDS, AND TO HOLD HIM IN MY ARMS! BUT AS QUICKLY, HE PUSHED ME AWAY ROUGHLY, AND LOOKING IN HIS EYES, I SAW NOTHING BUT HATE!

LEAVE ME ALONE!

"HE STRODE PAST ME WITHOUT ANOTHER GLANCE! AND PART OF ME DIED IN THAT MOMENT! I REMEMBERED THAT A SHORT TIME AGO, I HAD SLAPPED HIM, AND I KNEW THAT ANY FEELING HE HAD HAD FOR ME WAS GONE BY NOW! WHY SHOULD HE LET ME CARE FOR HIM AFTER WHAT I HAD DONE?

OH, DAN!

"THE FUNERAL FOR SETH MERIWELL WAS HELD THE FOLLOWING MONDAY, AND ALTHOUGH EVERY INSTINCT WITHIN ME WAS AGAINST IT, I FORCED MYSELF TO GO! ALL AROUND ME I COULD HEAR THE MEN MUTTERING THAT FRANK'S DEATH HAD BEEN UNNECESSARY!

IF WE KNEW A LITTLE ABOUT FIRE-FIGHTING SETH'D BE HERE TODAY!

THE TOWN NEEDS SOME DECENT EQUIPMENT!

"I WAS BUSY ALL THE NEXT WEEK, BUT I COULD NEVER GET MRS. MERIWELL OUT OF MY MIND! WHAT WOULD SHE DO WITH THE FAILING RANCH NOW THAT SETH WAS DEAD? THERE WAS NO WAY I COULD HELP, BUT I RODE OVER TO SEE HER ANYWAY!

I CAME OVER TO SEE IF THERE'S ANYTHING I CAN DO FOR YOU!

THERE'S NOTHING YOU CAN DO, KATHY! DAN ADAMS HAS TAKEN CARE OF EVERYTHING!

"I WANTED TO SCREAM-- 'YOU FOOL!' POOR MRS. MERIWELL-- SHE HAD NO WAY OF KNOWING THE MAN SHE WAS UP AGAINST! ONCE AGAIN, HE HAD TAKEN ADVANTAGE OF SOMEONE IN THEIR TIME OF WEAKNESS!

YOU KNOW, HE PAID FOR ALL THE FUNERAL EXPENSES HIMSELF! THEN HE OFFERED TO HANDLE THE SALE OF THE CATTLE FOR ME-- HE KNOWS SOME BUYERS WHO'LL PAY MUCH BETTER PRICES! WELL, IT DIDN'T SEEM FAIR--- HE'S DOING ALL THE WORK, SO I OFFERED HIM HALF-- HE PAID ME CASH TOO!

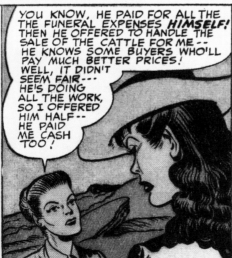

I WISH YOU HADN'T DONE THAT-- HE'S NO GOOD! HE'LL TRICK YOU SOMEHOW!

YOU GOT HIM ALL WRONG, KATHY! HE'S ORGANIZING A VOLUNTEER FIRE SQUAD IN TOWN, AND GETTING EQUIPMENT FROM THE CITY! PEOPLE HAVE CHANGED THEIR MINDS ABOUT HIM!

"I COULD SEE NOW, HIS ENTIRE SCHEME! HE WAS WINNING OVER THE PEOPLE! AND AFTER HE HAD THEIR CONFIDENCE, HE WOULD BUY THEM OUT, ONE BY ONE, UNTIL HE OWNED EVERYTHING AROUND HERE! AND THERE WAS NO WAY OF STOPPING HIM!

THERE'S NOTHING WE CAN DO-- HE'S GOT US ALL BY THE THROATS!

"AND PERHAPS THE WORST PART OF IT ALL WAS THE KNOWLEDGE THAT I, TOO, WOULD HAVE TO PLAY INTO HIS HANDS! WEEK BY WEEK THE MONEY HAD DWINDLED DOWN, UNTIL FINALLY IT WAS GONE. CATTLE STILL HAD TO BE FED AND THE MEN PAID, AND THERE WAS NO POINT IN TRYING TO GET A LOAN FROM THE BANK! THERE WAS ONLY DAN ADAMS TO TURN TO!

THERE'S NOT A CENT LEFT! WELL, I CAN'T LET THE STOCK STARVE! I'LL HAVE TO GO TO HIM!

"EARLY THE NEXT MORNING, I SADDLED A HORSE TO GO TO TOWN! I FELT LIKE I WAS BETRAYING DAD AND EVERYONE WHO HAD EVER WORKED TO BUILD THE RANCH UP INTO SOMETHING-- BUT I HAD NO CHOICE!

I'M GOING INTO TOWN TO TRY TO GET A LOAN, BILL!

ALL RIGHT, MISS KATHY!

"AS I ENTERED HIS STORE I WONDERED WHAT HAD FILLED MY THOUGHTS BEFORE THEY WERE FULL OF HATE FOR HIM! THEN, WHEN I SAW HIM STANDING IN THE STORE, SO BIG AND STRONG, THE FEELING THAT HAD COME OVER ME THE NIGHT OF THE FIRE BESEIGED ME, LEAVING ME WEAK AND EVEN MORE CONFUSED!

WELL, I WAS BEGINNING TO WONDER WHETHER YOU STILL LIVED IN THESE PARTS OR NOT!

I CAME TO ASK YOU IF YOU WANTED TO BUY HALF OF MY RANCH!

"HE LOOKED AT ME FOR A LONG MOMENT AS THOUGH HE WERE THINKING IT OVER, AND I WONDERED IF HE WERE CONSIDERING TURNING ME DOWN! I COULDN'T MEET HIS STEADY GAZE, AND EMBARRASSEDLY I TURNED AWAY!

I DON'T WANT YOUR RANCH, KATHY, BUT I'LL LEND YOU THE MONEY, IF YOU'LL TAKE MY ADVICE ABOUT SELLING YOUR CATTLE!

I TOLD YOU BEFORE, I DON'T WANT ANY FAVORS FROM YOU! I WANT THE SAME OFFER YOU MADE EVERYONE ELSE!

YOU'VE HEARD MY OFFER TO YOU! YOU'LL DO IT THAT WAY OR NOT AT ALL!

THEN I DON'T WANT IT!

"I TURNED AWAY TO LEAVE, BUT BEFORE I GOT TO THE DOOR, I BEGAN TO CRY! I DIDN'T KNOW WHICH WAY TO TURN OR WHAT TO DO! RIGHT THEN, MORE THAN ANYTHING ELSE IN THE WORLD I WANTED DAN TO PUT HIS ARMS AROUND ME AND TELL ME EVERYTHING WOULD BE ALL RIGHT!

KATHY! YOU LITTLE FOOL! **COME HERE!**

"IT WAS A COMMAND, AND I OBEYED HIM, FEELING FOR THE FIRST TIME SINCE WE MET, THAT I WAS DOING THE RIGHT THING! HE TOOK ME IN HIS ARMS AND SAID ALL THE THINGS I HAD WANTED TO HEAR!

DRY YOUR EYES KATHY! I'M GOING TO TAKE GOOD CARE OF YOU FROM NOW ON!

OH, DAN! I WANT YOU TO!

AND JUST TO RELIEVE ALL YOUR CRAZY IDEAS ABOUT ME -- I'M NOT INTERESTED IN OWNING ANY OF THE RANCHES AROUND! BUT THERE'S NO EXCUSE FOR THEIR NOT PAYING OFF! I CAN TAKE CARE OF THAT ANGLE BY A FEW MODERN RANCHING TECHNIQUES AND BY SELLING CATTLE DIRECTLY TO EASTERN PLANTS INSTEAD OF LOCAL DEALERS WHO TAKE ALL THE PROFIT! I ONLY BOUGHT PART INTEREST BECAUSE THAT WAS THE ONLY WAY I COULD GET MONEY FROM THE BANK! PERSONALLY I'LL MAKE PLENTY IN THIS STORE IF THIS IS A PROSPEROUS COMMUNITY!

"IT HAD BEEN OUR OWN IGNORANCE AND BACKWARDNESS THAT HAD HELD US BACK, AND WE HAD SCORNED DAN BECAUSE HE WANTED TO SHOW US THE WAY OUT OF OUR POVERTY! I HAD BEEN THE WORST OF THEM ALL, BUT I WOULD SPEND THE REST OF MY LIFE, MAKING IT UP TO HIM!"

Produced by SIMON & KIRBY

Was it right for a girl to spend months of lonliness and anxiety --waiting for a man who is sailing every ocean of the globe?

Could a man expect to find his sweetheart brimming with laughter and undimmed affection when he returned from his frequent voyages? These were among the many problems I faced when I became a...

SAILOR'S GIRL!

"THE SEA NOT ONLY GAVE THE PEOPLE OF CAPE MANCASSET THEIR LIVELIHOOD, BUT ALSO THEIR BAD WEATHER... I WAS COMPLETING AN ERRAND FOR MY FATHER WHEN THE STORM LADEN CLOUDS ROLLED IN FROM THE BEACHES...

HERE YOU ARE, MISTER BANKS. THOUGHT I'D DELIVER THIS FOR DAD WHILE I WAS IN THIS PART OF TOWN!

ALDEN FISHERIES NEVER HAD A PRETTIER MESSENGER, THANK YOU, SARI!

I'D HURRY HOME IF I WERE YOU CHILD.. LOOKS LIKE THE BIG BLOW IS ABOUT DUE!

I'M GOING THIS MINUTE! GOOD-BYE, MISTER BANKS!

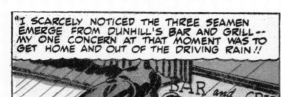

"I SCARCELY NOTICED THE THREE SEAMEN EMERGE FROM DUNHILL'S BAR AND GRILL -- MY ONE CONCERN AT THAT MOMENT WAS TO GET HOME AND OUT OF THE DRIVING RAIN!!"

NOW *THERE'S* A TRIM LITTLE CRAFT, MATES! WHATCHER SAY WE HELP HER FIND A PORT IN THIS STORM!

HEAVE TO, HONEY! WEATHER'S MIGHTY ROUGH TONIGHT! HOW ABOUT JOININ' OUR CONVOY AND SETTIN' COURSE WITH US?

PLEASE LET ME PASS! I'M IN A HURRY!

NOW DON'T BE THAT WAY, BABY! LET'S DO THE TOWN! LET'S HAVE SOME LAUGHS, EH?

SEE HERE, SAILOR! YOU'RE BEING VERY ANNOYING!

LET HER ALONE, LUKE!

SAVE YOUR ORDERS, RED! WE'RE NOT ABOARD SHIP! I'VE LITTLE STOMACH FOR YOUR TIGHT-LIPPED COMPANY AS IT IS! NOW, GET LOST!

LET ME GO, DO YOU HEAR? LET ME GO OR I'LL HAVE YOU ARRESTED!

DON'T MIND THAT KILL-JOY, BABY! HE'S *ALWAYS* BEEN JEALOUS OF MY TALENT FOR PLEASING THE LADIES! COME ON! DON'T PLAY "HARD TO GET!" LET'S BE *FRIENDLY*, EH?

"I DIDN'T SEE THE DESCENDING BLOW! ITS DEVASTATING IMPACT WAS TRANSMITTED TO ME THROUGH ITS UNFORTUNATE RECIPIENT. MY ASSAILANT'S FINGERS RELAXED THEIR HOLD ON MY ARMS -- AND I FELT MYSELF FREE...

CRACK!

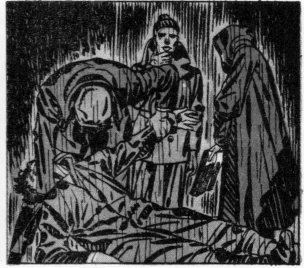

I - I'D LIKE TO THANK YOU FOR COMING TO MY AID! YOU DON'T THINK YOUR FRIEND IS SERIOUSLY HURT--?

LUKE WILL COME OUT OF IT SOON... HE'S REALLY A GOOD EGG, BUT HIS FATAL CHARM ALWAYS GETS HIM INTO TROUBLE... FORGET THIS HAPPENED, MISS...

"FORGET THIS HAPPENED!" HE SAID THAT EVEN AS I STOOD ENCHANTED BY EVERY FEATURE OF HIS HANDSOME, UNSMILING COUNTENANCE--FASCINATED BY THE SUPPLE POWER IN THE TALL, LEAN FRAME. FORGET THIS MEETING? OH, NO...*I WAS PLANNING TO SEE THIS MAN, RED, AGAIN...*

SARI! HAVE YOU BEEN LISTENING TO WHAT I'VE JUST SAID?

OH, I'M SORRY, DAD! GUESS I MUST HAVE BEEN DAYDREAMING...I BELIEVE I DID HEAR YOU MENTION BOSTON!

DARN RIGHT I DID! I WANT YOU TO VISIT AWHILE WITH YOUR AUNT DEBORAH! SHE KNOWS ALL THE RIGHT PEOPLE-- SAY, *WHAT ON EARTH IS WRONG WITH YOU, GIRL?*

3

I'M HAUNTED BY A SHOCK OF RED HAIR AND TWO STEADY BLUE EYES! DO YOU LIKE BLUE EYES, DAD?

SO *THAT'S* IT! WHO *IS* THE MAN? WHAT'S HIS NAME? WHERE DID YOU MEET HIM?

HIS NAME IS ERIC THE RED... A VIKING SEARAIDER WHO COMMANDS A DRAGON SHIP MANNED BY A FIERCE AND TERRIBLE CREW. HIS SKIN IS THE COLOR OF BRONZE --- HIS GREAT STRENGTH HAS BEEN TEMPERED IN THE FIRE OF MANY BATTLES... WE MET IN A STORM -- AND NOW -- I'M HIS CAPTIVE.

JUMPING CATFISH!

DAD, YOU KNOW EVERYBODY IN THIS TOWN? WHAT CAN YOU TELL ME ABOUT THIS MAN I DESCRIBED?

HE MUST BE DEAD AT LEAST A THOUSAND YEARS!

HOWEVER, I DO KNOW A RED-HEADED SEAMAN WHO MIGHT FIT YOUR PICTURE IN A PIG-HEADED, MOROSE SORT OF WAY! ... WORKS ABOARD ONE OF MY FISHING SMACKS!

HIS *NAME*, DAD! WHAT'S HIS NAME?

IT'S NOT ERIC THE RED! - ALTHOUGH EVERYONE DOES CALL HIM "RED"! HE'S LISTED IN MY LEDGERS AS JONAS PIKE!

JONAS PIKE? OH, NO! THAT NAME COULDN'T *POSSIBLY* FIT THE MAN I HAVE IN MIND!

I WOULDN'T SAY THAT! PIKE'S A COLD, UNAPPROACHABLE PERSONALITY! BUT HE'S A FINE SEAMAN! BUILT LIKE AN OAK MAST -- HITS LIKE A TEAM OF MULES. HE CAN BE A PRETTY ROUGH CUSTOMER!

DAD- IF YOU DON'T OBJECT, I'D LIKE TO INVITE THIS JONAS PIKE TO DINNER TO-MORROW EVENING ... I-I'VE SIMPLY GOT TO FIND THIS GORGEOUS MAN AGAIN.!

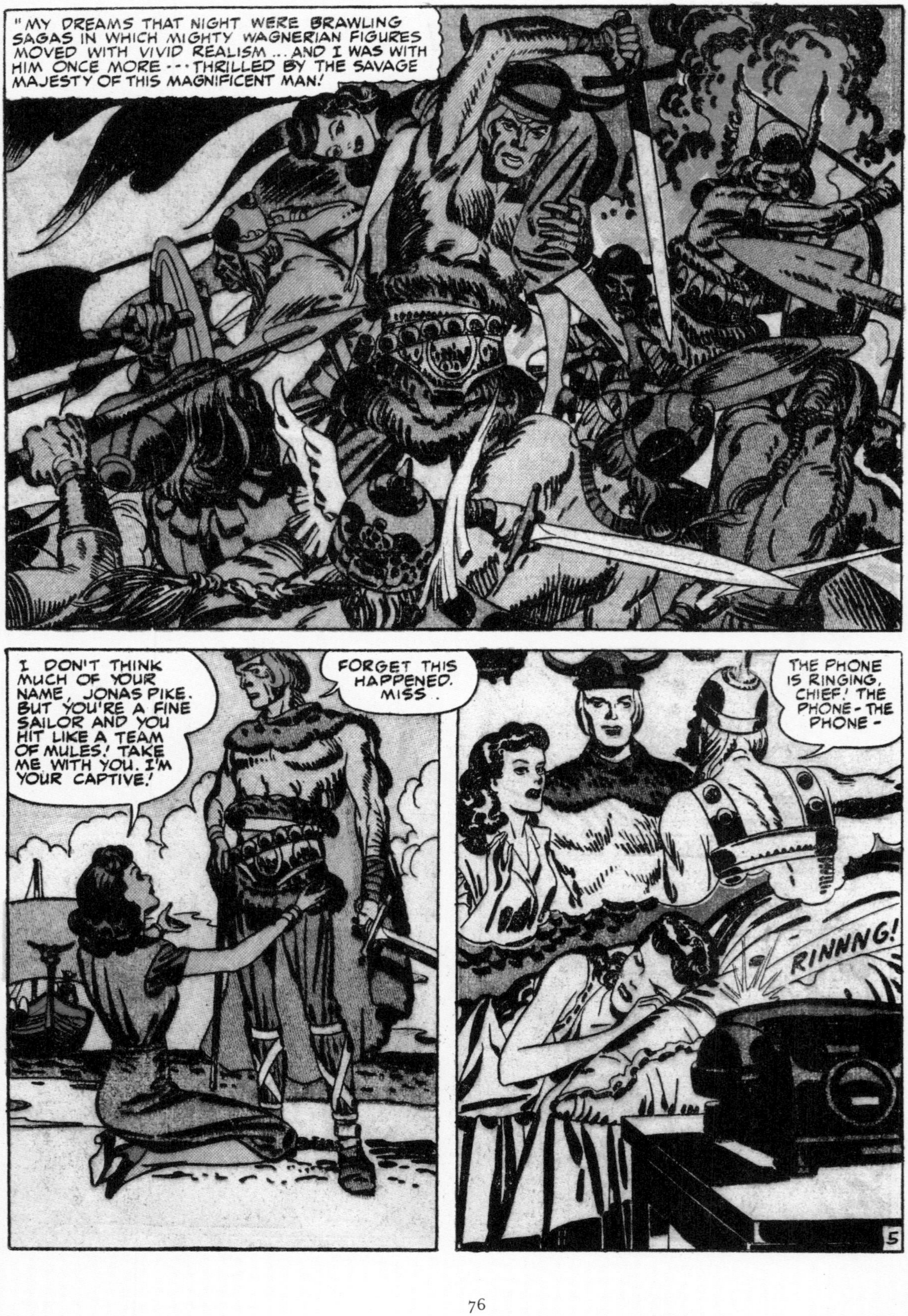
"MY DREAMS THAT NIGHT WERE BRAWLING SAGAS IN WHICH MIGHTY WAGNERIAN FIGURES MOVED WITH VIVID REALISM ... AND I WAS WITH HIM ONCE MORE --- THRILLED BY THE SAVAGE MAJESTY OF THIS MAGNIFICENT MAN!
I DON'T THINK MUCH OF YOUR NAME, JONAS PIKE. BUT YOU'RE A FINE SAILOR AND YOU HIT LIKE A TEAM OF MULES! TAKE ME WITH YOU. I'M YOUR CAPTIVE!
FORGET THIS HAPPENED, MISS..
THE PHONE IS RINGING, CHIEF! THE PHONE - THE PHONE -
RINNNG!
5

"THE LANGUOR OF SLEEP WAS STILL WEARING OFF WHEN I LIFTED THE PHONE RECEIVER TO MY EAR... DAD'S VOICE SOUNDED MUFFLED AND INDISTINCT -- UNTIL HE MENTIONED RED'S NAME... THEN I SAT BOLT UPRIGHT!

DAD! YOU *SAW* JONAS PIKE? DID YOU INVITE HIM TO DINNER?

YES, I DID, GIRL... HE WASN'T INTERESTED.. HAD OTHER PLANS... PERHAPS IT'S JUST AS WELL THAT HE DECLINED... RED'S NOT YOUR TYPE! HE'S NOT *ANYBODY'S* TYPE! YOU'D PROBABLY FIND HIM A BORE! NOW, COME DOWN TO EARTH AND WE'LL DISCUSS THAT TRIP TO BOSTON THIS EVENING!

"I KNEW WHAT DAD WAS REALLY SAYING! ONLY HE COULDN'T RISK BEING DIRECT WITHOUT MAKING ME FEEL LIKE A NAIVE ADOLESCENT. WAS IT JUST AN ILLUSION I WAS PURSUING? PERHAPS IT WAS. BUT THE TEARS IT BROUGHT TO MY EYES WERE VERY, VERY REAL ... THAT AFTERNOON I STRUCK OUT FOR THE SEASHORE. I DECIDED IF I HAD TO SULK I WOULD CHOOSE AN APPROPRIATE ATMOSPHERE..

THAT AROMA -- SMELLS LIKE TOBACCO SMO-- SMO--
AAACHOOOO!

BLESS YOU!

6

"I WATCHED HIM RISE SLOWLY TO HIS FULL HEIGHT WITH A LAZY, CAT-LIKE GRACE..THIS WAS NO ELUSIVE VISION I FACED... THIS WAS BEAUTIFUL, JOYOUS REALITY...I AVERTED MY GAZE TO CONCEAL MY TRUE REACTION TO HIS SUDDEN APPEARANCE...

SO WE MEET AGAIN... YOU'RE THE GIRL IN THE RAIN!

AND YOU'RE THE KNIGHT ERRANT! IT SEEMS WE'RE FATED FOR SURPRISE MEETINGS!

DO YOU COME TO THIS SPOT VERY OFTEN?

ONLY WHEN MY MIND IS DISTURBED. AND YOU?

STRANGELY ENOUGH, I'M HERE FOR A REASON VERY SIMILAR TO YOURS!

THEN PERHAPS WE CAN FIND THE ANSWER TO THIS UNREST-- TOGETHER--

I-I DON'T UNDERSTAND WHAT YOU MEAN?

DON'T YOU-?

"THE WAVES RUSHED IN UPON THE SHORE LIKE ROARING CATARACTS. AND RETREATED FROM THE WET SANDS IN FOAMY POOLS... IN THE COOL BREEZE WAS THE BREATH OF THE SEA -A SEAGULL'S CRY --- THE SIGH OF THE SPIRIT WINGING TOWARD THE SUN ...

WE'VE BOTH FELT IT, LADY OF THE RAIN-- IT'S STRONGER THAN THE CALL OF THE SEA... WE HAD TO ANSWER IT-- WE *HAD* TO!

"WE KISSED AGAIN... AND THE SEA LASHED OUT AGAINST THE SHORE WITH FUTILE FURY... EVERY ELEMENTAL FORCE OF NATURE WAS IMPOTENT AGAINST THIS GREAT AND WONDERFUL EMOTION WHICH SWEPT THROUGH EVERY ATOM OF OUR BEING... ONLY IN RED'S ARMS WOULD I EVER KNOW THE TRUE MEANING OF LOVE!

LADY-- LADY-- HOW I LOVE YOU!

"THE FOLLOWING DAY, RED PUT OUT TO SEA ONCE MORE... I WAVED RATHER FORLORNLY AT THE SHIP RECEDING RAPIDLY ACROSS THE WATERS... THE WARMTH OF HIS LOVE WAS STILL FRESH UPON ME-- AND I HURLED SILENT INVECTIVES AT THE WIDENING DISTANCE BETWEEN US!

"I DREADED LOOKING FORWARD TO THE SWEET MOMENTS AHEAD, MADE BRIEF BY THESE FREQUENT PARTINGS... SOMETHING HAD TO BE DONE TO KEEP RED NEAR ME IN THE FUTURE... I SPOKE TO DAD ABOUT IT THAT EVENING...

YOU MEAN THAT YOU WANT ME TO GIVE RED A LAND-LUBBER'S JOB IN THE OFFICE? I'D BE GLAD TO!

YOU'RE SWELL, DAD! IT MEANS A LOT TO ME!

BUT YOU KNOW AS WELL AS I DO THAT RED WILL *NEVER* *ACCEPT* THAT KIND OF JOB! I OFFERED ONE TO RED BEFORE, AND HE TURNED IT DOWN!

WHEN YOU ASK A BORN SAILOR LIKE RED TO LEAVE THE SEA, YOU'RE TAMPERING WITH HIS SOUL! OF COURSE, I CAN IGNORE THAT FACT... *MY* INTEREST IN RED IS STRICTLY COMMERCIAL... BUT YOU APPARENTLY LOVE THE MAN... *HIS* HAPPINESS WILL AFFECT YOUR OWN. TREAD EASY, GIRL...

8

"DAD DIDN'T LIKE THIS SITUATION AT ALL. HE VIEWED MY EFFORT TO FIND A HAPPY MEDIUM FOR RED AND MYSELF AS A FOREGONE FAILURE. 'DON'T LET THIS GO ANY FURTHER!' WAS HIS FRANK COMMENT. 'YOU CAN'T BREAK THE SEA'S HOLD ON A MAN!'"

I'VE GOT TO TRY, DAD! I'VE GOT TO TRY! WITH YOUR HELP, I CAN WORK THIS THING OUT!

THE JOB WILL BE OPEN *IF* YOU CAN GET RED TO ACCEPT IT! GOOD LUCK, GIRL!

"IF IT WAS SELFISH TO WANT THE MAN YOU LOVE CONSTANTLY BY YOUR SIDE, THEN I WAS SELFISH! TO ME, THERE WAS NOTHING ON THIS EARTH AS IMPORTANT AS OUR LOVE... I KNEW NOTHING ABOUT THE SPELL OF THE SEA.. IT WAS EVIDENTLY A SPIRITUAL THING THAT WOVE ITSELF INTO THE INNER BEING OF A MAN UNTIL IT BECAME A PART OF HIS SUBSTANCE.. A GROWING FEAR OF THIS INTANGIBLE FORCE GNAWED AT MY CONFIDENCE -- FOR IT WAS A LOVE -- A LOVE WITH DEPTHS AT WHICH I COULD ONLY GUESS..."

HE'LL BE BACK WITH TOMORROW'S TIDE.. I-I-ALMOST *DREAD* HIS ARRIVAL! HOW WILL HE REACT TO FATHER'S OFFER!

"I WASN'T AT THE PIER WHEN RED'S SHIP DROPPED ANCHOR THE FOLLOWING AFTERNOON... INSTEAD I WAITED WITH TENSE EXPECTANCY AT MY HOME... THE RINGING OF THE DOORBELL BROUGHT ME FROM THE SOFA WITH A START. I ASSUMED WHAT I HOPED WOULD PASS FOR FIRM RESOLUTION AND WENT TO MEET RED... ."

RED--IT'S WONDERFUL TO SEE YOU BACK...

WELL, THIS IS A HEARTY WELCOME... I WAS HOPING YOU'D BE AT THE PIER!

HOWLING WINDS OF CAPE HORN, I WANT THAT SMILE I'VE BEEN DREAMING ABOUT ABOARD SHIP! WELL, THAT'S MORE LIKE IT! MISS ME, SARI?

OH, RED, YOU'LL NEVER KNOW HOW MUCH! I GUESS THAT'S WHY I WAS SO MOODY!

IT ISN'T FAIR, DARLING! I NEVER KNEW IT WOULD BE LIKE THIS! YOU DON'T REALIZE THE TORMENT THIS WAITING INFLICTS ON A GIRL AS DEEPLY IN LOVE AS I AM!

YOU'LL GET USED TO IT IN TIME, SARI.. YOU'RE A SAILOR'S GIRL NOW-- MY GIRL!

RED, I DON'T THINK THE PERSON EXISTS WHO COULD LOVE YOU THE WAY I DO... THAT'S WHY I COULDN'T GO THROUGH ANOTHER SUCH LONELY VIGIL... DON'T GO BACK, RED.. STAY ASHORE-- WITH ME-- I'LL TRY SO HARD TO MAKE YOU HAPPY..

BUT SARI..YOU'RE NOT AWARE OF WHAT YOU'RE ASKING! I'M A *SEA FARING MAN!* I EARN MY LIVELIHOOD FROM THE SEA! IT'S MY WAY OF *LIFE!*

9

I'M NOT ASKING YOU TO CHANGE YOUR WAY OF LIFE, RED! YOU CAN HELP FATHER OPERATE HIS FISHING FLEET AS AN EXECUTIVE IN HIS OFFICE...IT'S A MARVELOUS OPPORTUNITY FOR A MAN WITH YOUR CAPABILITIES!

AN OFFICE HAS NO ROLLING DECK.. THE GREEN SWELLS AND COOL SPRAY ARE BARRED BY **WINDOWS** AND THERE'S A CEILING BETWEEN A MAN AND THE SKY!

AND DOES THE SEA PLANT KISSES LIKE MINE ON YOUR LIPS? DOES THE SPRAY CARESS YOUR CHEEK WITH THE TENDERNESS OF MY HAND? ARE THE GREEN SWELLS DEEPER THAN OUR LOVE?

"A HEAVY SILENCE PERVADED THE ROOM, I ANXIOUSLY SEARCHED THE TAUT, WEATHER-BEATEN FACE FOR A CLUE TO THE THOUGHTS RACING BEHIND ITS FROWNING MASK. RED'S COLD, BLUE EYES SLOWLY TURNED FULL UPON ME --- AND THE KNOT INSIDE ME COILED TIGHTER AS I WAITED FOR HIS REPLY."

I COULD NEVER DO WITHOUT YOU, SARI! I-I'LL STAY ASHORE IF THAT'S WHAT YOU WANT!

DARLING! DARLING! I'M SO HAPPY I COULD SHOUT WITH JOY! YOU'LL **NEVER** REGRET THIS, RED! NEVER! NEVER!

"ALTHOUGH, DAD WAS PLEASED TO HAVE RED ON HIS EXECUTIVE STAFF, I OCCASIONALLY FOUND HIM EYEING RED WITH NEW UNDERSTANDING ...AS FOR RED, HE MADE A SINCERE EFFORT TO TO ADJUST HIMSELF TO A LAND BOUND EXISTENCE.. AND I WAS ALWAYS NEARBY TO INTERRUPT THE SIREN SONG WHEN IT LURED RED FROM HIS WORK..."

DAY DREAMING, DEAR?

SOMETHING LIKE THAT, SARI...I JUST NOTICED THE "SALLY ANN" LEAVING PORT! SHE'S A BEAUTY, THAT SHIP!

DON'T WORRY NONE.. I'M STILL SAILING UNDER **YOUR** COMMAND, CAPTAIN! WHAT BRINGS YOU TO THE BRIDGE, SIR?

PREPARE TO GET UNDER WAY FOR A SHOPPING TOUR, MISTER! IF YOU'RE FREE, WE'LL PULL ANCHOR AT ONCE!

SOUNDS LIKE A DULL CRUISE FOR A SEAMAN WHO'S SAILED THROUGH THE TYPHOONS OFF SINGAPORE... HOWEVER, IF THOSE ARE THE CAPTAIN'S ORDERS --

OH, NOT AN ORDER, MATE -- MERELY A DESIRE FOR YOUR COMPANY... PLEASE COME!

10

"SHOPPING PROVED TO BE AN EMBARRASSING CHORE TO RED...HIS DISCOMFORT WAS POORLY DISGUISED BY A THINLY VEILED DOCILITY...MY ATTEMPTS AT CLEVER SMALL-TALK DID LITTLE TO PUT RED AT EASE...

I'VE SIMPLY GOT TO BUY THIS ADORABLE LITTLE LAMP! IT'S JUST LIKE OUR MEETING-- LOVE AT FIRST SIGHT!

YEAH-- SURE IS!

"RED REMINDED ME OF A GREAT TRANSPLANTED TREE FROM THE RUGGED, STORM SWEPT TONDRA... STRAINING WITH DIFFICULTY TO SPREAD ITS ROOTS IN A GENTLER CLIMATE...IT WAS A CRUCIAL PERIOD FOR US BOTH...WOULD RED BOLT THIS ALIEN ELEMENT INTO WHICH I HAD DRAWN HIM? I DIDN'T THINK HE WOULD.-- THE INCIDENT ON COBB STREET PROVED IT...

BUT I THOUGHT YOU'D LIKE THE WALK, RED. IT'S SUCH A BEAUTIFUL DAY!

I-I JUST REMEMBERED SOME UNFINISHED WORK AT THE OFFICE. LET'S TAKE A CAB.

NO-- THAT CAN'T BE HIM!

WELL, SINK ME FIFTY FATHOMS! RED PIKE! WHAT ARE YOU DOING IN THAT LANDLUBBER'S GETUP?

W-WHY, CAPTAIN FYFE...I-I HAVEN'T SEEN YOU IN MONTHS...

YES, LOTS OF TIME FOR MANY THINGS TO HAPPEN-- EVEN MIRACLES. I MUST SAY THOSE TOGS FIT YOU RIGHT SMART, LAD!

Y'KNOW, I'VE ALWAYS BEEN A GRUMPY OLD DOG, RED...WORKED MY CREWS LIKE OLD SATAN HIMSELF...HATED EVERY SCURVY MAN-JACK! YET, I NEVER DROVE YOU, RED... DIDN'T HAVE TO! YOU WERE THE KIND OF SEAMAN WHO SAILED FOR MORE THAN PAY AND GRUB ALONE... I FELT THIS SORTA MADE US KIN...

THERE'S BRINE IN YOUR BLOOD, LAD... YOU BELONG ON A BRIDGE OF A GOOD SHIP! IT'S FAR BETTER TO FLOUNDER IN THE HEART OF A STORM THAN ROT IN DRYDOCK!

I'M CERTAIN THAT YOU MEAN WELL, CAPTAIN... BUT THE LIFE I'M LEADING ISN'T AS DISAGREEABLE AS YOU IMAGINE..MY WORK IS IMPORTANT... MY FUTURE ...WELL, MEET MISS ALDEN...

"I MADE A RATHER SMALL IMPRESSION ON CAPTAIN FYFE.. HE APPRAISED ME BRIEFLY AS HE WOULD A BOTTLE OF WINE OR A NEW CIGAR--AND OUT OF HIS REGARD FOR RED, I WAS FAVORED WITH A CURT TIP OF THE CAPTAIN'S CAP... AFTER A FEW FRIENDLY EXCHANGES, WE WERE ONCE MORE ALONE ... RED HAD FACED HIS PAST WITHOUT ANY SIGNS OF REGRET...I WAS VERY PLEASED..."

DAD AND I WILL EXPECT YOU AT DINNER THIS EVENING, RED.. WE'RE HAVING FRIED CHICKEN!

I'M YOUR MAN FOR THAT DISH, HONEY.. I'LL BE THERE!

"THAT NIGHT, A BAD STORM OF UNPRECEDENTED *VIOLENCE* STRUCK THE COAST.. THE CONVERSATION AT THE DINNER TABLE WAS REPEATEDLY PUNCTUATED BY VIVID LIGHTNING FLASHES AND EXPLOSIVE BLASTS OF THUNDER ...FATHER AND RED EXCHANGED OCCASIONAL GLANCES OF GRIM FOREBODING, WHICH LIKE THE HOWLING RAIN OUTSIDE PROVED EXTREMELY DISCONCERTING..."

WHAT'S *WRONG* WITH YOU TWO? SURELY YOU'RE NOT ALLOWING THE *STORM* TO UPSET YOU--

"SUDDENLY, THE PHONE RANG! BOTH MEN WERE OUT OF THEIR CHAIRS SIMULTANEOUSLY.. FATHER WAS FIRST TO REACH THE RECEIVER."

YES-YES-- THE "SALLY ANN"? GET THE EQUIPMENT OUT, RIGHT AWAY!.

THE STORM HAS THROWN THE SALLY ANN ON DEAD MAN'S REEF! SHE'S GOT *TWENTY MEN* ABOARD HER!

YOU'VE GOT OIL SKINS, SIR! I WANT THEM! THERE'S NO TIME TO LOSE!

RED! PROMISE ME YOU'LL DIRECT THAT RESCUE FROM SHORE! YOU MUSTN'T TRY ANYTHING HAZARDOUS!

I'LL TRY WHATEVER I HAVE TO! THOSE MEN MUST BE BROUGHT TO SAFETY!

NO, RED, *NO!* I COULDN'T STAND IT IF ANYTHING HAPPENED TO YOU! DON'T GO, RED-- DON'T GO--

HAVE YOU GONE MAD, SARI? A SHIP'S BEING POUNDED TO PIECES ON THOSE ROCKS! WE'VE GOT TO GET A LINE TO THE MEN ABOARD HER! I'M GOING!

12

"FRANTIC WITH ANXIETY, I DONNED PROTECTIVE CLOTHING AND FOLLOWED FATHER AND RED INTO THE RAGING MADNESS OF WIND AND WATER THAT TORE FURIOUSLY AT EVERYTHING ABOUT US! I CLUNG TO THE STREAMING ROCKS ON THE BEACH -- WATCHING THE SCURRYING FIGURES AT THE WATER'S EDGE, TRYING TO OUTSHOUT THE GALES ALL PREVADING VOICE!

WE CAN'T SHOOT A LINE OUT TO THE SHIP! TOO FAR! IF WE REACH THEM AT ALL, IT'LL HAVE TO BE BY BOAT!

THEN WE'LL TAKE THE BOAT, MISTER ALDEN!

"MY TEETH DUG DEEPLY INTO MY LOWER LIP WHEN I SAW THE LIFEBOAT LAUNCHED INTO THE HEAVING MOUNTAINS OF WATER! THE ATTEMPT SEEMED LUDICROUS IN THE FACE OF THE CYCLOPEAN ANGER HURLED AT THESE MEN! THEY HUDDLED LIKE ANTS IN THE HOLLOW OF A BOBBING TOY! WITH THE DANGER OF CAPSIZING EVER WITH THEM, RED AND HIS MEN MANAGED TO MAKE HEADWAY!

"IT WAS IMPOSSIBLE TO WITNESS THE DARING RESCUE WORK, BUT I WAS CERTAIN THAT RED'S HERCULEAN FIGURE WAS IN THE FOREGROUND OF WHATEVER OCCURRED!!

" WHEN THE LAST BOATLOAD OF SURVIVORS WAS BATTLING ITS WAY TO SHORE, THE SALLY ANN WAS TORN BY THE SEA FROM HER ROCKY CRUCIFIXION, AND SHE VANISHED IN THE BOILING FURY...

13

PULL ON THOSE OARS, MEN! PULL HARD! THIS NIGHT'S WORK IS ALMOST DONE!

WE **MADE** IT, RED! SAVED THE WHOLE CREW! SURE THOUGHT WE WERE COMMITTING SUICIDE!

"RED WAS STILL BELLOWING ORDERS TO THE MEN WHISKING THE SALLY ANN'S HALF-DROWNED CREW TO SHELTER, WHEN I FOUGHT MY WAY THROUGH THE WIND TO HIS SIDE! ONE OF RED'S GREAT ARMS DREW ME CLOSE AS THE OTHER CONTINUED TO GESTICULATE WITH AUTHORITATIVE MOTIONS!!"

"HIS FACE WAS AS I HAD SEEN IT IN MY DREAMS- FIERCE AND CONTORTED BY THE WET BITE OF THE RAIN!!! IT WAS THE TERRIFYING MAJESTY OF ERIC THE RED I GAZED AT --- THE SAME FACE THAT FIRED MY EMOTIONS *ANOTHER* NIGHT IN ANOTHER STORM..."

"IT CAME TO ME THEN, THAT THIS WAS THE MAN I LOVED AS I REALLY WANTED TO SEE HIM! --- THAT I WAS FOOLISHLY TRADING THIS INSPIRING MAN FOR A RESIGNED, UNHAPPY CREATURE BEHIND A DESK... I HELD ON TIGHTLY TO THIS *RED* I HAD ALMOST DESTROYED..."

CHICKEN! YOU SHOULDN'T HAVE COME OUT IN THIS STORM!

RED, I'VE NEVER BEEN SO FRIGHTENED OR THRILLED IN ALL MY LIFE! YOU WERE WONDERFUL!

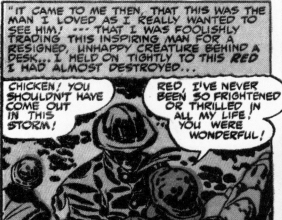

YOU KNOW, SARI- THERE'S A MAGIC IN THE STORM AND THE SWEEPING SEA THAT NEVER TOUCHES MOST MEN! BUT IT DOES ME! I HAVEN'T FELT SO FREE AND ALIVE IN WEEKS!

AND WHEN YOU'RE LIKE THIS, I SENSE THE MAGIC TOO, RED! IT'S A GIFT FROM THE SEA! WE'LL **SHARE** IT WITH THE SEA --- TOGETHER! WE'LL NEVER LOSE IT AGAIN!

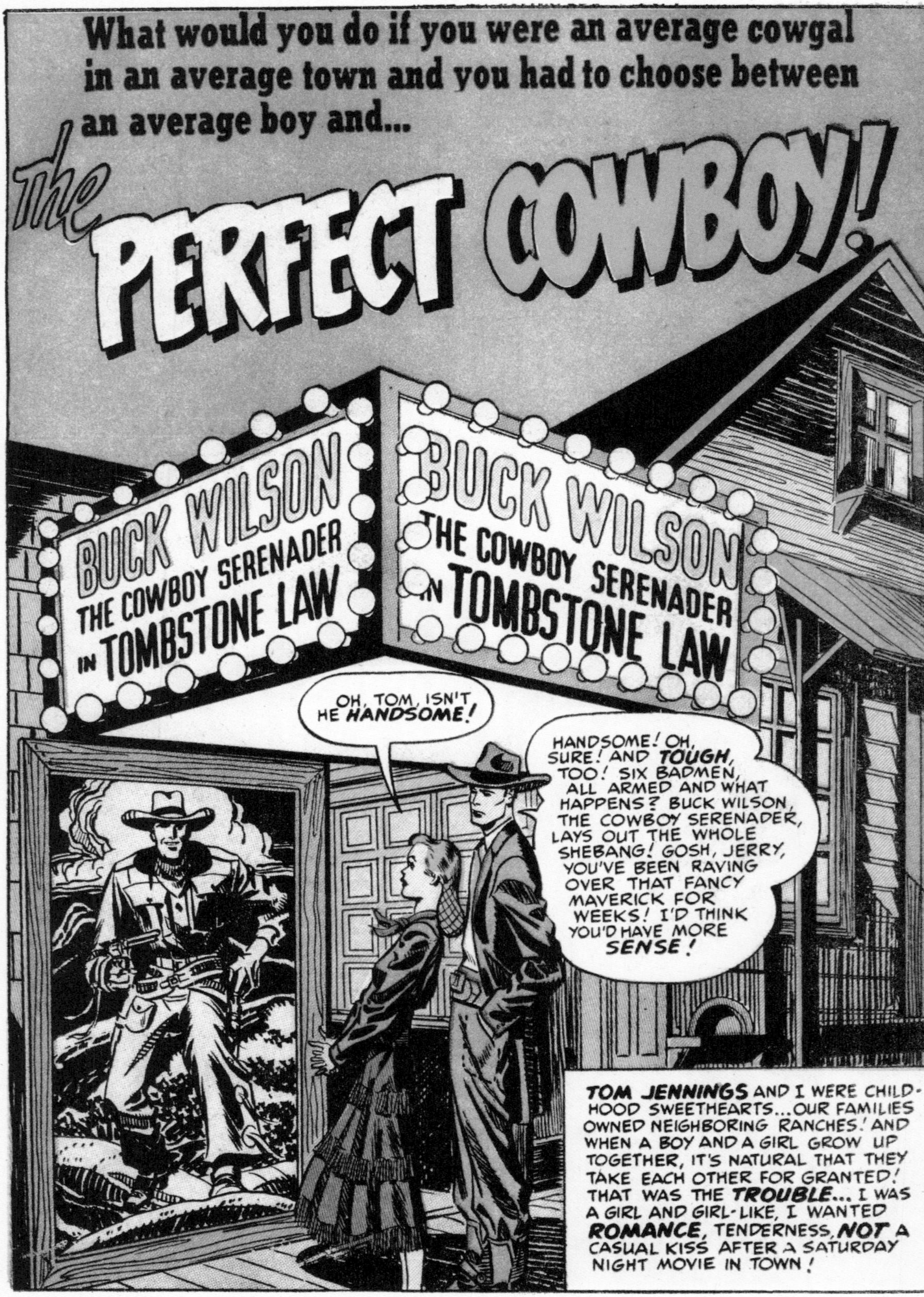

What would you do if you were an average cowgal in an average town and you had to choose between an average boy and...
The PERFECT COWBOY!
BUCK WILSON THE COWBOY SERENADER IN TOMBSTONE LAW
BUCK WILSON THE COWBOY SERENADER IN TOMBSTONE LAW
OH, TOM, ISN'T HE HANDSOME!
HANDSOME! OH, SURE! AND TOUGH, TOO! SIX BADMEN, ALL ARMED AND WHAT HAPPENS? BUCK WILSON, THE COWBOY SERENADER, LAYS OUT THE WHOLE SHEBANG! GOSH, JERRY, YOU'VE BEEN RAVING OVER THAT FANCY MAVERICK FOR WEEKS! I'D THINK YOU'D HAVE MORE SENSE!
TOM JENNINGS AND I WERE CHILDHOOD SWEETHEARTS... OUR FAMILIES OWNED NEIGHBORING RANCHES! AND WHEN A BOY AND A GIRL GROW UP TOGETHER, IT'S NATURAL THAT THEY TAKE EACH OTHER FOR GRANTED! THAT WAS THE TROUBLE... I WAS A GIRL AND GIRL-LIKE, I WANTED ROMANCE, TENDERNESS, NOT A CASUAL KISS AFTER A SATURDAY NIGHT MOVIE IN TOWN!

THE TROUBLE WITH YOU, TOM JENNINGS, IS THAT YOU CAN'T *UNDERSTAND ANYTHING*. YOU CAN'T ROPE AND BRAND! MAYBE IF YOU'D SPEND A LITTLE MORE TIME COURTING ME, LIKE... LIKE *BUCK WILSON* DOES IN HIS PICTURES, INSTEAD OF TREATING ME LIKE AN OLD SADDLE, I'D BE RAVING ABOUT *YOU!*

WELL, SINCE YOU SEEM TO PREFER *HIM* MAYBE YOU'LL FIND OUT FOR *YOURSELF* IN A COUPLE OF WEEKS JUST HOW LOCO YOU'RE ACTIN'!

BUCK WILSON IS COMING HERE, TO LITTLE BEND! HE'S GOING TO MAKE A PICTURE ON OUR RANGE! MAYBE WHEN YOU SEE HIM IN THE FLESH, YOU WON'T BE MAKING SUCH A *FUSS* OVER A MOVIE HERO!

OH, TOM, NO! IT CAN'T BE TRUE! *NOTHING* EVER HAPPENS IN LITTLE BEND! NOTHING SO... SO *EXCITING!*

"BUT IT *WAS* TRUE! SUDDENLY, ON A DAY THREE WEEKS LATER, LITTLE BEND UNDERWENT A TRANSFORMATION... IN ONE DAY, WHAT HAD BEEN A SLEEPY LITTLE COW-TOWN BE-CAME AN INFERNO OF ACTIONS, TRUCKS, MICRO-PHONES, LIGHTS! *AND THROUGH IT ALL MOVED BUCK WILSON CALM AND UNRUFFLED AS THE STRONG, SILENT MEN HE PLAYED ON THE SCREEN!* WHEN I MET HIM AT LAST, IT WAS BY ACCIDENT, QUITE BY *ACCIDENT!*

ALL RIGHT, BUCK! IN THIS SHOT YOU'RE JUST RIDING INTO TOWN. YOU SPOT A PRETTY GIRL AND FLASH THE OLD PERSONALITY SMILE. THEN YOU.... *WAIT A MINUTE!* PRETTY GIRL! WE'LL NEED A *GIRL!*

YOU! THINK YOU CAN SMILE AND LOOK PRETTY FOR TWENTY-FIVE BUCKS? YOU'RE PRETTY, DRESSED RIGHT... PERFECT! HOW ABOUT IT?

"I STILL CAN'T SAY HOW IT ALL CAME ABOUT. ALL IN A MOMENT I HAD BEEN LED TO A SPOT, TOLD WHERE TO WALK AND WHEN, AND THE ORDER HAD BEEN GIVEN: *ROLL 'EM!* I WALKED DOWN THE BOARD-PAVED SIDEWALK AS IF IN A DREAM!

THAT'S IT, BUCK! SLOW, SLOW!

"AND AS IF IN A DREAM, I NEVER SAW THE PLANK WHICH REACHED OUT, TREACHEROUSLY, AND SEIZED MY FOOT!

NOW, MISS, YOU... *HOLY COW!* A PERFECT TAKE *RUINED!*

"FOR A "FANCY" COWBOY, BUCK WILSON MOVED WITH THE SPEED AND EASE OF A RATTLER! EVEN AS I FELL I COULD SEE HIM LEAVE HIS HORSE IN ONE SMOOTH MOTION AND IN A MOMENT LATER STRONG HANDS HAD SET ME BACK ON MY FEET...

2

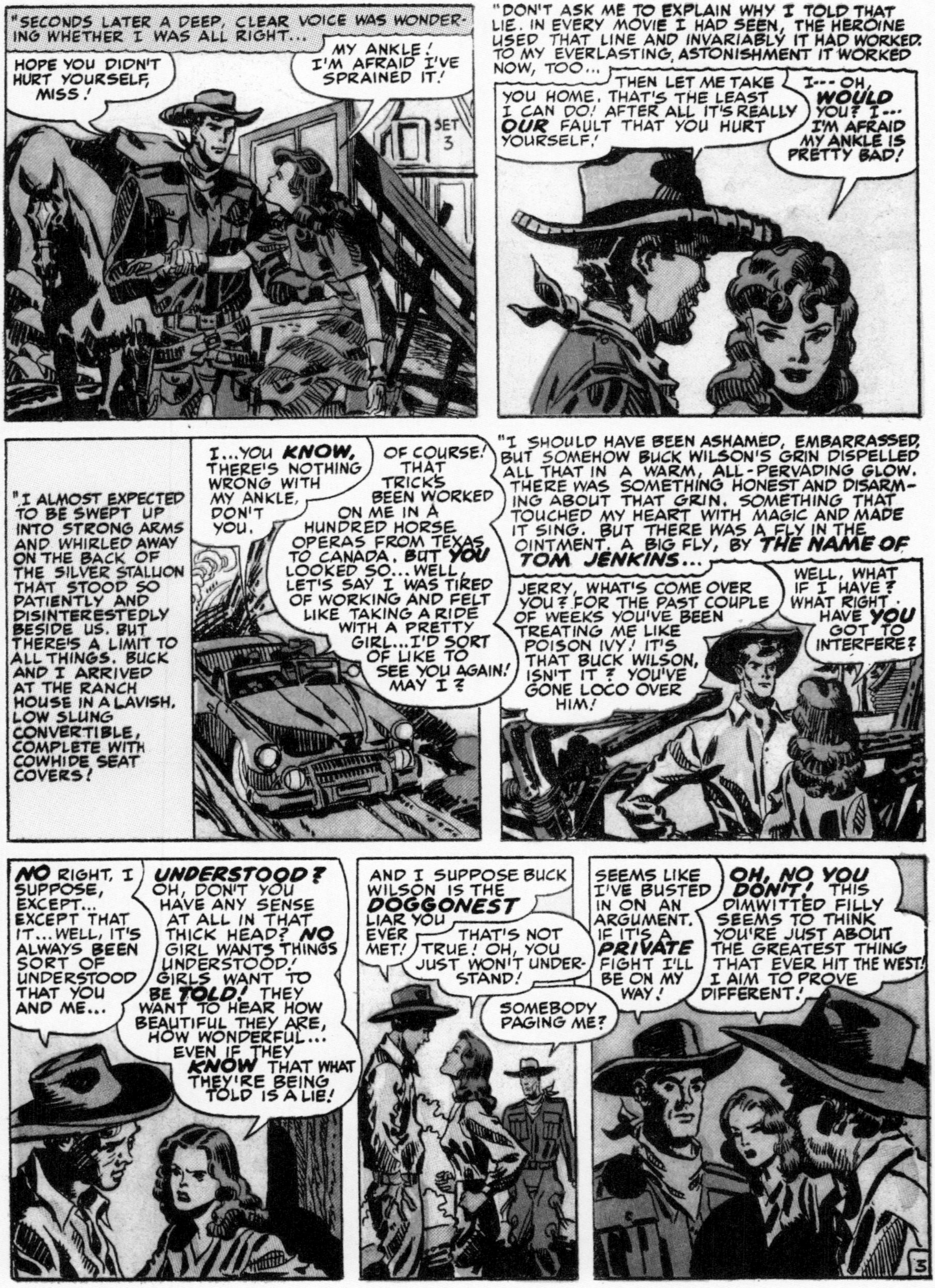
"SECONDS LATER A DEEP, CLEAR VOICE WAS WONDERING WHETHER I WAS ALL RIGHT...
HOPE YOU DIDN'T HURT YOURSELF, MISS!
MY ANKLE! I'M AFRAID I'VE SPRAINED IT!
SET 3
"DON'T ASK ME TO EXPLAIN WHY I TOLD THAT LIE. IN EVERY MOVIE I HAD SEEN, THE HEROINE USED THAT LINE AND INVARIABLY IT HAD WORKED. TO MY EVERLASTING ASTONISHMENT IT WORKED NOW, TOO...
THEN LET ME TAKE YOU HOME. THAT'S THE LEAST I CAN DO! AFTER ALL IT'S REALLY OUR FAULT THAT YOU HURT YOURSELF!
I--- OH, WOULD YOU? I--- I'M AFRAID MY ANKLE IS PRETTY BAD!
"I ALMOST EXPECTED TO BE SWEPT UP INTO STRONG ARMS AND WHIRLED AWAY ON THE BACK OF THE SILVER STALLION THAT STOOD SO PATIENTLY AND DISINTERESTEDLY BESIDE US. BUT THERE'S A LIMIT TO ALL THINGS. BUCK AND I ARRIVED AT THE RANCH HOUSE IN A LAVISH, LOW SLUNG CONVERTIBLE, COMPLETE WITH COWHIDE SEAT COVERS!
I...YOU KNOW, THERE'S NOTHING WRONG WITH MY ANKLE, DON'T YOU.
OF COURSE! THAT TRICK'S BEEN WORKED ON ME IN A HUNDRED HORSE OPERAS FROM TEXAS TO CANADA. BUT YOU LOOKED SO...WELL, LET'S SAY I WAS TIRED OF WORKING AND FELT LIKE TAKING A RIDE WITH A PRETTY GIRL...I'D SORT OF LIKE TO SEE YOU AGAIN! MAY I?
"I SHOULD HAVE BEEN ASHAMED, EMBARRASSED, BUT SOMEHOW BUCK WILSON'S GRIN DISPELLED ALL THAT IN A WARM, ALL-PERVADING GLOW. THERE WAS SOMETHING HONEST AND DISARMING ABOUT THAT GRIN. SOMETHING THAT TOUCHED MY HEART WITH MAGIC AND MADE IT SING. BUT THERE WAS A FLY IN THE OINTMENT. A BIG FLY, BY THE NAME OF TOM JENKINS...
JERRY, WHAT'S COME OVER YOU? FOR THE PAST COUPLE OF WEEKS YOU'VE BEEN TREATING ME LIKE POISON IVY! IT'S THAT BUCK WILSON, ISN'T IT? YOU'VE GONE LOCO OVER HIM!
WELL, WHAT IF I HAVE? WHAT RIGHT HAVE YOU GOT TO INTERFERE?
NO RIGHT, I SUPPOSE, EXCEPT... EXCEPT THAT IT...WELL, IT'S ALWAYS BEEN SORT OF UNDERSTOOD THAT YOU AND ME...
UNDERSTOOD? OH, DON'T YOU HAVE ANY SENSE AT ALL IN THAT THICK HEAD? NO GIRL WANTS THINGS UNDERSTOOD! GIRLS WANT TO BE TOLD! THEY WANT TO HEAR HOW BEAUTIFUL THEY ARE, HOW WONDERFUL... EVEN IF THEY KNOW THAT WHAT THEY'RE BEING TOLD IS A LIE!
AND I SUPPOSE BUCK WILSON IS THE DOGGONEST LIAR YOU EVER MET!
THAT'S NOT TRUE! OH, YOU JUST WON'T UNDERSTAND!
SOMEBODY PAGING ME?
SEEMS LIKE I'VE BUSTED IN ON AN ARGUMENT. IF IT'S A PRIVATE FIGHT I'LL BE ON MY WAY!
OH, NO YOU DON'T! THIS DIMWITTED FILLY SEEMS TO THINK YOU'RE JUST ABOUT THE GREATEST THING THAT EVER HIT THE WEST! I AIM TO PROVE DIFFERENT!
3

I SEE. AND JUST HOW DO YOU EXPECT TO DO THAT?

YOUR PRESS AGENT HAS BUILT YOU UP AS THE BEST MAN WITH A HOSS OR A GUN IN FORTY EIGHT STATES! THERE'S A HOSS IN THAT CORRAL THAT'S NEVER BEEN RIDDEN! LET'S SEE WHAT *YOU* CAN DO WITH HIM!

TOM! NOT CYCLONE! BUCK-- YOU WOULDN'T RISK YOUR LIFE TO TAKE UP A SILLY DARE!

WHAT'S THE MATTER, JERRY? AFRAID YOUR *MOVIE HERO* WON'T BE ABLE TO TAKE IT?

TOM! YOU'RE ACTING LIKE A SILLY SCHOOL-BOY!

NO, JERRY! *NOBODY* CALLS A DARE ON BUCK WILSON! I'LL RIDE CYCLONE!

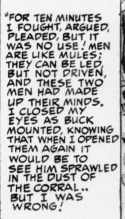

"FOR TEN MINUTES I FOUGHT, ARGUED, PLEADED, BUT IT WAS NO USE! MEN ARE LIKE MULES; THEY CAN BE LED, BUT NOT DRIVEN, AND THESE TWO MEN HAD MADE UP THEIR MINDS. I CLOSED MY EYES AS BUCK MOUNTED, KNOWING THAT WHEN I OPENED THEM AGAIN IT WOULD BE TO SEE HIM SPRAWLED IN THE DUST OF THE CORRAL.. BUT I WAS WRONG!

TOM, HE'S *RIDING* HIM!

"IT WAS A MAGNIFICENT RIDE! ANY GIRL BORN AND BRED IN THE WEST AS I HAD BEEN WOULD HAVE THRILLED TO IT. WHEN IT WAS OVER, BUCK WILSON RODE CYCLONE TOWARD US LIKE A CONQUERING HERO...

MAYBE I SHOULD HAVE TOLD YOU, JENNINGS-- I TOOK FIVE FIRSTS FOR BRONC BUSTING IN RODEOS BEFORE I TACKLED MOVIES!

TOM! WAIT!

LET HIM GO, JERRY! A JEALOUS MAN IS PRETTY TOUGH TO TALK SOME SENSE INTO! HE'LL BE BACK!

TOM AND I HAVE KNOWN EACH OTHER SINCE WE WERE KIDS. WE'VE NEVER QUARRELED BEFORE, I--I GUESS HE THINKS I--I'M IN LOVE WITH YOU!

MAYBE IT'S THE OTHER WAY AROUND. MAYBE HE THINKS *I'M* IN LOVE WITH *YOU!*

"THERE HADN'T BEEN MANY TENDER MOMENTS IN MY LIFE, BUT SOMETIMES ONE TENSE ECSTATIC MOMENT CAN TAKE THE PLACE OF *MANY*! BUCK DID NOT ANSWER AT ONCE! INSTEAD HE DREW ME *GENTLY* INTO HIS ARMS AND *KISSED* ME!

JERRY, I'VE KNOWN LOTS OF WOMEN IN LOTS OF PLACES BUT I'VE *NEVER* MET ONE LIKE YOU-- YOU'RE COOL, BLUE WATER IN THE DESERT. *I LOVE YOU, JERRY!*

"THIS WAS FULFILLMENT ALL AT ONCE. FATE HAD GIVEN ME EVERYTHING I HAD DREAMED OF FOR SO LONG-- IT WAS A BEAUTIFUL, *BEAUTIFUL* DAY -- BUCK AND I WERE TOGETHER UNTIL FAR INTO THE EVENING! WE FINALLY PARTED WITH SOFT SIGHS OF RELUCTANCE!

DAD! I DIDN'T KNOW YOU HAD COMPANY!

THIS IS MR. LEWIS, JERRY!

YOUR DAUGHTER AND I HAVE *MET*, MR. ANDERSON! I'LL COME RIGHT TO THE POINT, MISS ANDERSON! I'VE COME TO ASK YOU TO *STOP* SEEING BUCK WILSON!

BUCK WILSON IS HERE TO MAKE A PICTURE! IN *OUR* BUSINESS, MISS ANDERSON, *TIME* IS *MONEY*! AND SINCE BUCK MET YOU HE JUST HASN'T BEEN WORKING! SO, JUST AS A FAVOR, IF YOU'D STOP SEEING HIM--

BUCK ISN'T A *CHILD* AND NEITHER AM *I*! WHAT RIGHT DO YOU HAVE TO ASK A THING LIKE THAT! BUCK *LOVES* ME!

SO IT'S GONE AS FAR AS THAT ALREADY. WELL, YOU LEAVE ME NO CHOICE, MISS ANDERSON! YOU MAY AS WELL KNOW THE TRUTH! BUCK WILSON HAS MADE LOVE TO ONE GIRL ON *EVERY* LOCATION TRIP HE'S EVER TAKEN! *SURE* HE LOVES YOU, JUST AS HE LOVED THAT GIRL IN BUTTE-- AND THE ONE IN SAN ANTONIO! BUCK IS AN *ACTOR*! HE CAN NO MORE HELP MAKING LOVE TO A PRETTY GIRL THAN HE CAN HELP BREATHING!

YOU'RE *LYING*! YOU'RE *LYING*! GET *OUT*! *GET OUT*!

NOW HOLD ON, JERRY! MAYBE THERE'S MORE TO THIS THAN YOU *WANT* TO BELIEVE!

NEVER MIND, MR. ANDERSON! I'M LEAVING ANYWAY! JUST REMEMBER, MISS ANDERSON, I *WARNED* YOU!

"IT COULDN'T BE TRUE! IT *COULDN'T*! WOMAN-LIKE, I *SHUT* THE MEMORY OF THAT INTERVIEW FROM MY MIND! AND IF NOW OR THEN WHEN I WAS WITH BUCK, A TINY MAGGOT OF *SUSPICION* CRAWLED INTO MY BRAIN, I SOON FORGOT IN THE BEAUTY AND SWEETNESS OF HIS EMBRACE...

JERRY, JERRY! HOW DID I EVER MANAGE TO GO THROUGH LIFE BEFORE I MET YOU? THAT WASN'T *LIVING*! IT *COULDN'T* HAVE BEEN! ONLY *THIS* IS REAL!

TAKE ONE, SCENE ONE! VERY PRETTY!

5

TOM! HOW **COULD** YOU SPY ON US! YOU USED TO BE A GENTLEMAN!

I'M SORRY, JERRY. I GUESS THAT REMARK WAS UNCALLED FOR! BUT I **WASN'T** SPYING! I RODE OVER TO ASK YOU TO THE DANCE! TOWN'S THROWING A PARTY FOR THE PICTURE COMPANY, 'FORE THEY LEAVE TOWN!

SOMETIMES UNCALLED FOR REMARKS GET FOLKS INTO TROUBLE... ALL KINDS OF TROUBLE! LIKE A GOOD **SOCK** ON THE JAW, FOR INSTANCE!

I SAID I WAS SORRY! BUT IF YOU'RE HANKERIN' FOR TROUBLE, FANCY PANTS, MAYBE I CAN **OBLIGE!**

FAIR ENOUGH! THAT'S JUST WHAT I'M HANKERIN' FOR!

BUCK! STOP IT! YOU'RE BOTH BEHAVING LIKE **CHILDREN!**

ALL RIGHT, JERRY. I GUESS I--I **AM** A LITTLE OUT OF LINE! ABOUT THE DANCE, THOUGH... WILL YOU--

YOU'RE A LITTLE LATE, JENNINGS! JERRY'S GOING WITH **ME!**

"PERHAPS I WAS A **FOOL,** BUT I SAID NOTHING! BUCK HAD **NOT** ASKED ME TO THE DANCE! UNTIL THAT MOMENT I HAD NOT EVEN KNOWN THAT SUCH AN EVENT WAS TO TAKE PLACE! BUT SOMETHING, CALL IT A WOMAN'S INTUITION IF YOU WILL, HELD MY TONGUE UNTIL AFTER TOM JENNING HAD GONE!

YOU **WILL** GO WITH ME, WON'T YOU, JERRY?

YES, BUCK, I'LL GO WITH YOU! I WANT TO GO TO THAT DANCE! SOMEHOW I HAVE AN IDEA IT'S GOING TO BE IMPORTANT!

"INTUITION? YES, PERHAPS IT **WAS** INTUITION! BUT IT WAS **MORE** THAN THAT! DEEP DOWN INSIDE, I THINK I HAD ALWAYS KNOWN WHERE I STOOD! **NOW** I WAS TO FIND OUT FOR SURE! IT BEGAN WITH DAD'S ANNOUNCEMENT!

FOLKS, AS YOU ALL KNOW, ACME PICTURES HAVE **FINISHED** THEIR JOB IN THESE PARTS! I KNOW WE'LL ALL BE SORRY TO SEE THEM GO! BUT BEFORE THEY DO, THEIR STAR, BUCK WILSON, HAS VOLUNTEERED TO DO A NUMBER FOR US! OKAY, BOYS, **STRIKE UP THE BAND!**

"BUCK WAS **MAGNIFICENT!** THERE WAS POISE IN EVERY INCH OF HIS SIX FEET OF BONE AND MUSCLE! HE MOUNTED THE PLATFORM AND THE SMOOTH TONES FLOWED OUT OVER THE CROWD! I FELT A THRILL OF **PRIDE!** PRIDE AND-- SOMETHING ELSE! SOMETHING I COULD NOT DEFINE, BUT WHICH SENT A LITTLE CHILL OF APPREHENSION DOWN MY SPINE!

I GOTTA ADMIT THAT GUY CAN **SING!**

YES, HE **IS** GOOD, ISN'T HE?

YOU DON'T SOUND VERY *ENTHUSIASTIC!* WHAT'S THE MATTER? YOU AND ROMEO HAVE A SCRAP?

NOT THAT IT'S ANY OF *YOUR* BUSINESS, BUT THE ANSWER IS NO! BUCK AND I HAVE NEVER HAD A QUARREL! WE *COULDN'T!* WE--

"NO WE COULDN'T! IT WAS *TRUE!* HOW DOES ONE GO ABOUT QUARRELING WITH A MAN WHO IS PERFECTION? A VAGUE FEAR DRIFTED THROUGH MY MIND! HOW--? BUT THERE WAS NO TIME THEN TO THINK OF THAT! DAD WAS MAKING ANOTHER ANNOUNCEMENT!

ALL RIGHT, FOLKS! WE ALL KNOW THAT WAS A *GREAT* NUMBER AND MAYBE BUCK WILL OBLIGE US WITH ANOTHER, LATER ON! RIGHT NOW, EVERYBODY OUTSIDE FOR THE *PISTOL MATCH!*

"TOM JENNINGS WAS THE BEST SHOT WITH A SIX-SHOOTER THAT LITTLE BEND HAD *EVER* KNOWN! EVERYONE ADMITTED THAT! BUT I KNEW THAT TODAY HE WOULD BE *BEATEN!* IT WAS JUST-- JUST IN THE NATURE OF THINGS! AND AS HE HOLSTERED HIS GUN AFTER HIS CHANCE AT THE TARGET, I BEGAN TO UNDERSTAND, A LITTLE, WHAT WAS TROUBLING ME!

NOT BAD! *FOUR BULLS'-EYES* AND *TWO NEAR MISSES!* NOT BAD AT ALL!

ALL RIGHT, LET'S SEE WHAT YOU CAN DO, FANCY PANTS!

IT'S A *PLEASURE!*

BAM BAM BAM BAM BAM BAM

SIX BULLS'-EYES!! AND SO CLOSE TOGETHER THAT THE SPADE ON A PLAYING CARD COULD COVER THEM ALL! WAS IT ANY WONDER THAT TOM SLUNK AWAY! I SHOULD HAVE BEEN PUFFED WITH PRIDE IN BUCK'S ACCOMPLISHMENTS, BUT THAT WAS NOT WHAT I FELT! NOT EVEN WHEN HE SOUGHT ME OUT, LATER, AFTER THE OTHERS HAD DEPARTED TO THE BARN DANCE...

DREAMING, JERRY? ABOUT *ME*, I HOPE!

NO, BUCK! *THINKING!*

DON'T! IT PUTS FURROWS IN THAT PRETTY WHITE FOREHEAD. YOU KNOW, YOU SHOULD *ALWAYS* BE SEEN BY MOONLIGHT! IT BECOMES YOU! YOU'RE BEAUTIFUL, JERRY!

YOU ALWAYS SAY THE RIGHT THING, DON'T YOU, BUCK?

ONLY TO THE *RIGHT* PEOPLE, JERRY. AND YOU'RE THE RIGHT PEOPLE! DON'T YOU *WANT* ME TO SAY THINGS TO YOU? YOU KNOW I..

NO, BUCK, DON'T SAY IT! IT WOULD BE SOMETHING *BEAUTIFUL* I KNOW, BUT DON'T SAY IT! DO YOU WANT TO KNOW WHAT I WAS THINKING, BUCK? I WAS THINKING WHAT IT WOULD BE LIKE TO BE MARRIED TO AN INSTITUTION! THAT'S *YOU*, BUCK! WHATEVER YOU DO, YOU DO BETTER THAN ANYONE ELSE! NO QUARRELS, NO SPATS, JUST *PERFECTION!* I DON'T THINK I COULD STAND IT!

JERRY! ARE YOU TELLING ME YOU WOULDN'T *MARRY* ME? EVEN IF I ASKED YOU?

THAT'S JUST WHAT I'M TELLING YOU! YOU WERE NEVER INTENDED FOR MARRIAGE, BUCK! THERE'LL BE *OTHER* GIRLS.. IN BUTTE AND IN SAN ANTONIO, AND IN A HUNDRED OTHER TOWNS! YOU WERE MEANT TO CHARM *ALL* WOMEN, NOT JUST ONE! GOOD-BYE, BUCK! GOODBYE,-- AND *THANKS!*

"IT WAS A VERY AMAZED BUCK WILSON WHO REMAINED ROOTED IN HIS TRACKS AFTER I HAD *LEFT* HIM -- AMAZED, BUT NOT *TOO BADLY* DAMAGED! AS FOR ME, I HAD THINGS TO DO! ONE OF THE MUSICIANS TOLD ME WHERE TOM HAD GONE!

TOM! TOM! WAIT!

JERRY! WHAT ARE *YOU* DOING OUT HERE!

TOM, DO YOU REMEMBER *MILLER'S POND?* WE USED TO GO THERE, WHEN WE WERE KIDS--AND SKIP ROCKS ACROSS THE WATER! TAKE ME THERE NOW, TOM!

MILLER'S POND! NOW? HAVE YOU GONE OUT OF YOUR *MIND?*

NO, I'VE COME TO MY *SENSES!* DON'T ARGUE WITH ME, YOU BIG GOOF! I WANT YOU TO GO TO MILLER'S POND, JUST LIKE WE USED TO DO! BUT FIRST-- WILL YOU *KISS* ME, TOM?

WILL I-- YOU *HAVE* GONE OUT OF YOUR MIND! BUT I'M JUST *CRAZY* ENOUGH TO TAKE ADVANTAGE OF IT!

"THERE WAS NOTHING OF PERFECTION ABOUT THAT KISS... IT WAS ROUGH AND EAGER AND DEMANDING! BUT IT CAME FROM THE *HEART*, AND WE *DID* GO TO MILLER'S POND...

I'LL BEAT YOU THIS TIME!

OH, WILL YOU! WATCH THIS! BET IT BEATS YOURS BY THREE JUMPS!

THAT'S HOW IT *WAS!* THAT'S HOW IT'S GOING TO BE FOR ALWAYS AND ALWAYS! TOM ISN'T THE *HANDSOMEST* MAN IN THE WORLD, NOR THE *BEST* RIDER, NOR THE *FINEST* SHOT, BUT HE'S SOMETHING FAR MORE IMPORTANT! SOMETIMES WHEN WE QUARREL, I REMIND MYSELF OF THAT AND THEN I'M HAPPY AGAIN! YOU SEE-- HE'S *MINE!*

8

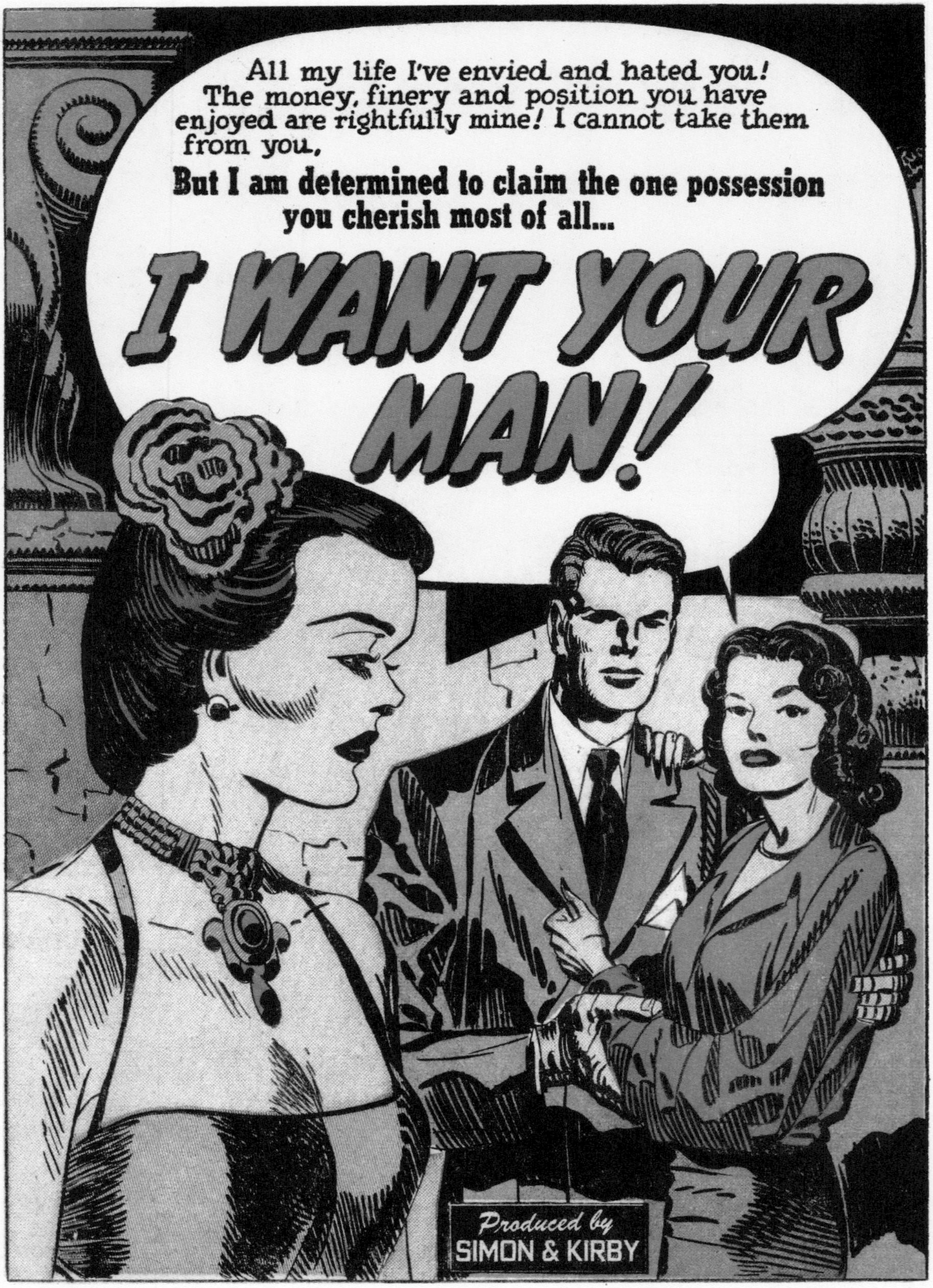
All my life I've envied and hated you! The money, finery and position you have enjoyed are rightfully mine! I cannot take them from you,
But I am determined to claim the one possession you cherish most of all...
I WANT YOUR MAN!
Produced by SIMON & KIRBY

"HATRED IS BORN OF ENVY... AND THERE WAS NOBODY IN TOWN I ENVIED MORE THAN JOANNE AINSWORTH.. IT SEEMED TO ME THAT HER EXISTENCE WAS A MALIGNANT ACT ON THE PART OF FATE TO MOCK ME TILL ETERNITY WITH THE THINGS I WANTED AND COULD NOT HAVE.. WE WERE BOTH OF MORTAL FLESH! BOTH SUBJECT TO THE SAME DESIRES! WHY WERE HERS FULFILLED AND NOT MINE? WHY? WHY? EVEN AS A LITTLE GIRL I SEETHED AGAINST THIS INJUSTICE! AND DETESTED ITS SYMBOL—JOANNE AINSWORTH!"

LOOK, MARSHA! A PONY!

WHAT OF IT?

SO JOANNE AINSWORTH HAS A PONY! SO WHAT? WHO CARES? WHO CARES? LOOK AT ME, BETTE! LOOK AT WHAT I CAN DO!

"I CARED, ALL RIGHT! JEALOUSY WAS INTENSE AND CHAOTIC INSIDE ME.. BUT I WAS TOO PROUD A CHILD TO HURL INVECTIVES.. INSTEAD I RELEASED MY RESENTMENT IN A WILD OUTBURST OF ENERGY! MY YOUNGER SISTER, BETTE, LOOKED ON, WIDE-EYED WITH CONCERN!"

HOW'S THAT?

MARSHA! COME DOWN! YOU'LL HURT YOURSELF!

"I GAVE LITTLE HEED TO BETTE'S SHRILL VOICE! NO MORE THAN A CHILD MYSELF, I WAS UNABLE TO FATHOM THE REASON FOR MY CAPERS... BUT I WAS AWARE OF UNPLEASANT FEELINGS! AND SOUGHT ESCAPE FROM THEM IN WHIRLING MOVEMENT!!!"

"MY ANTICS LACKED BOTH CAUTION AND GOOD JUDGMENT! WHILE COMPLETING A SHORT ARC I REACHED FOR A METAL BAR WHICH WASN'T THERE! THE EARTH SUDDENLY TILTED SHARPLY AND RUSHED AT ME..."

MARSHA!

"MINGLED WITH THE PANIC THAT GRIPPED ME AS I FELL, WAS JUST ONE THOUGHT! 'I HATE JOANNE AINSWORTH!' THEN IT WAS DARK FOR A LONG, LONG TIME!"

95

"WHEN I AWOKE, I WAS IN MY BED AT HOME — THE SUBJECT OF MY PARENTS' DEEP **CONCERN!**

THERE! SHE'S COMING TO NOW! SHE'LL BE **ALL RIGHT!**

MY POOR LITTLE GIRL! MY **POOR** MARSHA!

MAMA—

YES, DARLING — IT'S **MAMA!** YOU HURT YOURSELF, BABY... A POLICE-MAN BROUGHT YOU HOME!

MAMA -- COULD I HAVE A PONY? **JOANNE AINSWORTH** HAS A PONY—

A **PONY**—

I'LL NEVER UNDERSTAND THE MIND OF A CHILD... INSTEAD OF WAILING OVER THAT BRUISE, THE **ONLY** THING THAT CONCERNS HER IS A GIFT I CAN'T AFFORD TO BUY HER!

CHILDREN ARE LIKE THAT, MISTER BAKER! I SUGGEST YOU DON'T DISTURB HER NOW! LET HER **REST**... I'LL BE AVAILABLE IF I'M NEEDED! GOOD DAY!

"I DRIFTED IN A TWILIGHT WORLD OF SEMI-AWARENESS -- THE THROBBING OF MY WOUND PREVENTING COMPLETE RELAXATION... AND THROUGH THE HALF-OPENED DOOR OF MY ROOM THE LOW SOUND OF VOICES **HUMMED** ACROSS THE SILENCE TO WHERE I RESTED! IT WAS MOTHER AND DAD...

THREE DOLLARS FOR THE DOCTOR! AND A HALF DAY LOST AT THE TROLLEY LINE! WHY CAN'T THESE KIDS BE MORE **CAREFUL?**

I HAD TO CALL YOU HOME, STEVE! AFTER ALL MARSHA **IS** OUR CHILD, AND SHE IS HURT!

NOW DON'T BRAND ME AS BEING CALLOUS, DOLLY! I'M A MOTORMAN – NOT A BANK PRESIDENT! IT'S HARD ENOUGH MAKING ENDS MEET WITHOUT HAVING **EXTRA** EXPENSES!

BUT ACCIDENTS ARE BOUND TO HAPPEN, STEVE! YOU CAN'T EXPECT A CHILD TO USE ADULT CAUTION... PLEASE LET'S NOT QUARREL!!

3

AND WHERE ON EARTH DOES MARSHA PICK UP THESE NOTIONS ABOUT EXPENSIVE GIFTS? IT'S TIME SHE BEGAN TO LEARN THAT THE POOR MUST THINK ONLY OF *NECESSITIES*! AND TO LEAVE THE LUXURIES FOR THE RICH!

STEVE-- PLEASE DON'T--

FOR HEAVEN'S SAKE, *STOP CRYING*! YOU'RE *ALWAYS* CRYING! PROBABLY, BECAUSE YOU MARRIED ME-- WHEN YOU COULD HAVE ACCEPTED MADISON AINSWORTH! GO AHEAD! WHY DON'T YOU SAY IT? YOU'VE NEVER MISSED THE CHANCE ON PREVIOUS OCCASIONS!!

YES, YOU COULD HAVE HAD MAIDS, FURS AND YACHTS-- INSTEAD OF A MAN WHO CAN BARELY MAKE A LIVING! I KNOW ALL ABOUT IT!

NOTHING WAS FURTHER FROM MY MIND, STEVE BAKER! BUT SINCE *YOU* BROUGHT THIS SUBJECT UP--

--I COULD HAVE MARRIED MADISON AINSWORTH! AND IF I HAD-- IT WOULD HAVE BEEN *MARSHA* INSTEAD OF JOANNE WHO WOULD BE ENJOYING ALL THE BENEFITS OF THE AINSWORTH FORTUNE! HOWEVER, I LOVED YOU, STEVE-- I MARRIED YOU! NOW, DON'T MAKE ME SORRY I DID!

"THE AINSWORTH NAME HAD OFTEN BEEN USED IN THE QUARRELS BETWEEN MOTHER AND DAD! IT WAS A SOURCE OF BITTERNESS AND FRUSTRATION IN THEM BOTH! BUT NOT UNTIL I HEARD MOTHER'S WORDS THAT NIGHT, DID I UNDERSTAND AND FEEL FOR THE FIRST TIME, THE FULL INTENSITY OF THAT WHICH CONSUMED MY PARENTS!

I--I NEVER THOUGHT OF IT *THAT* WAY! IF MAMA HAD MARRIED MISTER AINSWORTH-- THEN I-- AND NOT JOANNE-- WOULD HAVE LIVED IN THAT BIG HOUSE-- AND HAD ALL THOSE PRESENTS--

EVERYTHING JOANNE AINSWORTH HAS WAS ALMOST MINE!--- SHOULD HAVE BEEN MINE-- *MINE*!

"AND THAT THOUGHT LODGED INSIDE OF ME... TO THRIVE AND FESTER ON THE ADVERSITY WHICH CLOUDED MY YEARS OF GROWTH.... JOANNE AINSWORTH! A DAY NEVER PASSED WITHOUT HER NAME ARISING IS SOME CONVERSATION OR ISSUE OF WHICH I WAS A PART...AT SEVENTEEN, I *HATED* JOANNE AINSWORTH MORE THAN EVER...

I SAY LET'S BE PRACTICAL ABOUT IT! IF WE ELECT JOANNE AINSWORTH AS QUEEN OF THE PROM, HER DAD IS BOUND TO DONATE TO THE SCHOOL-FUND, AND..

AS CHAIRMAN OF THIS COMMITTEE, I SAY "NO!" ANY SUGGESTIONS LIKE THAT SHOULD NOT BE CONSIDERED! THIS IS ONE TIME HER FATHER'S MONEY WILL NOT EARN ANY SPECIAL PRIVILEGES FOR JOANNE AINSWORTH!

"THE GIRLS HEEDED ME, TOO! I WAS AN OUT-STANDING AND *FORCEFUL* PERSONALITY IN MY HIGH SCHOOL STUDENT GROUP... MY DRIVE AND WIT WON ME POPULARITY AND RESPECT... BUT THE MANTLE OF LEADERSHIP WAS SCANT GARB FOR A DISCONTENTED SPIRIT SUCH AS MINE!

WHY, NONE OF US HAS EVER SO MUCH AS SPOKEN TO JOANNE AINSWORTH! SHE DOESN'T ATTEND OUR SCHOOL! SHE PROBABLY DOESN'T CARE TO *MINGLE* WITH US! I DON'T SEE WHY WE SHOULD BUTTER UP TO THAT SNOB FOR HER FATHER'S ENTIRE FORTUNE!

"FOR SOME UNACCOUNTABLE REASON, I TOOK THE LONG ROUTE HOME WHEN THE MEETING ADJOURNED! THE AINSWORTH HOUSE WAS LARGE AND STATELY... AND FRAMED IN A WINDOW ON AN UPPER FLOOR, JOANNE SAT *HAUGHTILY* AT HER VANITY WHILE HER PERSONAL MAID CAREFULLY COMBED THE GIRL'S BEAUTIFUL LUSTROUS HAIR...

"IT WASN'T FAIR! IT WASN'T FAIR! THAT LOVELY NEGLIGEE JOANNE WORE -- HER MAID -- THE SMART CLOTHES I KNEW WERE HANGING IN THE CLOSET -- THEY WERE RIGHTFULLY MINE! AND A TURN OF FATE HAD *CHEATED* ME OUT OF THEM! INCENSED BY THE FUTILITY OF MY THOUGHTS, I HURRIED THE REST OF THE WAY HOME...

YOU'RE HOME JUST IN TIME, MARSHA! LUNCH WILL BE READY IN *FIVE* MINUTES!

HI, SIS!

"I WAS TOO UPSET TO ANSWER EITHER MOM OR BETTE.. I RUSHED INTO MY ROOM AND *FLUNG* MYSELF ON MY BED IN A FIT OF TEARS ...

5

MARSHA! YOU'RE ACTING UP AGAIN! WHAT'S COME **OVER** YOU, CHILD?

PLEASE, MOM! LEAVE ME **ALONE**! I'LL BE ALL RIGHT!

IS LIFE REALLY SO **MISERABLE**, MARSHA?

YES... **YES**, IT IS!

OH, MOTHER, I CAN'T UNDERSTAND WHY YOU CHOSE THIS **SHABBY** EXISTENCE INSTEAD OF THE COMFORT AND SECURITY MADISON AINSWORTH OFFERED YOU!

I'LL TELL YOU **WHY**, MARSHA!

I FELL IN **LOVE**, MARSHA, JUST AS YOU WILL SOMEDAY! I KNEW THAT MARRYING YOUR DAD MEANT ENDURING YEARS OF HARDSHIP! WHY, STEVE BAKER DIDN'T EVEN HAVE A JOB THEN! YET, I REJECTED MADISON AINSWORTH AND MARRIED STEVE! I... I JUST KNEW HE WAS THE ONE... THAT'S ALL... THAT'S LOVE...

"I REMEMBERED MOTHER'S WORDS WHEN I FIRST SAW **TOD GARRET**.. I JUST KNEW HE WAS THE ONE. HE SEEMED TO THROW OFF RADIATIONS TO WHICH MY HEART RESPONDED GEIGER COUNTER!!! MY SISTER, BETTE, WAS RATHER STARTLED BY MY DAZED BEHAVIOR...

COME ON, MARSHA! WHAT'S **WRONG** WITH YOU, ANYWAY?

WHO IS THAT YOUNG **FELLOW** WITH MISTER AINSWORTH, BETTE?

NOBODY THAT WILL DO **YOU** ANY GOOD TO KNOW, SIS! HE'S EAR-MARKED FOR JOANNE AINSWORTH! HIS NAME'S TOD GARRET.. WORKS FOR JOANNE'S DAD!

"I COULDN'T SUPPRESS A SHORT BITTER LAUGH AT THE DIABOLICAL THOROUGHNESS WITH WHICH FATE HAD DONE ITS WORK! JOANNE HAD INDEED BEEN GIVEN EVERYTHING... *EVEN THE MAN I LOVED!* BUT I WOULD NO LONGER WATCH FROM A DISTANCE! TO HUNGER AND COVET! TOD GARRET WAS JOANNE'S ONE POSSESSION I WOULD STEP IN AND TAKE FOR MY OWN!

MARSHA! YOU DIDN'T LISTEN! I SAID TOD GARRET WAS JOANNE AINSWORTH'S *PERSONAL PROPERTY!*

NOT YET, HE ISN'T, JOANNE HAS AN OPTION ON TOD...BUT SHE DOESN'T *OWN* HIM!

ARE YOU CRAZY, MARSHA? DO YOU REALLY THINK YOU CAN MAKE TOD GARRET LEAVE JOANNE AINSWORTH AND A COZY FUTURE IN HER FATHER'S BUSINESS...FOR *YOU?* LET'S FACE IT, MARSHA...TOD WON'T EVEN *LOOK* AT YOU!

WE'LL SEE ABOUT THAT, BETTE! I *WANT TOD GARRET!!* AND I'LL MAKE HIM WANT ME... WANT ME ENOUGH TO GIVE UP JOANNE AND HER RICHES FOR MY LOVE! I'M A WOMAN.. I'LL MANAGE IT!

"THERE WAS NO POSSIBLE WAY OF MEETING TOD THROUGH SOCIAL CHANNELS...THAT WAS ACTUALLY AN ADVANTAGE...BECAUSE I WAS FORCED TO HURDLE THE ACCEPTED, FORMAL PRELIMINARIES AND EMPLOY A LESS SUBTLE BUT MORE EFFECTIVE METHOD...THE FOLLOWING DAY I *DELIBERATELY* PUT A RUN IN MY STOCKING AND WALKED TOWARD THE BANK WHEN I SAW TOD COMING OUT!

OOPS -

OH!

I'M TERRIBLY SORRY! ARE YOU *HURT?*

I-I THINK I *BRUISED* MY KNEE A BIT— THAT'S ALL!

"WHEN TOD HELPED ME TO MY FEET, I EXAMINED MY STOCKINGS AND FEIGNED HORROR AT THE RUN I KNEW WOULD BE THERE! THIS BIT OF PRETENSE BROUGHT MY EXPOSED LEGS UNDER TOD GARRET'S STARTLED GAZE! HE WAS NOT DISPLEASED...

OH, GOODNESS! I'VE GOT A *RUN* IN MY STOCKING! AND I JUST BOUGHT THIS PAIR YESTERDAY!

WHAT ROTTEN LUCK!

7

LOOK HERE! THIS REGRETTABLE INCIDENT HAS ALL BEEN DUE TO **MY** CARELESSNESS! SUPPOSE I PAY YOU WHAT THOSE STOCKINGS ARE WORTH... AND, WHAT'S MORE- I'LL DRIVE YOU TO WHEREVER YOU'RE GOING! MY CAR'S PARKED DOWN THE BLOCK!

YOU'RE VERY KIND.. BUT I...I COULDN'T ACCEPT EITHER OFFER... SUPPOSE WE JUST **FORGET** THIS HAPPENED AND --

OF COURSE! HOW **STUPID** OF ME! I'M TOD GARRET! I WORK IN THE BANK! OH, COME ON! LET'S GET SOME WARM FOOD... AND DRY OFF OUR COATS! SHALL WE?

YOU LOOK RESPECTABLE AND SOUND SENSIBLE! I'LL **JOIN** YOU, TOD GARRET! JUST FOR THE RECORDS, MY NAME IS MARSHA BAKER!

"MY OPENING OFFENSIVE TO CAPTURE TOD GARRET HAD GAINED CONSIDERABLE GROUND! I DECIDED TO CONSOLIDATE MY POSITION! THE FINAL SIEGE OF MY OBJECTIVE'S HEART WOULD COME **LATER**... TOD TOOK ME TO **THE CRILLON** -- THE FINEST RESTAURANT IN OUR TOWN...

I'M SURE YOU'LL LIKE THIS PLACE,' ALL ITS PATRONS RECOMMEND IT HIGHLY!

IT'S **LOVELY**, TOD!

" THE FOOD WAS WONDERFUL, AND THE ORCHESTRA PLAYED LOW AND HEADY MUSIC... TOD HELD ME **CLOSE** AS WE GLIDED ACROSS THE POLISHED DANCE FLOOR... HIS CHEEK WAS A SOFT CARESS UPON MINE... HIS ARMS, A HAVEN.' WE DIDN'T EXCHANGE A WORD...

"IT WAS DARK WHEN TOD'S CAR DREW UP BEFORE MY HOUSE. THE EVENING HAD LEFT ITS MARK ON **BOTH** OF US... WE WEREN'T STRANGERS ANY LONGER... NOR WOULD WE EVER BE AGAIN !!

GOOD NIGHT, TOD, I-I HAD A **SWELL** TIME!

MARSHA--

8

"TOD GARRET WAS MINE! I HAD REBELLED AGAINST DESTINY – FORAGED INTO JOANNE AINSWORTH'S DOMAIN -- AND HAD TAKEN HER MAN! EACH IDYLLIC MOMENT WITH TOD THAT FOLLOWED, MADE THE TRIUMPH MORE COMPLETE ... AND OUR LOVE MORE ECSTATIC...

DO YOU REALIZE, MISS BAKER - THAT YOU'VE MADE A MESS OF A MAN'S NEAT, ORDERLY, WELL PLANNED FUTURE --

HAVE I REALLY DONE THAT TO YOU, MISTER GARRET!

YOU'VE FALLEN FROM THE BLUE LIKE A BOMBSHELL, MARSHA... AND YOU'VE CAUSED RAGING FIRES WHERE THERE WAS ONCE CALM AND CERTAINTY! I'M IN LOVE WITH YOU, MARSHA!

LOVE EXPRESSED ISN'T LOVE PROVEN, TOD! LOVE IS FINAL AND ABSOLUTE... THERE ARE NO MIDDLE ROADS!

DOES THIS PROVE ANYTHING?

NO, IT DOESN'T, TOD! THERE IS STILL JOANNE AINSWORTH! YOU HAVEN'T FORGOTTEN JOANNE, HAVE YOU?

OH... YOU KNOW ABOUT JOANNE AND MYSELF -

OF COURSE I DO! THE ENTIRE TOWN KNOWS YOU TWO HAVE BEEN GOING STEADY FOR MONTHS! WOULD YOU LIKE TO PROVE WHAT YOU JUST SAID ABOUT LOVING ME?

I HAVEN'T BEEN INSINCERE WITH YOU, MARSHA! I DO LOVE YOU! ... MORE THAN YOU REALIZE!

I'VE TRIED TO TELL JOANNE ABOUT YOU... BUT WHENEVER I'M WITH HER -- I-I JUST SEEM TO GO SOFT INSIDE... IF YOU KNEW JOANNE, YOU'D UNDERSTAND WHY!

I ONLY UNDERSTAND THAT YOU CAN'T LOVE BOTH OF US! YOU MUST DECIDE FOR YOURSELF. I'LL KNOW WHEN YOU HAVE... I'D LIKE TO GO HOME NOW, TOD!

"I WAS SUPREMELY CONFIDENT THAT I WOULD HOLD TOD AGAINST ANY ODDS... IF JOANNE AINSWORTH WAS SAVING A TRUMP CARD, I KNEW IT COULDN'T BE TOD'S LOVE... FOR I HAD THAT! I WAS FIRMLY *CONVINCED* OF IT! TOD WOULD BREAK WITH JOANNE-- AND I HOPED IT WOULD GIVE HER PAIN -- THE DEEP, GNAWING KIND OF PAIN WHICH HAD BEEN MY LEGACY SINCE CHILDHOOD...

WELL! *YOU'RE* IN A GOOD MOOD THIS MORNING!

I'LL BET TOD GARRET'S GOT SOMETHING TO DO WITH IT! HE'S BEEN DATING YOU, HASN'T HE -- *WHAT ABOUT JOANNE AINSWORTH?*

POOF-TO JOANNE AINSWORTH! SHE DOESN'T EXIST ANYMORE! TOD AND I ARE IN LOVE, MY DEAR LITTLE SISTER! -- IN LOVE! JOANNE IS *OUT!* I'VE TAKEN HER MAN!

AND WHAT DO YOU THINK OF *THAT,* MY LITTLE DOUBTING THOMAS? WHAT DO YOU THINK *NOW* OF THE GIRL YOU SAID TOD WOULDN'T LOOK AT?

I ADMIRE HER SPUNK BUT NOT HER SPORTSMANSHIP! BE CONTENT WITH HAVING WON TOD, MARSHA... BUT DON'T CHEAPEN THAT LOVE BY USING IT TO TORMENT JOANNE! WHY, YOU DON'T EVEN *KNOW* THE GIRL!

THAT'S NO FAULT OF MINE! SHE'S ALWAYS KEPT TO HER IVORY TOWER-- LOOKING DOWN UPON US COM- MONERS WITH SMUG CONTEMPT! BUT THE TABLES HAVE TURNED ON MISS JOANNE AINSWORTH!

SHE'LL YEARN AND HUNGER AND TURN SICK INSIDE FROM WANTING, LIKE *I* DID! I'LL WALK WITH TOD WHERE JOANNE CAN SEE US -- AND SHE'LL SWEAR *ENVIOUSLY* EACH TIME TOD KISSES ME -- FOR TOD'S KISSES WOULD HAVE BEEN HERS-- IF I HADN'T COME ALONG!

AND OUT OF JOANNE'S FUTILE YEARNINGS WILL COME HATE -- *HATE* FOR ME -- A HATE I SHALL ACCEPT AS EAGERLY AS ONE DOES LOVE! FOR I SHALL KNOW WHAT THAT HATE IS DOING TO HER! THEN, I'LL NOT ONLY REALIZE HAPPINESS BUT *JUSTICE!*

OH, MARSHA-- HOW *HORRIBLE*--

"TOD CALLED AT THE HOUSE TWO DAYS LATER... HE HAD MADE THE BREAK WITH JOANNE... HE LOOKED LIKE A MAN WHO HAD REGRETFULLY STRUCK A CHILD! FORTUNATELY FOR ME, TOD KEPT HIS EYES AVERTED AS HE SPOKE.. ELSE, HE MIGHT HAVE SEEN THE JUBILANCE IN MY OWN..."

I- I'VE TOLD JOANNE ABOUT US, MARSHA... I FEEL LIKE A *HEEL*!

LOVE IS LIKE ANY OTHER GAME, TOD. *SOMEONE* HAS TO LOSE!

JOANNE WAS FINE ABOUT THE WHOLE THING... BUT TELLING HER WAS DIFFICULT... DIFFICULT!

YOUR LOVE FOR ME WAS GREATER THAN YOUR OBLIGATION TO JOANNE. YOU'RE *COMPLETELY* MINE NOW... AND I'VE NEVER WANTED ANYTHING IN THIS WORLD AS MUCH AS I HAVE YOU! OH, TOD- TOD--

"THE TASTE OF VICTORY WAS SWEET! BUT NOT ALL OF ITS FRUITS HAD BEEN SAVORED.. FOR THE *BIGGEST* PLUM OF ALL CAME BY MAIL... BETTE BROUGHT THE ENVELOPE TO ME THE NEXT DAY... IT WAS SMALL, SMART AND EXPENSIVE...I KNEW AT ONCE, THE IDENTITY OF THE SENDER..."

I GUESS THERE'LL BE NO END TO YOUR CROWING! THIS IS FROM *MISS BIG*, NO LESS!

WELL! DO TELL! THANK YOU, CHILD!

"THE PAPER WAS COLORED A SOFT, PASTEL SHADE. AND POSSESSED A QUALITY OF SERENE ELEGANCE., IT WAS LIKE A VISIT FROM JOANNE HERSELF. THE FEELING OF SURPRISE AND TRIUMPH WAS DECIDEDLY ELECTRIC!"

-FROM WHAT TOD HAS TOLD ME ABOUT YOU, I SEE NO REASON WHY WE SHOULDN'T BE FRIENDS. I'LL BE HOME TUESDAY. IF YOU SHOULD CARE TO CALL. I WOULD LIKE VERY MUCH TO MEET THE GIRL WHO EARNED TOD'S LOVE --

SO YOU'VE FINALLY CONDESCENDED TO INVITE ME TO YOUR HOME, HAVE YOU, MISS AINSWORTH? I'LL BE THERE - DON'T WORRY! I'VE WAITED YEARS FOR THIS MOMENT. WE'LL CHAT AND DRINK YOUR PINK TEA. AND WHEN YOU'RE DONE WITH YOUR BRAVE AND NOBLE SPEECH *I'M GOING TO SPIT RIGHT IN YOUR EYE!*

"I WAS DRESSED AND READY TO LEAVE FOR THE AINSWORTH HOUSE THAT FOLLOWING TUESDAY WHEN MY SISTER, BETTE, STOPPED ME AT THE DOOR.

MARSHA....DON'T GO TO JOANNE WITH MALICE IN YOUR HEART. SOMEHOW. IT SEEMS INDECENT TO TAKE YOUR VILE HATRED OF HER INTO HER OWN HOME!

IT WAS JOANNE WHO EXTENDED THE INVITATION. NOW THE CAT GOES TO LOOK AT THE QUEEN! DON'T DELAY ME, BETTE. IT'S PROPER TO BE PROMPT!

BE GRACIOUS, MARSHA! WIN HER RESPECT-- NOT HER UNDYING HATE!

THAT'S JUST WHAT I WANT FROM JOANNE! --HER HATE! THIS IS *MY* DAY, BETTE! AND DON'T THINK I WON'T MAKE THE MOST OF IT!

"IN YEARS PAST, THE GREAT IRON GATE HAD ADMITTED ME TO THE SPLENDOR BEYOND ONLY IN DREAMS... BUT THAT DAY, IT STOOD AJAR IN THE BRIGHT SUNLIGHT OF REALITY, AND ACROSS ITS THRESH-HOLD MY *VENGEANCE* WAITED...

"THE HOUSE WAS HUGE AND LAVISH! I FOLLOWED THE BUTLER THROUGH ROOMS BESIDE WHICH MY OWN HOME WAS NOTHING MORE THAN A *HOVEL*.. AWESTRUCK AND PRACTICALLY SPEECH-LESS, I GAZED IN SILENCE AT THE WONDERS ABOUT ME! *ALL THIS COULD HAVE BEEN MINE,* I TOLD MYSELF! I WAS CHEATED--*CHEATED!* AND THE ANGER MOUNTED RAPIDLY INSIDE ME-- FURIOUSLY BURNING ITS WAY TO THE EMOTIONAL POWDER CHARGE I WAS CERTAIN WOULD GO OFF ONCE THAT LITTLE SNOB JOANNE, ENTERED..

MISS AINSWORTH WILL SEE YOU *SHORTLY*, MISS.. MAY I TAKE YOUR COAT?

NO, THANK YOU! I WON'T BE STAYING LONG!

MISS MARSHA BAKER?

I'M JOANNE AINSWORTH. DO FORGIVE ME FOR KEEPING YOU WAITING MY, YOU *ARE* PRETTY. AREN'T YOU? I DON'T BLAME TOD A BIT FOR BEING ATTRACTED TO YOU.

12

OH, YOU POOR DEAR! TOD SHOULD HAVE *TOLD* YOU ABOUT ME! PLEASE DON'T BE ILL AT EASE!

Y-YOU'RE AN INVALID-- AN *INVALID!*

WELL, REALLY, MISS BAKER! I CAN COMPREHEND YOUR REACTION! BUT I CAN'T APPRECIATE YOUR LACK OF DISCRETION... THIS IS MOST *EMBARRASSING!* I DID SO LOOK FORWARD TO A PLEASANT CHAT WITH YOU!

YOU DON'T *UNDER-STAND!* OH-- MERCIFUL HEAVEN--

IF YOU'RE REMORSEFUL OVER THE FACT THAT YOU'VE WON TOD FROM AN INVALID, PLEASE REST ASSURED THAT YOUR VICTORY WAS NOT ONE-SIDED! I'M *NOT* AS HELPLESS AS I SEEM! HAD I WANTED TO HOLD TOD, HE'D HAVE NEVER BEEN YOURS! I CAN BE QUITE AS CAPABLE AND ALLURING AS THE NEXT GIRL!

TOD IS A WONDERFUL PERSON! FATHER THOUGHT TOD WOULD MAKE A FINE SON-IN-LAW! BUT TOD WAS NEVER MY CHOICE AS A HUSBAND! ODDLY ENOUGH, I WAS GOING TO TELL HIM THAT, WHEN INSTEAD--HE TOLD ME ABOUT YOU!

HOW *LONG* HAVE YOU BEEN THIS WAY-- HOW LONG?

YOUR POINTLESS SENSE OF GUILT IS MAKING YOU EXCESSIVELY *EMOTIONAL*, MISS BAKER! I-I WAS GIVEN A PONY AND CARRIAGE WHEN I WAS TEN... THERE WAS AN ACCIDENT! NOW, PLEASE, I --

AND ALL THESE YEARS-- I'VE BEEN ENVYING-- HATING-- SCHEMING AGAINST AN INVALID!

MISS BAKER! DO YOU MEAN TO SAY THAT THERE IS A *PERSONAL* ISSUE INVOLVED HERE?

IT'S MORE THAN THAT NOW! I'VE JUST HAD A GOOD LOOK AT MY SOUL, MISS AINSWORTH, AND I TELL YOU THAT I'M TERRIBLY *SHAKEN* BY THE UGLY, WARPED AND WICKED SIGHT OF IT!

13

106

"I BEGAN DISGORGING EVERY ROTTEN THOUGHT WHICH HAD FESTERED IN MY MIND SINCE CHILDHOOD. AND THEY FELL FROM MY TONGUE LIKE LONG SMOULDERING CINDERS-- BURNING AND SEARING BOTH JOANNE AND MYSELF... I WAS *CONDEMNING* MYSELF BEFORE HER FOREVER! AND I DID IT UNHESITATINGLY! FOR I WANTED TO MAKE AMENDS.. THIS SELF-IMMOLATION SEEMED THE ONLY WAY AT THE TIME..."

NOW YOU SEE WHY I CAME HERE -- TO TAUNT YOU -- INSULT YOU-- TO *LAUGH* AT YOU!

OH, MARSHA-- LET'S BE FRIENDS -- *GOOD* FRIENDS --

"I SANK NEXT TO HER ON MY KNEES! AND WEPT UNASHAMEDLY-- WEPT IN *GRATITUDE* FOR HER FORGIVENESS, WITHOUT WHICH, I COULD HAVE NEVER RETURNED TO TOD... I SOBBED OUT HER NAME AND THE HATRED WAS GONE..."

JOANNE--

I-I THINK WE SHOULD HAVE OUR *TEA* NOW!

THAT'S *WONDERFUL!* WONDERFUL! A LIFETIME OF LOVE-- IT'S WHAT I'VE BEEN SEARCHING FOR-- YEARNING FOR ALL THIS TIME, TOD-- TOD!

THERE'S NOTHING LIKE BEGINNING *NOW,* DARLING!

"I TOOK MY LEAVE OF JOANNE AINSWORTH SOON AFTER WE HAD OUR TEA... THE GREAT HOUSE WAS AN *ALIEN* PLACE NOW-- A PLACE WHERE I DIDN'T BELONG AT ALL! AND I ALMOST RAN ON MY WAY ACROSS THE GROUNDS!"

TOD! OH, I'M SO *GLAD* TO SEE YOU!

BETTE TOLD ME YOU WERE HERE! WELL, NOW YOU *KNOW* ABOUT JOANNE!

I KNOW ABOUT MYSELF TOO, TOD... HOW MUCH I NEED TO *LOVE* -- TEACH ME HOW TO LOVE, TOD! TEACH ME HOW TO LOVE!

THAT'S A *BIG* ASSIGN- MENT, HONEY! IT MAY LAST ALL OUR LIVES!

Nancy Hale's PROBLEM CLINIC

Treatment for the troubled heart

Nancy Hale, our authority and consultant on social affairs, will review the most important problems she receives each month and analyze them on these pages.

OUR CASE THIS MONTH CONCERNS MISS *RITA S.*--A PRETTY GIRL OF TWENTY WHO *RISKED HAPPINESS FOR A LOVE THAT DIDN'T EXIST!* LISTEN TO WHAT SHE WRITES:

"WE WERE VERY YOUNG, BRUCE AND I, WHEN WE FELL IN LOVE-- AND WITH ALL THE EARNESTNESS OF YOUTH WE WERE SURE, IN OUR HEARTS, THAT THIS LOVE OF OURS WOULD LAST THROUGH ALL ETERNITY!

IT WON'T BE SACRED, RITA, UNLESS YOU REPEAT AFTER ME: *I SOLEMNLY PLEDGE MY LOVE-- NOW AND FOREVER!*

OH, I DO, BRUCE, I DO!

"SOON AFTER THAT BRUCIE'S FATHER DECIDED TO ACCEPT A BUSINESS OFFER IN ANOTHER TOWN--THE DAY BRUCE LEFT, I FELT AS IF THE WORLD HAD BEEN SNATCHED FROM UNDER ME---

DON'T LOOK SO GLUM, RITA--JENKINS PRAIRIE ISN'T SO FAR AWAY! BESIDES, I'LL WRITE YOU EVERY DAY!

AND I'LL WRITE TO YOU, BRUCIE! I'LL *NEVER FORGET* YOU!

"BRUCE WROTE FAITHFULLY-- FOR A WHILE! THEN THE LETTERS CAME LESS AND LESS FREQUENTLY-- THREE YEARS PASSED---

IS--IS THERE A LETTER FOR ME?--FROM JENKINS PRAIRIE?

SORRY, RITA-- NOTHING FROM BRUCE TODAY!

"I BEGAN TO DATE OTHERS-- BUT NEVER ONCE DID I GIVE UP *HOPING* THAT SOME DAY BRUCE WOULD COME BACK FOR ME!

IT'S ABOUT *TIME* YOU DECIDED TO GIVE ME A BREAK, YOU BEAUTIFUL HERMIT!

GOODNESS KNOWS, YOU *ARE* PERSISTENT, GREG!

"GREG WAS NICE TO KNOW, NICE TO BE WITH! I SAW MORE AND MORE OF HIM --

DON'T LAUGH AT ME, RITA, WHEN I TELL YOU THAT I CAN'T IMAGINE WHAT LIFE WOULD HAVE BEEN LIKE IF I'D NEVER MET YOU!

PLEASE, GREG, DON'T! I'VE TOLD YOU HOW I FEEL ABOUT *BRUCE!*

"BUT TIME WILL HAVE ITS WAY--- *BRUCE STOPPED WRITING* --AND GREG LOVED ME!

I COULDN'T WAIT ANY LONGER, RITA! *PLEASE* SAY YOU'LL ACCEPT MY RING!

OH, GREG! YOU'VE BEEN SO PATIENT-- SO UNDERSTANDING! I'LL BE *PROUD* TO WEAR IT, DARLING!

"THEN THE INEVITABLE HAPPENED! I WAS AT THE RAILROAD STATION -- SEEING DAD OFF ON ONE OF HIS BUSINESS TRIPS ... WHEN I SAW A HANDSOME, FAMILIAR FIGURE DESCENDING FROM THE TRAIN --

BRUCE!!

WELL, BY GOSH.! IF IT ISN'T LITTLE RITA! ALL GROWN UP NOW AND MORE BEAUTIFUL THAN EVER.!

"SHAMELESSLY I BROKE MY ENGAGEMENT TO GREG! DELIRIOUS WITH JOY, I DEVOTED EVERY MINUTE, EVERY THOUGHT TO BRUCE!... BUT STRANGELY ENOUGH, THE OLD FEELING FOR HIM WAS GONE-- I REALIZED IT ABOUT A WEEK LATER --

BUT BRUCE, YOU PROMISED ME AN HOUR AGO THAT WE'D LEAVE EARLY! MY HEAD ACHES AND -- *OH, WHAT'S THE USE!*

LOOK, RITA-- THIS IS A *BIG* AFFAIR! THERE ARE IMPORTANT PEOPLE HERE! I *MUST* STAY!

BRUCE AND I JUST *DON'T* BELONG TOGETHER ANY MORE! I CLUNG TO A *MEMORY* AND IT RUINED MY HAPPINESS.!.. *WHAT SHALL I DO NOW, MISS HALE?*

NOW YOU KNOW, RITA, HOW DANGEROUS IT IS TO ACT WITHOUT CONSULTING *BOTH* YOUR HEART AND MIND! YOU WANTED A MEMORY -- AND YOU THREW AWAY *REAL LOVE!*.. FORGET YOUR PRIDE.. *GO TO GREG!* EXPLAIN EVERYTHING AND ASK HIM TO FORGIVE YOU!

AS USUAL, MISS HALE'S ADVICE PROVED A HAPPY SOLUTION TO MY DILEMMA-- I SHUDDER WHEN I THINK HOW CLOSE I CAME TO LOSING GREG BECAUSE OF IMMATURE EMOTIONS! SO, READER, IF *YOUR* HEART IS IMPRISONED BY THE GHOST OF AN OLD LOVE, TAKE HEED! YOU MAY BE PASSING UP YOUR CHANCE FOR *TRUE* HAPPINESS!

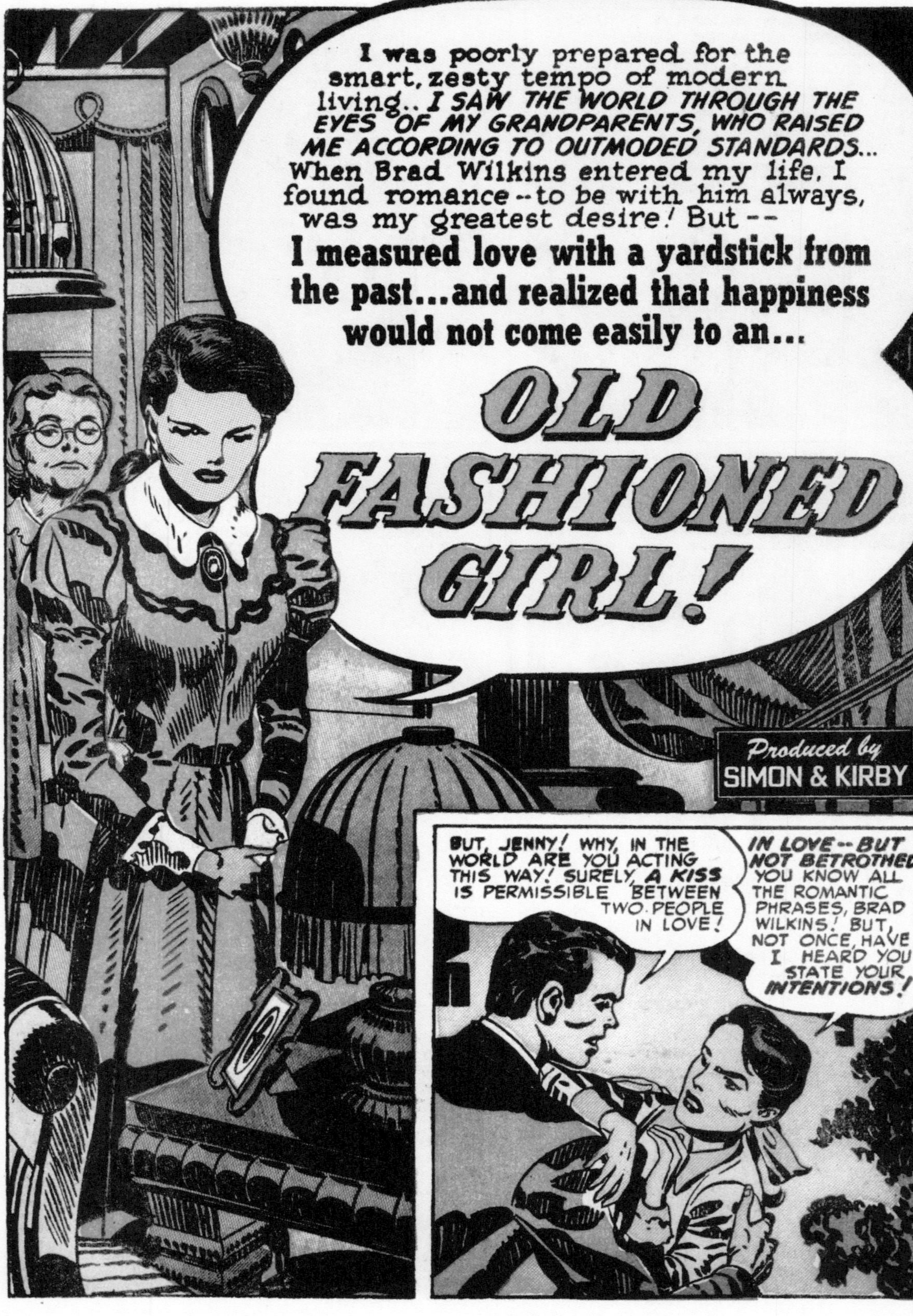
I was poorly prepared for the smart, zesty tempo of modern living.. I SAW THE WORLD THROUGH THE EYES OF MY GRANDPARENTS, WHO RAISED ME ACCORDING TO OUTMODED STANDARDS... When Brad Wilkins entered my life, I found romance--to be with him always, was my greatest desire! But--
I measured love with a yardstick from the past...and realized that happiness would not come easily to an...
OLD FASHIONED GIRL!
Produced by SIMON & KIRBY
BUT, JENNY! WHY, IN THE WORLD ARE YOU ACTING THIS WAY! SURELY, A KISS IS PERMISSIBLE BETWEEN TWO PEOPLE IN LOVE!
IN LOVE--BUT NOT BETROTHED! YOU KNOW ALL THE ROMANTIC PHRASES, BRAD WILKINS! BUT, NOT ONCE, HAVE I HEARD YOU STATE YOUR INTENTIONS!

"I WAS SIX WHEN MOTHER PASSED AWAY. FATHER WASN'T EARNING ENOUGH TO AFFORD HELP, SO THERE WAS ONLY ONE PERSON HE COULD TURN TO.. I STILL REMEMBER THE DAY DAD BUNDLED ME UP AND TOOK ME TO GRANDMA'S HOUSE! I STOOD IN THE MUSTY OLD PARLOR, TRYING TO HOLD BACK THE TEARS-- LISTENING TO THEM PLAN MY FUTURE!

OF COURSE WE'LL TAKE HER IN! IT'S OUR CHRISTIAN *DUTY!*

SHE'S A GOOD GIRL, AREN'T YOU, JENNY! SHE WON'T BE ANY BOTHER!

DADDY! DADDY! YOU'RE *NOT* GOING AWAY! YOU'RE GOING TO LIVE WITH US, HERE, AREN'T YOU?

NO, BABY, DADDY HAS TO WORK. AND, THERE'S NOT MUCH ROOM HERE..BUT I'LL COME TO *SEE* YOU OFTEN!

"I REMEMBER THE YEARS OF GROWING UP, THE LONG COTTON STOCKINGS AND OLD FASHIONED DRESSES GRANDMA MADE ME WEAR- THAT THE OTHER CHILDREN MADE *FUN* OF--

LOOK AT JENNY! SHE LOOKS *SILLY* IN THAT FUNNY OUTFIT!

MY MOMMY SAYS CHILDREN USED TO DRESS THAT WAY WHEN SHE WAS A LITTLE GIRL!

WELL, I DON'T CARE! GRANDMA TOLD ME IT'S *FITTIN'* FOR A LITTLE GIRL TO WEAR PROPER CLOTHES ..AND BESIDES.. I *LIKE* THEM! SO THERE!

"THE CATTY COMMENTS BECAME BOLDER, THE GIGGLES, LOUDER, I FINALLY BROUGHT MY PROBLEM TO GRANDMA.

GRANDMA, WHY MUST I WEAR THESE LONG STOCKINGS? WHY CAN'T I BE LIKE THE OTHER KIDS?

THERE'S *TIME ENOUGH* FOR PRIMPIN' AND FUSSIN' WITH CLOTHES, JENNY! YOU HAVE MORE IMPOR- TANT THINGS TO CONCERN YOURSELF WITH!

IF PARENTS, NOWADAYS, WOULD TAKE *MORE* TIME TO TEACH LITTLE GIRLS HOW TO BECOME GOOD, FUTURE *HOMEMAKERS*, INSTEAD OF FILLING THEIR HEADS WITH NONSENSE, THIS WORLD WOULD BE A *HEAP* BETTER OFF!

"OH, YES, GRANDMA SHOWED ME HOW TO COOK AND KEEP HOUSE..AND GRANDPA TAUGHT ME ALL ABOUT MANNERS AND MAINTAINING THE FAMILY BUDGET! WHEN I WAS SEVENTEEN, I WAS WELL PREPARED TO BE A PERFECT WIFE. THE ONLY TROUBLE WAS--I WASN'T EVER TOLD ABOUT *LOVE!*

I'M BRAD WILKINS! I BELIEVE YOUR GRANDMOTHER IS EXPECTING ME!

WON'T YOU COME IN, MISTER WILKINS--

GRANDMA WILL BE HERE PRESENTLY, MISTER WILKINS... WON'T YOU SIT DOWN?

"I SAT OPPOSITE HIM, FEELING UNCOMFORTABLE, AS HIS EYES SWEPT OVER ME. I DON'T THINK HE WAS AWARE THAT HE WAS STARING.. I TRIED TO MAKE CONVERSATION BUT, FOUND MYSELF TOO BUSY LOCATING A PLACE FOR MY HANDS TO SETTLE...

I MUST *APOLOGIZE* FOR MY APPEARANCE, MISTER WILKINS! AS YOU CAN SEE — I'VE BEEN CLEANING HOUSE,- AND—

OH! I'M SORRY, MISS! IT WAS *RUDE* OF ME TO STARE LIKE THAT!

AS A MATTER OF FACT, I NEVER EXPECTED TO FIND ANYONE SO *YOUNG* AND *ATTRACTIVE* IN THIS OLD FASHIONED HOUSE!

THIS HOUSE MAY SEEM OLD FASHIONED TO *YOU*, MISTER WILKINS—

BUT, IT HAS A *CHARM* ABOUT IT WHICH YOU DON'T FIND IN THE BARE, SIMPLICITY OF THE MODERN PLACES THEY BUILD TODAY!

OH, I *AGREE!* I HEARTILY *AGREE!*

YOU NEEDN'T DEFEND YOUR HOME, MY DEAR...HE KNOWS ALL ABOUT THIS PLACE..THAT'S WHY HE'S HERE!

HELLO, GRANDMA. IF YOU HAVE BUSINESS WITH MISTER WILKINS, I'LL LEAVE..

NONSENSE, CHILD! YOUNG BRAD DEALS IN *ANTIQUES*.. I'VE GOT TOO MANY.. I SHALL *SELL* HIM SOME! BRAD, THIS IS MY GRANDDAUGHTER, JENNY..

HELLO, JENNY—

"GRANDMA MADE HER SALE AND DEPARTED, LEAVING ME TO TAKE CARE OF THE DETAILS OF MOVING... THE YOUNG MAN, HOWEVER, WAS IN NO HURRY AND, IN NO MOOD FOR BUSINESS -- AND, I WAS MUCH TOO FLUSTERED...

I'LL REMOVE THE SHADE FROM THIS LAMP-- THERE'S A LITTLE TRICK TO IT!

WE CAN DO THAT SOME OTHER TIME-- RIGHT NOW, I'M MORE INTERESTED IN YOU!

WILL YOU GO OUT WITH ME, JENNY ? -- TONIGHT !

OH, MISTER WILKINS-- I NEVER--

THE NAME IS BRAD! AND, I'LL PICK YOU UP AT EIGHT! AS FOR THE FURNITURE -- I'LL SEND SOMEONE AROUND TO PICK THAT UP, TOO! -- SOMEONE HOMELIER THAN MYSELF!

"I MEANT TO TELL HIM THAT I'D NEVER REALLY HAD A DATE BEFORE... BUT FOR SOME STRANGE REASON, I HELD MY TONGUE... I WAS READY AT 7:30! HE CAME AT 8:30! IT WAS MY FIRST LESSON IN MEN! MY SECOND OCCURRED THAT VERY EVENING!

YOU WALTZ BEAUTIFULLY, JENNY-- I'M SORRY I DON'T!

IT'S THE ONLY DANCE STEP I KNOW, BRAD! I SUSPECT IT MUST BE QUITE BORING TO YOU!

WHO GIVES A DARN ABOUT DANCING, ANYWAY-- WHEN A GUY HAS A LOVELY YOUNG THING LIKE YOU IN HIS ARMS!

BRAD! YOU'RE HOLDING ME TOO CLOSELY! EVERYONE IS LOOKING AT US!

LET THEM!-- WHO CARES! ALL I CAN SEE IS YOU, JENNY! YOU'RE ALL I'VE SEEN SINCE I FIRST BARGED INTO YOUR HOME!

PLEASE, BRAD! YOU-- YOU MUSTN'T-

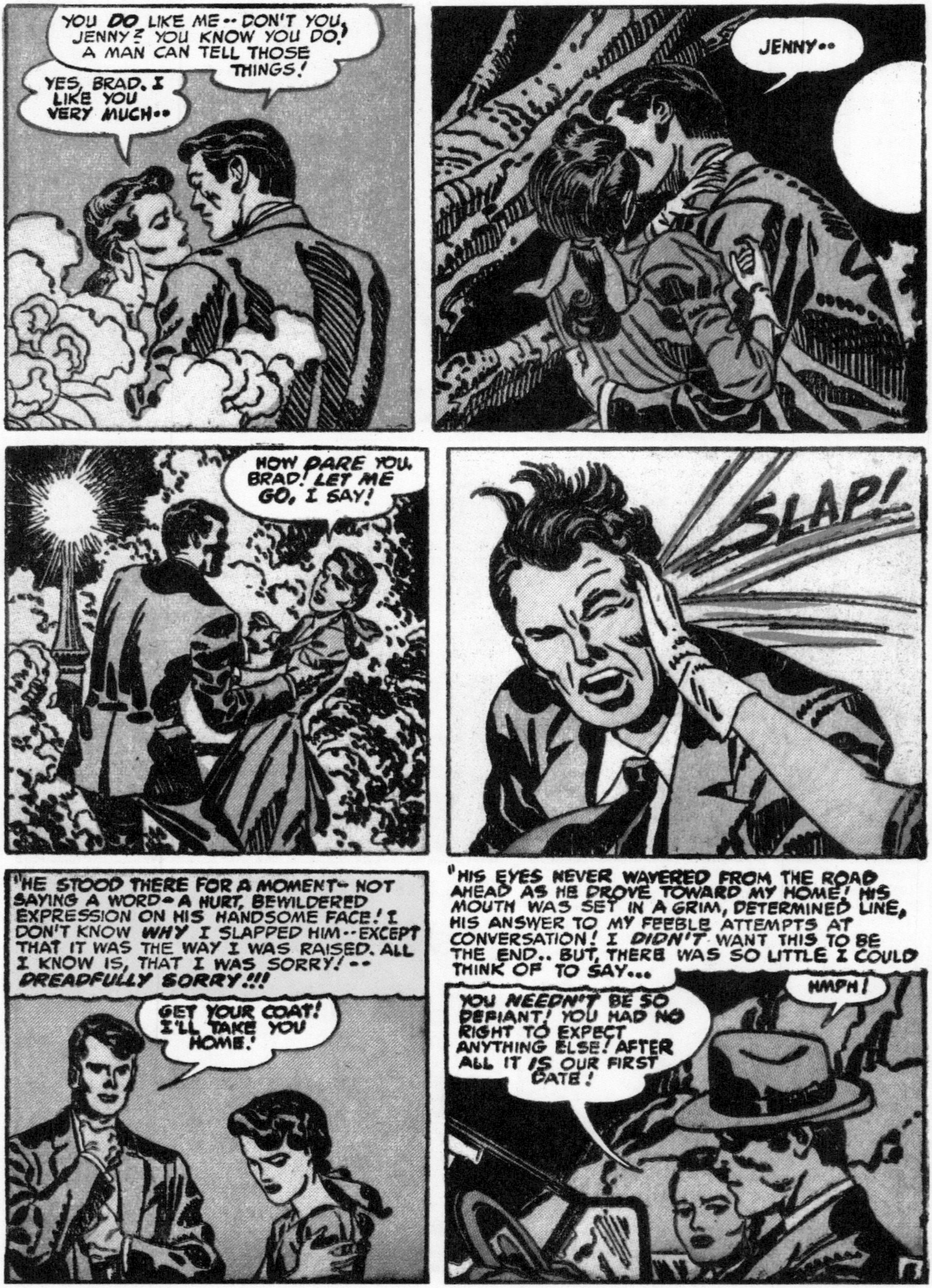
YOU DO LIKE ME -- DON'T YOU, JENNY? YOU KNOW YOU DO! A MAN CAN TELL THOSE THINGS!
YES, BRAD. I LIKE YOU VERY MUCH..
JENNY..
HOW DARE YOU, BRAD! LET ME GO, I SAY!
SLAP!
"HE STOOD THERE FOR A MOMENT-- NOT SAYING A WORD-- A HURT, BEWILDERED EXPRESSION ON HIS HANDSOME FACE! I DON'T KNOW WHY I SLAPPED HIM -- EXCEPT THAT IT WAS THE WAY I WAS RAISED. ALL I KNOW IS, THAT I WAS SORRY! -- DREADFULLY SORRY!!!
GET YOUR COAT! I'LL TAKE YOU HOME!
"HIS EYES NEVER WAVERED FROM THE ROAD AHEAD AS HE DROVE TOWARD MY HOME! HIS MOUTH WAS SET IN A GRIM, DETERMINED LINE, HIS ANSWER TO MY FEEBLE ATTEMPTS AT CONVERSATION! I DIDN'T WANT THIS TO BE THE END.. BUT, THERE WAS SO LITTLE I COULD THINK OF TO SAY...
YOU NEEDN'T BE SO DEFIANT! YOU HAD NO RIGHT TO EXPECT ANYTHING ELSE! AFTER ALL IT IS OUR FIRST DATE!
HMPH!

I THINK *YOU'RE* THE ONE WHO SHOULD APOLOGIZE! GRANDMA *ALWAYS* SAID THAT..

GRANDMA! IN GRANDMA'S TIME IT WAS *UNTHINKABLE* FOR A FELLOW TO KISS A GAL ON THEIR DATE! *BUT TIMES HAVE CHANGED, BABY!*

SURELY YOU CAN'T BE THAT NAIVE TODAY! -- THAT *OLD FASHIONED!*

IT'S THE ONLY CODE OF BEHAVIOR I KNOW, BRAD!

BUT I DON'T WANT YOU TO THINK I DISLIKE YOU! I-- I'M *VERY FOND* OF YOU..

ALL RIGHT, JENNY.. I'LL PLAY ALONG! I'LL TEACH YOU TO BE A MODERN, UP-TO-DATE, YOUNG LADY!

"BRAD DIDN'T TRY TO KISS ME GOOD NIGHT.. I'D HAVE BEEN EMBARRASSED IF HE HAD!" AND, IN THE DATES THAT FOLLOWED--THE WEEKS AND MONTHS OF FALLING IN LOVE, I CONTINUED MY RULE OF THE UNKISSED WONDER..

WE'VE BEEN GOING TOGETHER FOR SIX MONTHS NOW, JENNY..

AND, AM I SHOWING SIGNS OF ADVANCEMENT, BRAD?

SUPPOSE I JUST SAY THAT YOU LOOK SLICK.. DRESS SMART.. AND, SAY! YOU'RE EVEN USING *LIPSTICK!*

IT'S-- *KISSPROOF,* BRAD--

IS THAT AN INVITATION, JENNY--?

YOU SAID YOUR-SELF--THAT I'M *NOT OLD FASHIONED* ANYMORE!

JENNY--

"I CLUNG TO HIM--TO HIS *COOL* AND *GENTLE* LIPS-- WHILE WAVE AFTER *RAPTUROUS* WAVE OF LOVE SURGED *VIOLENTLY* AGAINST THE BARREN SHORES OF MY HEART--SWEET THUNDER BREAKING OVER BLEAK WASTES-- THE SOUND OF *SHATTERED* CONTINENTS IN THE MOMENT OF *CATACLYSM!* I WAS SUDDENLY OVERWHELMED BY *PANIC*--

STOP IT, BRAD! *STOP IT!*

WHAT IS IT, JENNY? WHAT'S WRONG?

IT'S *DISGUSTING!* WHAT CAN YOU *THINK* OF ME--

WHAT ARE YOU TRYING TO DO TO ME, JENNY! WHAT KIND OF SHAMEFUL TAG ARE YOU TRYING TO PIN ON A *NORMAL HUMAN EMOTION!* WE'RE NOT SAINTS! WE'RE MAN AND WOMAN!

DON'T TOUCH ME, BRAD! I-I DON'T *TRUST* YOU! I DON'T TRUST *ANY MAN!*

--NOT UNTIL I GET THAT *RING* ON MY FINGER! GRANDMA *TOLD* ME ABOUT MEN LIKE YOU! I SHOULD HAVE LISTENED TO HER! YOU'RE NOT SERIOUS ABOUT ME. IF YOU WERE YOU'D HAVE MENTIONED IT BEFORE THIS!

SO, I'VE TAKEN YOUR SWEET KISSES AND PROMISED NOTHING! PARDON ME, WHILE I TWIRL MY MOUSTACHE AND GIVE OUT WITH A *SNEER,* LITTLE NELL! GET WISE! I AM! YOU NEEDN'T WORRY ABOUT *ME* ANYMORE!

AFTER THAT, WE WERE *STRANGERS* IN THE SAME TOWN.. WHEN WE PASSED EACH OTHER ON THE STREET, WE CAREFULLY AVOIDED DIRECT CONTACT...

7

"THE YEARS FLEW BY...MY GRANDPARENTS PASSED AWAY! I WAS TWENTY-ONE, NOW, ABLE TO SUPPORT MYSELF! I SECURED A JOB AS A SALESGIRL...THAT'S WHERE I MET AL BEDFORD! IT WAS STRANGE, THE WAY WE MET!

PSST! ON YOUR TOES, JENNY! HERE COMES BEDFORD!

SOUNDS LIKE A TRAIN! WHO OR WHAT'S BEDFORD?

HE'S THE FLOOR MANAGER...TOUGH TO FOOL! HE CAN SPOT A SLACKER TEN MILES OFF!

MISTER BEDFORD MAY BE TOUGH... BUT HE CERTAINLY IS GOOD LOOKING!

"AL BEDFORD WASN'T AS HARD-BOILED AS HE WANTED THE HELP TO BELIEVE. ON THE CONTRARY, HE WAS ALL TOO EAGER TO PLEASE! IN A FEW WEEKS, AL WAS BEGGING ME FOR DATES -- HE DIDN'T HAVE TO BEG TOO HARD...

I'M FLATTERED, MISTER BEDFORD, TO THINK THAT YOU EVER NOTICED ME WHEN THERE ARE SO MANY PRETTY GIRLS AT THE STORE!

I DON'T USUALLY MIX BUSINESS WITH PLEASURE, JENNY! BUT IN YOUR CASE, I THREW THE RULES OUT OF THE WINDOW!

"BEFORE OUR FIRST DATE WAS HALF OVER, THIS CHARAC-TER WAS ACTUALLY GETTING MAUDLIN! I LEARNED AN INTERESTING FACT ABOUT MEN THAT NIGHT! THERE WAS A TYPE THAT DIDN'T GROW BOLD ON THE FIRST DATE...AL WAS A TYPICAL SPECIMEN...

OF COURSE, I'LL SEE YOU AGAIN, AL...IN THE STORE--TOMORROW--

I DON'T MEAN IT THAT WAY, JENNY-- TOMORROW NIGHT, I'LL PICK YOU UP AFTER WORK!

"AL WAS RIPE FOR CONQUEST! BUT, I'D MADE A FIRM RESOLUTION TO AVOID ANYMORE ENTANGLEMENTS LIKE THE BRAD WILKINS FIASCO! I SAW AL AND - OTHER MEN - OFTEN! EVEN ONE OTHER MAN WOULD HAVE BEEN TOO OFTEN TO AL'S LIKING!

YOU WERE OUT AGAIN LAST NIGHT, JENNY!

YES, AL! I HAD A HEAVENLY TIME!

SETTLE DOWN, JENNY! YOU CAN'T RUN AROUND ALL HOURS OF THE NIGHT AND DO A GOOD SALES JOB THE NEXT DAY!

DON'T BE PETTY, MISTER BEDFORD! YOU NEVER NOTICED MY FAILINGS THE MORNINGS AFTER OUR DATES TOGETHER!

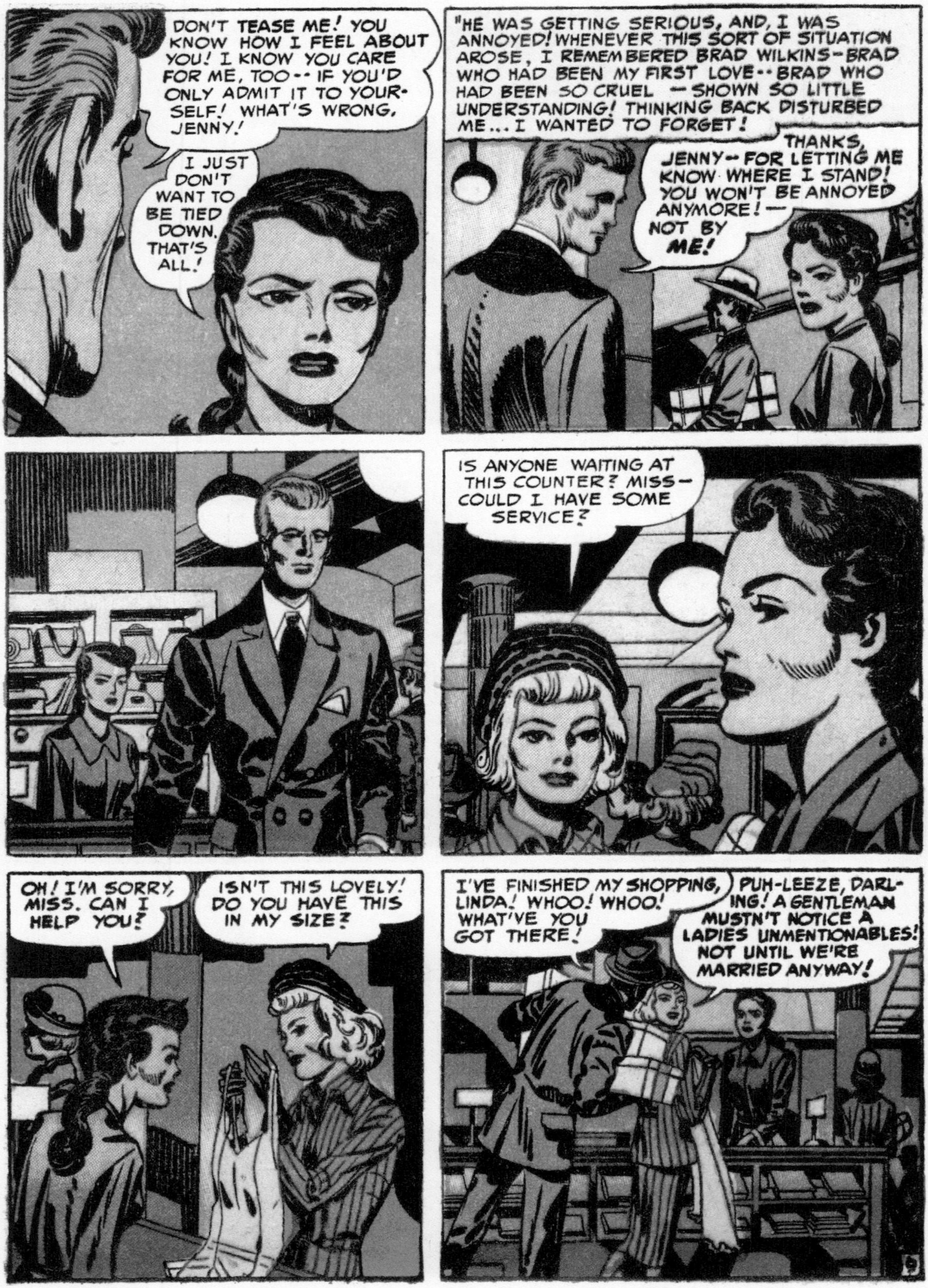

DON'T TEASE ME! YOU KNOW HOW I FEEL ABOUT YOU! I KNOW YOU CARE FOR ME, TOO -- IF YOU'D ONLY ADMIT IT TO YOURSELF! WHAT'S WRONG, JENNY!
I JUST DON'T WANT TO BE TIED DOWN. THAT'S ALL!
"HE WAS GETTING SERIOUS, AND, I WAS ANNOYED! WHENEVER THIS SORT OF SITUATION AROSE, I REMEMBERED BRAD WILKINS-BRAD WHO HAD BEEN MY FIRST LOVE -- BRAD WHO HAD BEEN SO CRUEL -- SHOWN SO LITTLE UNDERSTANDING! THINKING BACK DISTURBED ME... I WANTED TO FORGET!
THANKS, JENNY -- FOR LETTING ME KNOW WHERE I STAND! YOU WON'T BE ANNOYED ANYMORE! -- NOT BY ME!
IS ANYONE WAITING AT THIS COUNTER? MISS -- COULD I HAVE SOME SERVICE?
OH! I'M SORRY, MISS. CAN I HELP YOU?
ISN'T THIS LOVELY! DO YOU HAVE THIS IN MY SIZE?
I'VE FINISHED MY SHOPPING, LINDA! WHOO! WHOO! WHAT'VE YOU GOT THERE!
PUH-LEEZE, DARLING! A GENTLEMAN MUSTN'T NOTICE A LADIES UNMENTIONABLES! NOT UNTIL WE'RE MARRIED ANYWAY!

JENNY!

H-HELLO, BRAD—

"WE WERE FACE TO FACE IN THE SUDDEN SHOCK OF RECOGNITION! WE SPOKE TO EACH OTHER FOR THE FIRST TIME IN MANY YEARS... *MY HEART BEAT WILDLY AT THE SOUND OF HIS VOICE*--EVEN THOUGH, WHAT HE SAID WAS CONTROLLED AND FORMAL..."

NICE TO SEE YOU, JENNY. ER--YOU LOOK FINE!

THANK YOU, BRAD, YOU'RE LOOKING WELL, YOUR-SELF.

"THERE WAS A BRIEF INTRODUCTION TO THE GIRL BRAD WAS WITH... AND BEFORE I KNEW IT, THEY WERE LEAVING..."

WELL, GOTTA RUSH! BE SEEING YOU, JENNY!

GOOD-BYE, BRAD-

"I WATCHED THE TWO OF THEM VANISH IN THE BUSTLING CROWD, THEN I TURNED TO FIND *AL BEDFORD* AT THE COUNTER... HE'D BEEN WATCHING, TOO..."

SO *THAT'S* IT, JENNY.. YOU'RE CARRYING A *TORCH*--AND YOU DON'T WANT TO GET BURNED AGAIN! YOU MUST HAVE HAD IT PRETTY *BAD* TO BE AFFECTED BY IT SO LONG!

OH, AL—AL! I *HATE* HIM! AFTER ALL THESE YEARS I *STILL HATE HIM!*

DON'T CRY, HONEY. GET YOUR COAT.. I'LL TAKE YOU OUT OF HERE!

"I OFTEN THINK BACK AND THANK HEAVEN FOR AL— THAT HE WAS THERE WHEN I NEEDED HIM! HE HELD ME CLOSELY AS WE DESCENDED THE STAIRS TO THE EMPLOYEES' EXIT!"

IT'S ALMOST LUNCH HOUR, ANYWAY! COME ON, WE'LL TALK IT OUT OVER SOME COFFEE AT MAXWELL'S DRUG STORE!

"THE FOOD AND COFFEE WAS UNUSUALLY GOOD AT MAXWELL'S DRUG STORE... IT SOMEWHAT EASED MY EMOTIONAL STRESS. IT WAS MEDICATION FOR THE MIND. AND, I FOUND IT EASIER TO TALK TO AL ABOUT BRAD.

AND AFTER THAT DAY -- WELL, BRAD AND I WERE MORE OR LESS -- STRANGERS--

THAT WAS MANY YEARS AGO, JENNY, WHEN YOU MET BRAD TODAY, YOU SPOKE --

WHAT I WANT TO KNOW, JENNY, IS, -- WHAT ABOUT TOMORROW? HOW WILL YOU FEEL ABOUT BRAD IF YOU SHOULD SEE HIM TOMORROW?

I'M VITALLY INTERESTED IN THAT QUESTION! MIND IF I JOIN YOU?

OH! IT'S YOU! I'M GLAD YOU'RE HERE.. THIS CAN BE SETTLED-- RIGHT NOW!

I SAW YOU TWO COME IN HERE WHEN I CAME BACK TO SEE JENNY!

AND, I SAW YOU WHEN YOU LEFT THE STORE.. YOU DIDN'T SEEM SO CONCERNED ABOUT JENNY!

I AM! I-I THOUGHT I'D GOTTEN OVER HER -- BUT, SEEING JENNY AGAIN -- WELL, IT'S JUST NO USE!

WHAT ABOUT THE GIRL YOU WERE WITH --

I HEARD HER MENTION -- MARRIAGE!

LINDA PRESUMED TOO MUCH! IT WAS STRICTLY HER IDEA! I DON'T LOVE HER... SHE MUST HAVE KNOWN THAT!

IT'S JENNY I LOVE! I ALWAYS HAVE! I ALWAYS WILL! I'D LIKE TO KNOW HOW *SHE* FEELS ABOUT IT... THAT'S WHY I'M HERE!

ANYONE CAN SEE HOW SHE FEELS ABOUT IT..

SHE *HATES* YOU! SHE'S HATED YOU FOR YEARS! GO AHEAD! ASK HER YOURSELF!

DO YOU, JENNY? REALLY AND *TRULY?*

"HIS ARMS REACHED FOR ME..AND, I MOVED INTO THEM. THEY WERE STRONG AND WARM! *OUR LIPS MET--HEALING A TORN WOUND OF EMPTY YEARS!* ANGUISH AND TORMENT WERE FORGOTTEN.

MARRY ME, JENNY!

OH, BRAD— BRAD!

PARDON ME, WON'T YOU – OF COURSE!

WELL, SINCE NOBODY SEEMS INTERESTED.. THAT LEAVES *ME* TO PAY THE *CHECK!* HAVE FUN!

"I WAS NO LONGER THE SCARED, CONFUSED KID WHO NOW HELD BRAD SO CLOSELY.. I WAS A *WOMAN* NOW! BUT WANT TO KNOW A SECRET? I'M STILL AN OLD FASHIONED GIRL--AND BRAD'S THE ONLY MAN I EVER KISSED!"

The END

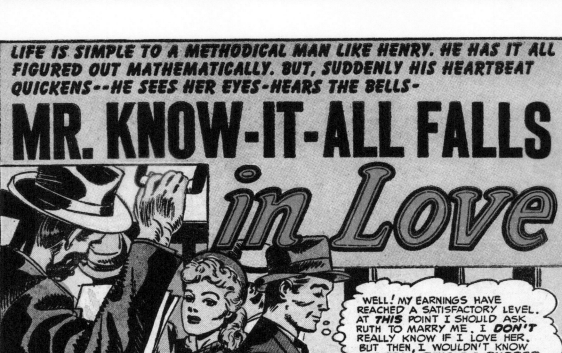

LIFE IS SIMPLE TO A METHODICAL MAN LIKE HENRY. HE HAS IT ALL FIGURED OUT MATHEMATICALLY. BUT, SUDDENLY HIS HEARTBEAT QUICKENS--HE SEES HER EYES--HEARS THE BELLS--

MR. KNOW-IT-ALL FALLS in Love

WELL! MY EARNINGS HAVE REACHED A SATISFACTORY LEVEL. AT *THIS* POINT I SHOULD ASK RUTH TO MARRY ME. I *DON'T* REALLY KNOW IF I LOVE HER. BUT THEN, I WOULDN'T KNOW THE REAL THING IF I *RUBBED SHOULDERS* WITH IT!

"LITTLE DID I THINK THAT MORNING AS I DROPPED MY ANNUITY PAYMENT INTO THE MAIL BOX THAT MY ENTIRE LIFE WAS TO BE CHANGED BY AN EVERYDAY OCCURRENCE. FOR I LIVED A SANE, RATIONAL EXISTENCE, WITH EVERY MOVE PLANNED WELL AHEAD OF TIME...

HMMM. IT'S THREE AND A HALF MINUTES TO THE *STATION* AND I'VE GOT FIVE TO MAKE IT IN -- JUST ABOUT RIGHT FOR ME TO PICK UP A PAPER AND GET SETTLED IN MY SEAT.

"I HAD CHOSEN THE GIRL I WAS GOING TO MARRY, THE HOUSE I WAS GOING TO LIVE IN, THE COMPANY I WAS GOING TO WORK FOR... EVEN THE VARIOUS STEPS I HAD TO TAKE TO GET TO THE THE TOP. YES SIR, I FELT *QUITE SECURE* THAT MORNING ...

OH! I ... ER ... I BEG YOUR PARDON!

THAT'S QUITE ALL RIGHT... NO DAMAGE DONE!

"I HARDLY *LOOKED* AT THE GIRL, AND YET ALL THE WAY DOWN TO THE STATION I COULDN'T GET HER OFF MY MIND! PERHAPS IT WAS THE SLIGHT TRACE OF *PERFUME* THAT REMAINED ON MY LAPEL, I THOUGHT.

THIS IS *SILLY!* HERE I HAVE THE MOST WONDERFUL GIRL IN THE WORLD IN LOVE WITH ME AND I GO THINKING ABOUT SOME DAME WHO JUST HAPPENS TO PASS ON THE STREET.

"IN THE COURSE OF MY DAYS WORK, I THOUGHT I HAD SUCCEEDED IN DRIVING HER COMPLETELY FROM MY MIND -- BUT THAT NIGHT, AS I DROVE TO PICK UP MY DATE...

NOW, WHY AM I IN *THIS* DIRECTION? IT'S FAR OUT OF MY WAY... AND *THAT GIRL* BY THE MAIL BOX? CAN IT BE THAT SHE...?

"THE MORE I THOUGHT ABOUT IT, THE MORE I REALIZED THAT IT WAS NOTHING MORE THAN A SUBCONSCIOUS LONGING FOR FEMALE COMPANIONSHIP! AFTER ALL, I *WASN'T* GETTING ANY *YOUNGER*... SO, WHEN I REACHED *RUTH'S* HOUSE, I DECIDED IT WAS TIME TO TAKE THE FATAL STEP!

YOU'RE *TWO MINUTES LATE*, HENRY! THIS ISN'T *LIKE* YOU AT ALL!

I WAS ER... HELD UP A FEW MINUTES! I HOPE IT DIDN'T INCONVENIENCE YOU!

HENRY, IT DID MY HEART GOOD TO SEE YOU LATE JUST *ONCE* IN YOUR LIFE! IT PROVES YOU'RE *HUMAN!* NOW, COME ON, WHERE ARE WE GOING?

WELL, IF YOU DON'T MIND, I THOUGHT MAYBE WE'D JUST SIT HERE AND TALK FOR AWHILE... I... HAVE SOMETHING RATHER *IMPORTANT* TO TELL YOU...

YOU COULDN'T HAVE PICKED ON A BETTER NIGHT! IT'S LOVELY OUT HERE... NOW SIT DOWN AND TELL ME ALL ABOUT IT!

I'VE BEEN FIGURING THINGS OUT, RUTH, AND IT SEEMS TO ME THAT I'M IN ABOUT AS COMFORTABLE A *FINANCIAL* POSITION NOW AS I'LL *EVER* BE IN... PARTICULARLY WITH RESPECT TO *THE FUTURE*... MY POSITION AS ACCOUNTANT WITH THE FIRST NATIONAL IS QUITE SECURE AND...

...I HAVE A TIDY SUM IN THE BANK! WELL, I THINK YOU'RE A SWELL GIRL, RUTH... JUST THE TYPE I'D WANT FOR A *WIFE!* YOU'RE PRETTY, NEAT, EASY-GOING... IN FACT, I THINK WE TWO WOULD BE QUITE COMPATIBLE!

HENRY WATTLE, ARE YOU TRYING TO PROPOSE?

OF COURSE, I'M PROPOSING! I SUPPOSE I *SHOULD* HAVE GOTTEN DOWN ON MY KNEE OR SOMETHING OF THAT SORT!

WELL, WHY DIDN'T YOU *SAY* SO WITHOUT ALL THAT DIALOGUE? COME HERE, YOU BIG *LUG!*

NOW WHAT'S ALL THIS ABOUT *MONEY IN THE BANK* AND *COMPATIBLE... AND WHAT NOT!*

RUTH, YOU'RE TAKING THIS ENTIRELY *TOO LIGHTLY!* THOSE THINGS ARE *IMPORTANT* WHEN ONE IS CONTEMPLATING A BIG STEP LIKE *MARRIAGE!*

CERTAINLY THEY ARE! BUT A LOVE AFFAIR ISN'T PREPARED LIKE A *BALANCE SHEET!* TWO PEOPLE MEET EACH OTHER, FALL IN LOVE... *THEY GET MARRIED!*

YOU'VE BEEN READING TOO MANY NOVELS! PEOPLE FALL IN LOVE BECAUSE THEY'RE ECONOMICALLY AND SOCIALLY COMPATIBLE! IT'S INEVITABLE... THE *ONLY* THING THAT'S INEVITABLE ABOUT *LOVE!*

I MUST SAY I'M NOT OVERLY IMPRESSED BY YOUR ROMANTIC ARDOR... BUT YOUR *LOGIC* OVERWHELMS ME! DO YOU THINK A *KISS* COULD THROW THE BOOKS OUT OF BALANCE AT THE MOMENT?

I DON'T KNOW ABOUT THE *BOOKS,* BUT IT'S MAKING *ME* A LITTLE *SHAKY!*

"I SUPPOSE I WOULD HAVE MARRIED RUTH, RAISED A FINE FAMILY AND LIVED HAPPILY EVER AFTER, EXACTLY AS I HAD PLANNED! BUT THE NIGHT AFTER I PROPOSED TO RUTH, I HAD TO WORK LATE, AND THAT STARTED THE MOST UNFORESEE-ABLE CHAIN OF CIRCUM-STANCES EVER!

HMMM... TEN-THIRTY! I SHOULD BE HOME BY... SAY! ISN'T THAT THE GIRL WHO....SURE, IT IS! AND ALL BY HERSELF IN THIS LONELY SECTION AT SUCH A LATE HOUR!

I HOPE YOU WON'T THINK I'M BOLD, MISS, BUT...WELL, WE'RE PRACTICALLY NEIGHBORS...AND IT'S AWFULLY LATE! PERHAPS YOU'LL LIKE ME TO WALK YOU TO YOUR DOOR?

WALK ME TO MY DOOR? BUT I... OF COURSE! THAT'S VERY NICE OF YOU, MR... ER...MR?

WATTLE... HENRY WATTLE! I'M AN ACCOUNTANT WITH THE FIRST NATIONAL...

I'M PLEASED TO MEET YOU, MR. WATTLE! I'M LORETTA HELM...A SCULPTRESS, WITH NO NATIONAL, OR STATE EITHER, FOR THAT MATTER! IN FACT I HAVEN'T EVEN SOLD A STATUE YET...

YOU HAVEN'T? BUT HOW DO YOU MAKE A LIVING? I MEAN... I HOPE YOU DON'T THINK I'M TOO IN—

...NOT AT ALL...THAT'S A GOOD QUESTION! I LIVE ON A SMALL IN-COME MY FATHER LEFT ME! THE ONLY REASON I HAVEN'T SOLD A STATUE YET IS THAT I'M NOT SURE WHAT I WANT TO DO!

BUT THAT'S SILLY. EVERY MATURE PERSON SHOULD HAVE A COURSE TO FOLLOW... A PATTERN FOR THE FUTURE! IT ISN'T RATIONAL TO JUST... DRIFT!

BUT IT'S FUN...WHEN THE BILLS ARE PAID... WHICH ISN'T OFTEN! GOSH, I'M HOME ALREADY! WOULD YOU LIKE TO COME IN FOR A MOMENT AND SEE SOME OF MY WORK?

WELL IT'S RATHER LATE! SOME OTHER TIME, PERHAPS!

SWELL! HOW'S TOMORROW NIGHT?

TOMORROW NIGHT? BUT I'VE ...WHY YES! TOMORROW NIGHT WOULD BE PERFECT!

GOOD! I'LL SEE YOU THEN...

"SHE WAS QUITE IMPULSIVE... HARDLY THE TYPE OF GIRL I WOULD BE INTERESTED IN... NOT AT ALL LIKE RUTH! AND YET, WHEN I CALLED RUTH THE NEXT DAY TO TELL HER I COULDN'T MAKE OUR DATE THAT NIGHT, I HAD A BIT OF A GUILTY CONSCIENCE!

I HATE TO CALL YOU ON SUCH SHORT NOTICE RUTH, BUT SOMETHING HAS COME UP...

THAT'S QUITE ALL RIGHT, HENRY! I UNDERSTAND! EVERYTHING DOESN'T ALWAYS WORK OUT AS PLANNED!

"I DECIDED I'D LOOK AT HER STATUES AND TAKE THE FIRST OPPORTUNITY TO LEAVE! IT WAS ONLY FAIR TO RUTH... AND THEN WHY SHOULD I WANT TO DALLY WITH THIS GIRL ANYWAY? BUT THE MOMENT I SAW HER STANDING IN THE DOORWAY, I REALIZED HOW FOOLISH THAT PLAN WAS!

MR. WATTLE! HOW PROMPT YOU ARE! COME RIGHT IN... AND DON'T MIND THE MESS! I NEVER SEEM TO GET TO ALL THE THINGS I WANT TO!

"IT WASN'T THAT SHE WAS PRETTY! BUT THERE WAS SOMETHING ABOUT HER FACE... HER MANNER... SOMETHING THAT MADE ME WANT TO STAY, EVEN THOUGH HER STUDIO WAS NOT THE SORT OF ORDER I WOULD HAVE LIKED TO HAVE SEEN!

THIS IS ENTITLED "BIRD AT REST" AS YOU CAN SEE, IT ISN'T FINISHED YET... AND I DON'T KNOW WHEN I'LL GET AROUND TO WORKING ON IT!

BUT HOW DO YOU EXPECT TO SELL IT IF YOU DON'T FINISH IT!

PERHAPS I'LL NEVER FINISH IT... WHO KNOWS! I THINK THE UNCERTAINTY OF IT IS ALL THE FUN, DON'T YOU?

WELL, IT'S HARDLY PRACTICAL! BUT I SUPPOSE AS LONG AS IT MAKES YOU HAPPY... WELL, IT'S YOUR LIFE!

LIFE ITSELF IS UNCERTAINTY, DON'T YOU THINK? YOU AND I, FOR INSTANCE... BEFORE LAST NIGHT, WE HAD NEVER MET! AND NOW, HERE WE ARE!

YES, HERE WE ARE, AREN'T WE?

"AND THEN I DID THE STRANGEST THING...

YOU... YOU'LL HAVE TO EXCUSE ME... REALLY... I... I'VE NEVER DONE A THING LIKE THAT BEFORE! GOSH, IF YOU DON'T MIND, I'LL BE LEAVING NOW!

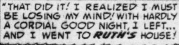

"THAT DID IT! I REALIZED I MUST BE LOSING MY MIND! WITH HARDLY A CORDIAL GOOD NIGHT, I LEFT... AND I WENT TO *RUTH'S* HOUSE!

HENRY! WHAT ARE YOU DOING HERE? I THOUGHT YOU HAD A BUSINESS APPOINTMENT!

I CALLED IT OFF! I'VE GOT SOMETHING MORE *IM-PORTANT*

RUTH... *LET'S GET MARRIED*... WHY STALL IT OFF ANY LONGER! IT'S ALWAYS BEEN IN THE CARDS FOR US!

WELL! WHAT BROUGHT *THIS* ON?

WE'VE DISCUSSED IT MANY TIMES BEFORE! WHY THE SURPRISE ACT? TELL YOU WHAT... WE'LL GET THE LICENSE AT LUNCH TOMORROW... WE'LL BOTH BE *FREE* THEN!

WE *CERTAINLY WILL BE!* AND *AFTER* LUNCH TOO!

WHAT'S THE MATTER WITH YOU RUTH? I NEVER THOUGHT YOU'D *OBJECT* TO THE IDEA!

I *DON'T!* IT'S JUST YOUR SUDDEN BULL-IN-THE-CHINA-SHOP APPROACH THAT SCARES ME! IT *ISN'T* LIKE YOU!

WELL, WHAT DO I HAVE TO DO? STRIKE A ROMANTIC POSE? SPOUT A MESS OF SENTIMENTAL HOGWASH? IS *THAT* WHAT YOU WANT?

YES... I MEAN, *NO!* IT'S NOT THAT EITHER! YOU'RE THE *METHODICAL* TYPE, HENRY! YOU'D NEVER MARRY... *UNLESS IT WAS READY TO FIT INTO YOUR SCHEDULE...*

NOW, SOMETHING'S FORCED YOU TO MAKE A *HURRIED* DECISION! I WON'T HAVE IT THAT WAY! I CAN WAIT UNTIL YOU'VE THOUGHT THINGS OUT WITH CALM AND REASON...

ALL RIGHT, ANYTHING YOU SAY, RUTH...

6

"THAT NIGHT, I HARDLY SLEPT AT ALL ...

LIFE IS A UNCERTAINTY, HENRY, BUT THAT'S WHAT MAKES IT FUN! EVERY DAY IS A *SURPRISE*...A NEW HORIZON TO BE MET AND CROSSED!

"I COULDN'T GET LORETTA OFF MY MIND! EVERY-WHERE I WENT, EVERYTHING I DID OR SAW, CON-TAINED SOMETHING OF HER!

I HAVEN'T SOLD A STATUE YET, BUT I DON'T CARE!

THIS TRIAL BALANCE IS TWENTY CENTS SHORT MR. WATTLE! THE UNCERTAINTY OF IT IS FUN, ISN'T IT?

I'M NOT SURE WHAT I WANT TO DO... I NEVER AM!

"I COULDN'T EAT, COULDN'T SLEEP, COULDN'T WORK! FINALLY, IN DESPERATION, I DECIDED TO TELL RUTH ABOUT IT! SHE WAS INFINITELY WISER ABOUT THESE THINGS!

I CAN'T UNDERSTAND IT, RUTH! I HARDLY KNOW THE GIRL... AND YET, I... I CAN'T GET HER OUT OF MY MIND!

NO WONDER YOU ACTED LIKE THE FOOL YOU DID! HENRY... DON'T YOU KNOW THE *SYMPTOMS*?

THE SYMPTOMS OF WHAT? I'M *NOT* SICK!

OH, YES YOU ARE! *LOVESICK!* HA! HA! HA! REALLY, HENRY... I CAN'T HELP IT... IT'S SIMPLY... *HYSTERICAL!*

IN LOVE WITH *HER?* BUT THAT'S *RIDICULOUS!* I'M IN LOVE WITH *YOU!*

NONSENSE, YOU IDIOT! I'M ONLY A FIGURE THAT SEEMS TO ADD UP IN YOUR GREAT PLAN! BUT LOVE IS THE *UNKNOWN* QUANTITY WHICH KNOCKS ALL PLANS FOR A LOOP!

HENRY... IF YOU DON'T TAKE THAT *CONFUSED* LOOK OFF YOUR FACE... I'LL LAUGH FIT TO BURST!

WHAT'S SO FUNNY ABOUT ALL THIS? YOU SOUND ALL TOO WILLING TO HAND ME OVER TO THIS GIRL! I *DON'T* FEEL VERY FLATTERED!

MAYBE NOT, HENRY! BUT WHEN THINGS STRAIGHTEN THEM-SELVES OUT, YOU'LL BE *HAPPY!* OH, I'D ACCEPT YOU, HENRY... YOU'RE A GOOD MAN, BETTER THAN MANY I KNOW! THAT'S WHY I WANT TO SEE YOU MARRY... *FOR LOVE!*

RUTH, I... I NEVER REALIZED WHAT A REALLY FINE GIRL YOU ARE!

"IN A FEW MOMENTS, MY WHOLE WORLD HAD TURNED UPSIDE DOWN! ALL MY SELF-CONFIDENCE WAS SHAKEN... I WAS DOING SOMETHING *WITH-OUT* A PLAN! WHEN LORETTA OPENED THE DOOR FOR ME, I FOUND MYSELF SHY OF COURAGE OR WORDS...

WHY, MR. WATTLE! THIS IS A PLEASANT SURPRISE! DO COME IN!

MISS HELM... LORETTA... I... I'VE GOT SOME-THING TO SAY TO YOU THAT... THAT...

DO YOU REMEMBER YOUR SAYING YOU NEVER PLANNED ANYTHING... THAT YOU *LIKED* SURPRISES?

YOU... HAVE A... SURPRISE... FOR *ME*...

WOULD IT SURPRISE YOU IF I... I TOLD YOU THAT I LOVED YOU?

I'D SAY IT'S THE REALIZATION OF A *FOND HOPE*... THAN A SURPRISE, MR. WATTLE...

IF THAT MEANS YOU LOVE ME... CALL ME... HENRY...

HENRY... DARLING...

"OF ALL THE UNFORESEEN, ILLOGICAL AND *REMARKABLE* THINGS TO BEFALL A MAN, I THOUGHT TO MYSELF... AS HER KISSES LOOSENED HEAVENLY CHAOS THROUGHOUT MY VERY BEING!

DESTINY OR COINCIDENCE... *LOVE IS TERRIFIC!*

OH, IT'S MORE THAN THAT! IT'S A PLOT! A SCHEME... A PLAN!

Y-YOU MEAN... A PLAN? LIKE FIGURES... AND DECIMALS... AND STATISTICS WORKED... OUT... ON... PAPER...

NO, SILLY! *MY* PLAN! A WOMAN'S PLAN! THAT NIGHT WHEN I LET YOU ESCORT ME HOME FROM THE STATION... WELL... AFTER YOU'D GONE I HAD TO RETURN TO THE STATION...

Y-YOU DID? WHY?

... FOR MY *CAR*! I ALWAYS PARK IT AT THE STATION TO DRIVE HOME IN! BUT, I DIDN'T THAT NIGHT! I'D MET YOU, DARLING... AND YOU LOOKED SO... INTEREST-ING! SO HANDSOME... JUST LIKE THE MAN I'D ALWAYS DREAMED OF MARRYING!

The END

He was the missing guest at their wedding, his was the tortured heart that filled each thought of them with hate. Yet, of all the gifts showered on the happy couple, not one of them was more highly valued than his---

Wedding Present!

BABY, THIS SCENERY HAD NOTHING UNTIL YOU GOT HERE. A LITTLE MORE SMILE, NOW. THAT'S IT!

HANK, YOU MAKE IT EASY TO SMILE, YOU LOOK SO COMICAL WHEN YOU FUSS WITH THAT CAMERA!

Produced by **SIMON & KIRBY**

"I REMEMBER *KAY MASTER'S* BEAUTIFUL IMAGE SMILING UP AT ME IN THE CAMERA FINDER--AND WHAT HER RADIANT SMILE WAS DOING TO THE COMPOSURE OF ONE *HANK WILEY.* THAT'S ME. I'D BEEN DATING HER MORE AND MORE FREQUENTLY, AND THE REASON WAS BEGINNING TO DAWN ON ME.

WELL, THAT'S THE LAST OF THE FILM. I SHOULD HAVE BROUGHT ANOTHER PACK!

AND *ANOTHER MODEL* AS A REPLACEMENT. I'M STIFF AS A BOARD FROM ALL THAT POSING!

HERE. LET OLD *"DOC" WILEY* TAKE SOME OF THOSE *KINKS* OUT. I COME FROM A LONG LINE OF CHIROPRACTORS, YOU KNOW!

YOU'RE DOING *WELL* BY YOUR FAMILY TRADITIONS. THAT FEELS WONDERFUL--

AH, BUT YOU HAVEN'T HAD THE *FULL ADVANTAGE* OF THE TREATMENT. *THIS* IS GUARANTEED TO RELAX YOU THOROUGHLY

DOCTOR-- YOU'RE A *WOLF!*

THAT WAS SOMETHING TO *HOWL* ABOUT. I LIKED THAT. DID YOU?

I'M NOT GOING TO FLATTER YOUR MALE EGO BY REVEALING MY REACTION!

130

"WHEN WE DROVE HOME FROM THAT PICNIC, HER IMAGE WAS STILL BEFORE ME...IN THE REAR VIEW MIRROR...RADIANT AS THE SUN AND WARM IN MY HEART! I WAS MAD ABOUT KAY MASTERS!"

OH, HANK, I FEEL JUST GRAND! IT'S BEEN SUCH A WONDERFUL DAY!

THERE'S *ANOTHER* ONE DUE TOMORROW, ACCORDING TO THE WEATHERMAN! SHALL I CALL FOR YOU?

OH, GOSH, I'M TERRIBLY SORRY, HANK! *BUT, I PROMISED CHARLIE GOODWIN* I'D GO OUT WITH HIM, TOMORROW...

OH, *THAT* GUY, AGAIN! I'M GOING TO HATE HIM FOR EVERY MINUTE HE'S WITH YOU... CAN'T YOU *BREAK* THE DATE, KAY?

NOW, DON'T BE A BIG BABY! CHARLIE IS A *FINE* FELLOW! IN FACT, I THINK QUITE A LOT OF HIM...

THAT DOESN'T MAKE *ME* VERY HAPPY... CONSIDERING HOW I *FEEL* ABOUT YOU...

WELL, THAT'S VERY INTERESTING! NOW, WE'VE GOT *SOMETHING TO TALK ABOUT* WHEN I SEE YOU AGAIN...

WE SURE HAVE, BABY...

"I WAS HAPPY WHEN I GOT HOME! THE WORLD LOOKED LIKE A GREAT PALACE! BUT, FROM THE SERIOUS EXPRESSION ON DAD'S FACE, HE DIDN'T SEEM TO THINK SO!"

HI, DAD... WHY SO GLUM? YOU GET ANOTHER *BILL* IN THE MAIL?

WE *DID* GET A LETTER ...IT WAS FOR *YOU*...

"THE *DRAFT NOTICE* SOBERED ME UP QUITE A BIT! I SUPPOSE, I'D BEEN EXPECTING ONE! BUT, NOT KNOWING WHEN IT WOULD ARRIVE, I WENT ABOUT MY NORMAL ROUTINE WITHOUT GIVING IT MUCH THOUGHT! NOW, THAT IT WAS HERE, I READ IT WITH SERIOUS INTENT! I WAS *THINKING* ABOUT *KAY*!"

WELL, THIS PUTS A NEW LIGHT ON THINGS FOR ME! I'VE GOT TO MAKE SOME HURRIED PLANS!

YOU'LL MAKE A *FINE* SOLDIER, SON! I'M SURE YOU'LL ACQUIT YOURSELF LIKE A MAN!

YES, AND I'M READY TO SHOULDER A MAN'S RESPONSIBILITIES! DAD, BEFORE I LEAVE FOR THE ARMY... *I'M GOING TO ASK KAY MASTERS TO MARRY ME!*

THIS DAY IS *FULL* OF SURPRISES, ISN'T IT! WELL, I KNOW KAY WON'T FIND A BETTER HUSBAND ANYWHERE! YOU'VE GOT MY BLESSINGS, BOY...

"I COULDN'T SLEEP THAT NIGHT! THIS NEW PHASE OF MY LIFE HAD BEGUN WITH LOVE AND WAR...DANGER AND ECSTACY...THE DRAMA OF IT ELECTRIFIED MY THOUGHTS! I COULD SEE KAY'S EYES LOOKING INTO MINE...SOFT AND PROUD ...AND WITH THE LOVE THAT WOULD OUTLIVE THE RIFLE'S ROAR! THE FOLLOWING EVENING, WITH MY HEART BEATING WILDLY, I WENT TO SEE KAY MASTERS..."

KAY...I'VE GOT SOME-THING VERY IMPORTANT TO TELL YOU...

I...I THINK I KNOW WHAT IT IS YOU HAVE TO SAY, HANK...

HANK, I'VE SPENT SOME OF MY HAPPIEST MOMENTS IN YOUR COMPANY! BUT WE'VE REACHED THE STAGE WHERE OUR DATES HAVE TAKEN ON A DEEPER MEANING...

THAT'S WHAT I'VE COME TO TALK TO YOU ABOUT, KAY...THAT DEEPER MEANING... AND ITS BEARING ON OUR IMMEDIATE FUTURES...

LISTEN TO ME, HANK! WE CAN SEE EACH OTHER AGAIN...ONLY AS FRIENDS! IT'S A DECISION I MADE LAST NIGHT! IT WAS A HARD DECISION TO MAKE! BUT, A NECESSARY ONE! YOU SEE....I'M GOING TO MARRY CHARLIE GOODWIN!

KAY! WHAT ARE YOU SAYING? I...I CAN'T BELIEVE YOU MEAN THAT...

"I WAS TELLING THE TRUTH! MY MIND JUST REFUSED TO ACCEPT THE VISION OF A FUTURE WITHOUT KAY! I JUST COULDN'T FACE THAT KIND OF FUTURE! NOT WITHOUT FEAR AND LONELINESS AND CONFUSION..."

I WON'T GIVE YOU UP, DO YOU HEAR? YOU BELONG TO ME! I LOVE YOU AS NO OTHER MAN EVER COULD!

HANK...PLEASE, IF YOU HAVE ANY REGARD FOR MY FEELINGS, DON'T MAKE A SCENE! LET ME GO, HANK!

I'LL NEVER LET YOU GO, KAY! YOU DON'T KNOW WHAT YOU MEAN TO ME!

HANK... FOR PETE'S SAKE...

ALL RIGHT, WILEY! YOU CAN CUT OUT THE ROUGH STUFF!

CHARLIE!

SO IT'S CHARLIE, IS IT! IT'S YOUR FAULT, YOU SMOOTH TALKING PUNK! YOU FED HER A FAST LINE AND SHE FELL FOR IT!

"I HIT HIM AGAIN AND AGAIN... AS THE HATE INSIDE ME POURED FROM MY TONGUE AND LEAPED INTO EACH OF MY KNOTTED FISTS! I WAS REALLY STRIKING OUT IN A FRENZIED EFFORT TO REGAIN SOMETHING FOREVER LOST TO ME... CRYING INSIDE WITH FUTILE TEARS OF FRUSTRATION AND SORROW...

STOP IT, HANK! STOP IT!

KAY!

GET OUT, HANK! GET OUT! I NEVER HAD ANY IDEA YOU WERE LIKE THIS! THERE'S NO EXCUSE FOR WHAT YOU'VE DONE!

TAKE IT EASY, HONEY! HE JUST CAN'T TAKE A LOSS LIKE A MAN. THAT'S ALL!

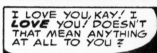

I LOVE YOU, KAY! I LOVE YOU! DOESN'T THAT MEAN ANYTHING AT ALL TO YOU?

OH, HANK! I...I FEEL SO TERRIBLY SORRY FOR YOU! PLEASE, GO, NOW...

"SHE FELT SORRY FOR ME! IT WAS ANOTHER WOUND TO LICK ON MY WAY HOME! THIS NIGHT, WHICH I'D LOOKED FORWARD TO SO EAGERLY, HAD LAIN IN WAIT FOR ME LIKE AN ASSASSIN AND MADE ME ITS VICTIM!

SON! HOW DID IT... OH! I SEE! THINGS DIDN'T TURN OUT AS YOU EXPECTED! COME IN, BOY!

I DON'T WANT TO TALK ABOUT IT, DAD...

HANK...YOU DIDN'T MAKE A FOOL OF YOURSELF? I MEAN...YOU DIDN'T MAKE THINGS DIFFICULT THERE, DID YOU?

WHAT'S THE DIFFERENCE WHAT I DID! I DON'T GIVE A HOOT FOR ANYTHING ANY MORE...

ALL BROKEN UP ABOUT IT, ARE YOU? WELL, THE ARMY'S GOT A SURE CURE FOR AN ACHING HEART... THEY CALL IT ACHING FEET!

YEAH... SURE.. A YEAR FROM NOW, I'LL LOOK BACK ON IT ALL, AND LAUGH MYSELF SICK!

"THE NEWS ABOUT KAY'S ENGAGEMENT TO CHARLIE WAS IN THE LOCAL PAPER THAT WEEK! SOON AFTER, I GOT AN INVITATION TO ATTEND A BACHELOR PARTY FOR CHARLIE! IRVING ARNOLD, WHO DELIVERED IT IN CHARLIE'S NAME, BARELY GOT AWAY WITH HIS LIFE! ON THE DAY OF THE WEDDING I LEFT FOR ARMY SERVICE ... AND, GLAD TO GET OUT OF TOWN!"

SON... MAKE YOUR PEACE WITH KAY AND CHARLIE! I KNOW YOU CAN'T ATTEND THE WEDDING ...BUT...

WHAT DO YOU WANT ME TO DO? SEND THEM A *TELEGRAM*?

YES! A TELEGRAM ... A PRESENT... ANYTHING TO SHOW THEM THAT YOU'RE THEIR FRIEND... AND YOU BEAR NO GRUDGES! IT'S *A MAN'S WAY*, HANK! I'D BE PROUD OF YOU IF YOU DID IT!

THERE'S NO TIME LEFT, DAD! I... IM GOING TO BE BUSY FROM NOW ON! THINGS MAY BE DIFFERENT WHEN I GET BACK, WHO KNOWS...

"THE WOUND DIDN'T HEAL! IT HURT MORE THAN EVER! NEWS FROM HOME REVEALED THE HAPPY PROGRESS OF THE MARRIED COUPLE! IT MADE ME SULLEN AND ALMOST VICIOUS IN TRAINING!"

THAT'S GOOD! WILEY! DON'T *KILL* THE POOR GUY...

"THEN CAME MY ASSIGNMENT TO THE MEDICS AND THE LONG JOURNEY TO KOREA... TENDING TO THE WOUNDS OF OTHERS, I ALMOST FORGOT MY OWN!"

EASY, FELLA! DON'T MOVE NOW! WE'LL PATCH IT UP!

"THE SOUND AND THE FURY INCREASED UNTIL IT CRUSHED THE PAST WITH ITS VIOLENCE ... I MARCHED, I RAN, I FROZE, I SWEATED... IN A NIGHTMARE THAT WOULDN'T END..."

"SOMEWHERE ALONG THE WAY, I WAS TRANSFERRED TO A FIELD HOSPITAL... CLOSE ENOUGH TO THE FIGHTING TO RECEIVE CASUALTIES! THERE WAS EVEN A *NURSE NAMED NELLIE* WHO ENJOYED THE NOVELTY OF MY COMPLETE INDIFFERENCE TO HER!"

HEY, *STRONG AND SILENT!* HURRY WITH THAT HYPO WILL YOU?

OKAY... OKAY...

THANKS! SAY DON'T YOU EVER *SMILE?* THESE BOYS MIGHT *APPRECIATE* A SMILE! THEY NEED ALL THE COMFORT WE CAN GIVE THEM ...

I'M A *MEDIC*.. NOT A COMEDIAN! THE GUYS KNOW THE SCORE! YOU DON'T HEAR *THEM* BEEFING, DO YOU?

"ONE NIGHT, THE RUCKUS ON THE LINE GREW SUDDENLY LOUDER... THE SPORADIC CRACKLE OF SMALL ARMS FIRE VANISHED IN THE FRIGHTENING DIN OF HEAVIER STUFF! *THE ACTION WAS BIG... SO WERE THE CASUALTIES!*

BRING THIS DOGGIE OVER HERE! THE TENT'S CROWDED! HEY! THIS GUY'S FACE... *I KNOW... HIM!*

"THE WAR HAD COVERED HIS FACE WITH GRIME AND BEARD AND STAMPED HIM, LIKE ALL THE OTHERS, WITH THE SHOCK OF BATTLE! BUT IT COULDN'T HIDE CHARLIE GOODWIN FROM MY HATE!

GOOD OLD CHARLIE! SO *YOU* WERE DRAFTED TOO...

THIS BOY NEEDS PLASMA AND WE'VE USED UP OUR SUPPLY! HE'LL DIE BEFORE A FRESH BATCH GETS HERE! WILEY! YOU'RE HIS BLOOD-TYPE! WILEY, ARE YOU LISTENING?

"SHE LOOKED AT ME... READING MY FACE... AND AS SHE RECOILED FROM WHAT SHE SAW THERE, I COULD FEEL THAT SHE KNEW THE WHOLE STORY!

HANK WILEY! *YOU WANT HIM TO DIE!* OH, NO, HANK!

I DON'T CARE *WHAT* HAPPENS TO HIM! I WOULDN'T LIFT A FINGER TO HELP HIM!

A GUY WITH *A SCORE* TO SETTLE! I MIGHT HAVE KNOWN IT! HANK, YOU FOOL! IT'S *YOUR* LIFE THAT NEEDS SAVING! NO MATTER WHAT HE'S DONE TO YOU... IF HE DIES... *YOU* DO TOO! YOU CAN NEVER LIVE AGAIN WITH HIS DEATH ON YOUR CONSCIENCE!

"BLAST HER! SHE HAD A KNACK FOR BEING RIGHT! I *WAS* DYING! I'D BEEN KILLING MYSELF INSIDE FOR A YEAR NOW... OVER A HOPELESS, FOOLISH, CHILDISH GRUDGE! DISGUSTED WITH MYSELF, I TOOK OFF MY FIELD JACKET!

OKAY, DRACULA! *TAKE* YOUR QUART OF BLOOD!

HANK, I'M PROUD OF YOU! YOU'RE MY BOY!

"AND, SO, THE TRANSFUSION TOOK PLACE.. *MY* BLOOD MINGLING WITH THAT OF THE MAN I NO LONGER HATED! LYING BY MY SIDE, HE WAS JUST A GUY I KNEW... MARRIED TO A GIRL FROM MY HOME TOWN... WHO WAS WAITING FOR *HIM* TO COME BACK IN ONE PIECE...

HE'S COMING AROUND! HE'LL LIVE TO SHOW OFF ALL OF HIS CITATIONS TO KAY!

"I MUST HAVE SMILED UP AT NELLIE, BECAUSE SHE SMILED BACK AT ME! NOW, THERE WAS A GREAT KID... *PRETTY* TOO... NOW, THAT I WAS BEGINNING TO *NOTICE* HER!

"I THINK, OF ALL THE PRESENTS KAY AND CHARLIE RECEIVED, MINE MUST HAVE BEEN THE MOST GRATIFYING! I GAVE THEM *A FUTURE!* IT WAS A YEAR LATE FOR THE WEDDING, BUT RIGHT ON TIME FOR THEIR *FIRST ANNIVERSARY!* AS FOR ME, I FOUND MY REWARD IN LIFE AND MANHOOD... *AND A SWELL GAL NAMED NELLIE!*

THE END

Norma didn't want much out of life—just everything that a big bank roll could buy. So she got an idea—a ridiculous idea for a classy gal like Norma. It smelled of sauerkraut and mustard and lots of money! But what has all this to do with love, you say? Well, it will be as big a surprise to you as it was to

NORMA THE QUEEN OF THE HOT DOGS!

MMMM — *REAL* MINK! IT SURE FEELS GOOD TO THE TOUCH—

OH, *NORMA!* TURN AROUND FOR A SECOND—

"IN A WAY, I SUPPOSE, I'D *ACHIEVED* WHAT I'D SET OUT TO DO — TO WEAR EXPENSIVE CLOTHES AND BE LOOKED AT AND ADMIRED. BUT, THE MINKS AND FINE FABRICS WEREN'T MINE. AND, THE LOOKS OF ADMIRATION USUALLY CAME FROM MY BOSS, 'MISTER FASHION' HIMSELF, *ERNEST TULLMAN,* FOR WHOM I WORKED AS A CLOTHES MODEL.

YOU'RE A *KNOCKOUT,* NORMA. EVEN A CRAZY QUILT WOULD LOOK GOOD ON YOU!

YOU'RE *MUCH* TOO KIND, MISTER TULLMAN—

KIND, KIND — I WANT TO MEAN *MORE* THAN THAT TO YOU, NORMA. BUT, YOU ALWAYS FREEZE UP ON ME—

I'M SURE YOU *WOULDN'T* WANT ME TO STEP OUT OF LINE, SIR. I'M ONLY ONE OF YOUR EMPLOYEES—

THAT'S A GOOD ANSWER. THE KIND THAT HELPS YOU KEEP YOUR JOB. LOOK, NORMA, I'M TOO OLD TO FENCE AROUND. AND, I'M YOUNG ENOUGH TO FEEL I CAN MAKE YOU HAPPY. I WANT TO *MARRY* YOU—

THAT WAS A REAL PROPOSAL, NORMA. IT'S A *BETTER* DEAL THAN YOU'LL GET FROM A YOUNG HOOLIGAN WITH "LOOKS" AND NO MONEY, BELIEVE ME. THINK IT OVER. NO RUSH. I'M A PATIENT MAN — UNDERSTANDING TOO —

"SURE, I WAS CYNICAL ENOUGH TO GIVE IT SOME THOUGHT! THERE WAS COMFORT AND SECURITY INVOLVED! BUT, THE EAGER, LITTLE EYES OF ERNEST TULLMAN, BURNING BRIGHT IN THEIR FLESHY POUCHES, CHANGED MY MIND! I'D TRIED FOR AND MISSED THE RIGHT ROAD TO MINK AND HAPPINESS! SOMEWHERE, IT WAITED FOR ME... WAS I SMART ENOUGH TO FIND IT?"

AH, THE QUEEN! WELCOME TO THE HOME OF THE HOG DOG!

HI, JERRY! FRY ME TWO! HOW'S BUSINESS?

"I MADE IT A HABIT TO STOP AT JERRY CAIN'S HOT DOG STAND ON MY WAY TO THE SUBWAY EACH DAY! HE WAS SUCH A SWEET, AMIABLE LITTLE GUY!"

BUSINESS JUMPS EVERY TIME YOU SHOW UP, MISS HOWARD! YOU KNOW THAT!

FLATTERER! DID IT EVER OCCUR TO YOU THAT THERE ARE MORE PEOPLE ON THE STREET DURING THE RUSH HOUR?

NAH! LISTEN, THERE WAS A RUSH HOUR EVERY DAY BEFORE YOU BECAME MY CUSTOMER... AND IT NEVER HELPED MUCH! IT'S YOU, MISS HOWARD... WHEN YOU STOP BY, IT GIVES THE DOGS A LITTLE CLASS!

WELL, THANK YOU, JERRY! I MUST SAY IT'S RATHER AN ODD DISTINCTION!

IT SELLS 'EM! THAT'S WHAT COUNTS! IF I HAD YOU AROUND ALL DAY I COULD MAKE THIS JOINT SHOW A PROFIT!

"THAT'S WHEN THE IDEA HIT ME! A WILD, CRAZY IDEA! AND YET, THERE WERE VISIONS BEYOND IT WHICH HAD EXCITING IMPLICATIONS!"

BOY, WOULD I LOVE TO CUT YOU IN AS A PARTNER! YOU'D DRAW THEM IN LIKE FLIES!

YES, I COULD MODEL HOT DOGS.. MAKE THEM LOOK GOOD TO EAT...

"JERRY LAUGHED AT THAT! BUT, I DIDN'T! I KEPT THINKING OF ALL THE ADS IN WHICH PRETTY GIRLS WERE SELLING EVERYTHING FROM AUTOMOBILES TO CIGARETTE LIGHTERS... WHEN I TURNED TO JERRY AND ACCEPTED HIS OFFER, HE ALMOST KEELED OVER!"

SAY... DID I JUST HEAR YOU SAY YOU'D REALLY CONSIDER IT...

YOU BET! I'VE SAVED A LITTLE! WHAT WILL IT COST ME TO BUY AN EQUAL SHARE IN THIS STEAMY LITTLE HOT DOGGERY?

"IT FELT STRANGE TO LEAVE THE PLUSH AND REGAL SURROUNDINGS OF TULLMAN'S FASHION SALON FOR THE SIZZLE AND AROMA OF A HOT DOG STAND! BUT, I HAD BIG THINGS IN MIND... AND, THE HOPE THAT THEY'D MATERIALIZE!"

GOOD MORNING PARD— WOW! WHERE'D YOU GET THAT OUTFIT? YOU... YOU'RE DYNAMITE IN IT!

SO ARE OUR DELICIOUS, DOGGIES, SIR! FRIED TO A ROYAL, GOLDEN BROWN ... OBVIOUSLY A PRODUCT WITH A PEDIGREE, SIR!

2

"SOMEHOW, IT SEEMED TO WORK. I BROUGHT THE *SWANK* SHOWMANSHIP OF TULLMAN'S SALON TO JERRY'S LOWLY STAND. AND THE CUSTOMERS WENT FOR IT — REMEMBERED IT — AND TALKED ABOUT IT. IN A FEW MONTHS JERRY AND I WERE RUNNING A *PROSPERING* BUSINESS."

ONE MORE FOR THIS GENTLEMAN, JERRY!

COMING RIGHT UP--

"JERRY AND I SOON BOUGHT OUT THE STORE NEXT TO US AND ENLARGED OUR FACILITIES. WE HIRED SOME HELP--*PRETTY GALS*—MODELS IN THE ROUGH!"

NORMA, WHAT *WONDERFUL* NEW WRINKLES YOU'VE INTRODUCED TO THIS BUSINESS!

I REALIZE THIS IS JUST A BEANERY, GIRLS. BUT, WE'LL PAY A LITTLE MORE TO GET A LITTLE MORE -- A LITTLE GRACE, CHARM -- POISE. IT'S OUR *POLICY!*

"THINGS WERE GATHERING MOMENTUM -- THE SPEED NECESSARY TO PUT US WITHIN REACH OF THE VISION I'D SEEN AT THE START. WE HAD TWO STORES WHEN I WENT TO SEE *TOM COOKE* OUR ACCOUNTANT AND CONSULTANT."

A CHAIN. THAT'S WHAT YOU WANT. *A CHAIN OF HOT DOG STANDS!*

YOU MAKE IT SOUND *FUNNY,* TOM--

WELL, IT SEEMS TO STRIKE ME THAT WAY! *"NORMA - QUEEN OF THE HOT DOGS."* YES, THAT'S A RIB TICKLER.

STOP ME IF I'M WRONG. BUT, THAT RIB TICKLING ACCOUNT HAS COME TO MEAN A PRETTY GOOD *FEE* FOR YOU!

"TOM WAS *IMPUDENT* BUT BRIGHT. I LEANED HEAVILY ON HIS GOOD SENSE. AT THIS TIME HE WAS SHOWING VERY LITTLE."

WHERE ARE YOU GOING, BABY? *WHAT* ARE YOU AFTER — MAY I ASK?

MONEY! MINK! INDEPENDENCE! AND I'M SWEATING BLOOD TO EARN THEM!

YOU'RE TRYING TOO HARD FOR THE *WRONG* THINGS, HONEY--

HEY! WHY YOU FRESH --

TOM COOKE! HAVE YOU GONE OUT OF YOUR MIND? WHAT IN BLAZES ARE YOU TRYING TO *PROVE?*

LOVE, MAYBE -- EVER HEAR OF THE WORD?

LOVE! PTAH... HA-HA-HA-HA-HA-HA! NOW, *THERE'S* SOMETHING REALLY FUNNY! FORGIVE ME, TOM! I JUST CAN'T HELP LAUGHING!

I DON'T KNOW WHY! LOVE'S A *GOOD* INVESTMENT! IT OUTLASTS MINK AND MONEY!

HONESTLY, TOM, IF YOU ARE SERIOUS ABOUT THIS, I'M SORRY I LAUGHED! YOU'RE REALLY A SWEET GUY! BUT LOVE ISN'T WHAT I'M AIMING FOR RIGHT NOW..

NORMA, YOU'LL WEAR OUT A HUNDRED MINKS BEFORE YOU REALIZE THEY'RE *NOT* WHAT YOU REALLY WANTED! IT MAY BE TOO LATE, THEN, TO LOOK INTO YOUR OWN HEART... IT MAY NOT BE THERE...

OKAY! LOVE IS IMPORTANT! BUT, *HOW* DO I KNOW I'M IN LOVE WITH YOU, TOM?

ALL I ASK IS THE CHANCE... TO *HELP* YOU FIND OUT...

"HE DREW ME TO HIM! THIS TIME, GENTLY, VERY TENDERLY... AND OUR LIPS MET IN A SOFT FIRE THAT GLOWED WITH GROWING BRIGHTNESS!"

"IT WAS LIKE EMERGING FROM THE WILD THICKETS OF A FOREST...INTO THE *SUNLIGHT*... WHERE, THE GROUND WAS GREEN AND LEVEL... AND THE VERY AIR HAD THE SPIRITUAL QUALITY OF PEACE! THIS WAS HOW I FELT IN TOM'S EMBRACE!"

"WE WENT STEADY AFTER THAT... EACH DATE LEADING US TOWARD THE INEVITABLE STEP! JERRY CAIN WAS BEST MAN AT OUR WEDDING! IT WAS VERY DISTURBING TO SEE HIM IN FORMAL ATTIRE AND WITHOUT AN APRON!

I NOW PRONOUNCE YOU MAN AND WIFE!

"IN TIME, CAME *MOTHERHOOD* AND NEW HORIZONS WHICH I'D NEVER SEEN BEFORE... UNTIL I'D RELEASED THE POWERS OF MY OWN HEART! THE OLD YEARNINGS AND DRIVES HAD BEEN REPLACED BY MORE WORTHWHILE AND FRUITFUL AMBITIONS!

"I'D FOLLOWED SO MANY DIFFERENT ROADS ...LOST MYSELF IN A HUNDRED BLIND ALLEYS... FOLLOWED THE *WILDEST* IDEAS... ALL IN PURSUIT OF THE THINGS THAT *DIDN'T* MATTER... THE RIGHT PATH WAS PART OF ME ALL THAT TIME... MY BABY'S FACE IS SOFT AGAINST MINE...SOFTER THAN THE FINEST MINK.. AND ABSOLUTELY *PRICELESS*! THIS KNOWLEDGE IS MY CONTENTMENT AND PEACE!"

The END

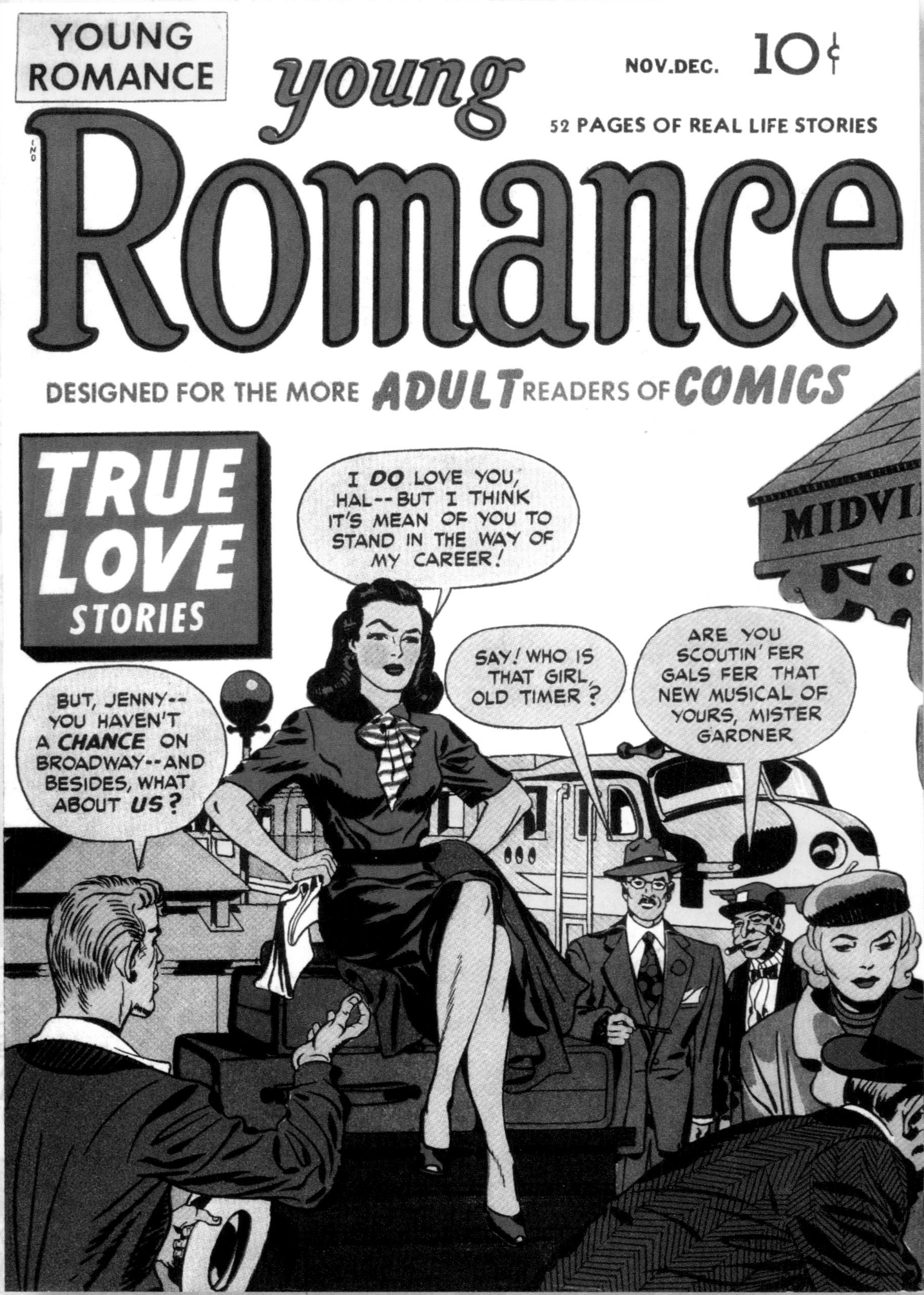
YOUNG ROMANCE
young Romance
NOV.DEC. 10¢
52 PAGES OF REAL LIFE STORIES
DESIGNED FOR THE MORE ADULT READERS OF COMICS
TRUE LOVE STORIES
I DO LOVE YOU, HAL--BUT I THINK IT'S MEAN OF YOU TO STAND IN THE WAY OF MY CAREER!
MIDVI
BUT, JENNY--YOU HAVEN'T A CHANCE ON BROADWAY--AND BESIDES, WHAT ABOUT US?
SAY! WHO IS THAT GIRL, OLD TIMER?
ARE YOU SCOUTIN' FER GALS FER THAT NEW MUSICAL OF YOURS, MISTER GARDNER

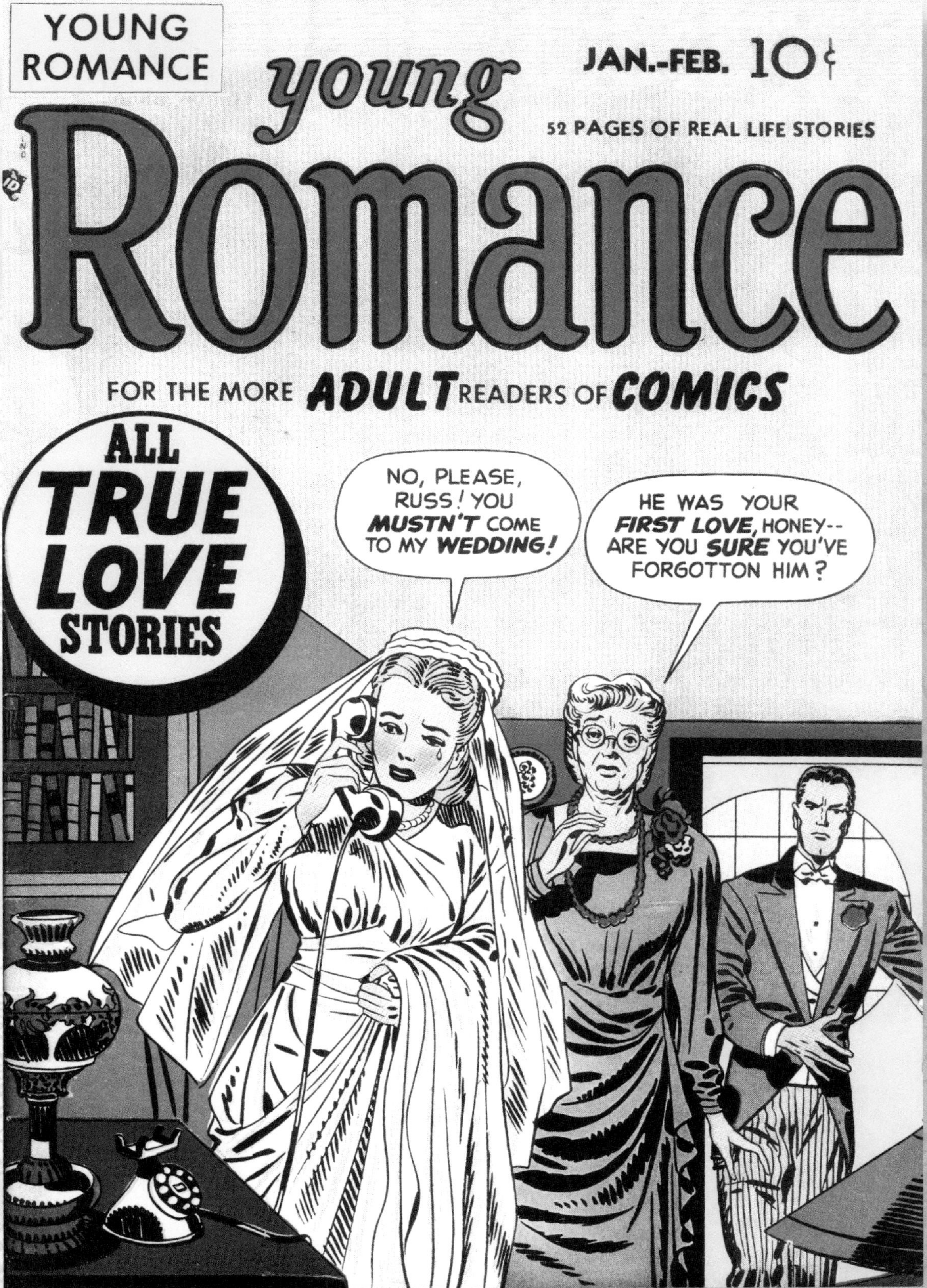
YOUNG ROMANCE
JAN.-FEB. 10¢
young Romance
52 PAGES OF REAL LIFE STORIES
FOR THE MORE ADULT READERS OF COMICS
ALL TRUE LOVE STORIES
NO, PLEASE, RUSS! YOU MUSTN'T COME TO MY WEDDING!
HE WAS YOUR FIRST LOVE, HONEY-- ARE YOU SURE YOU'VE FORGOTTON HIM?

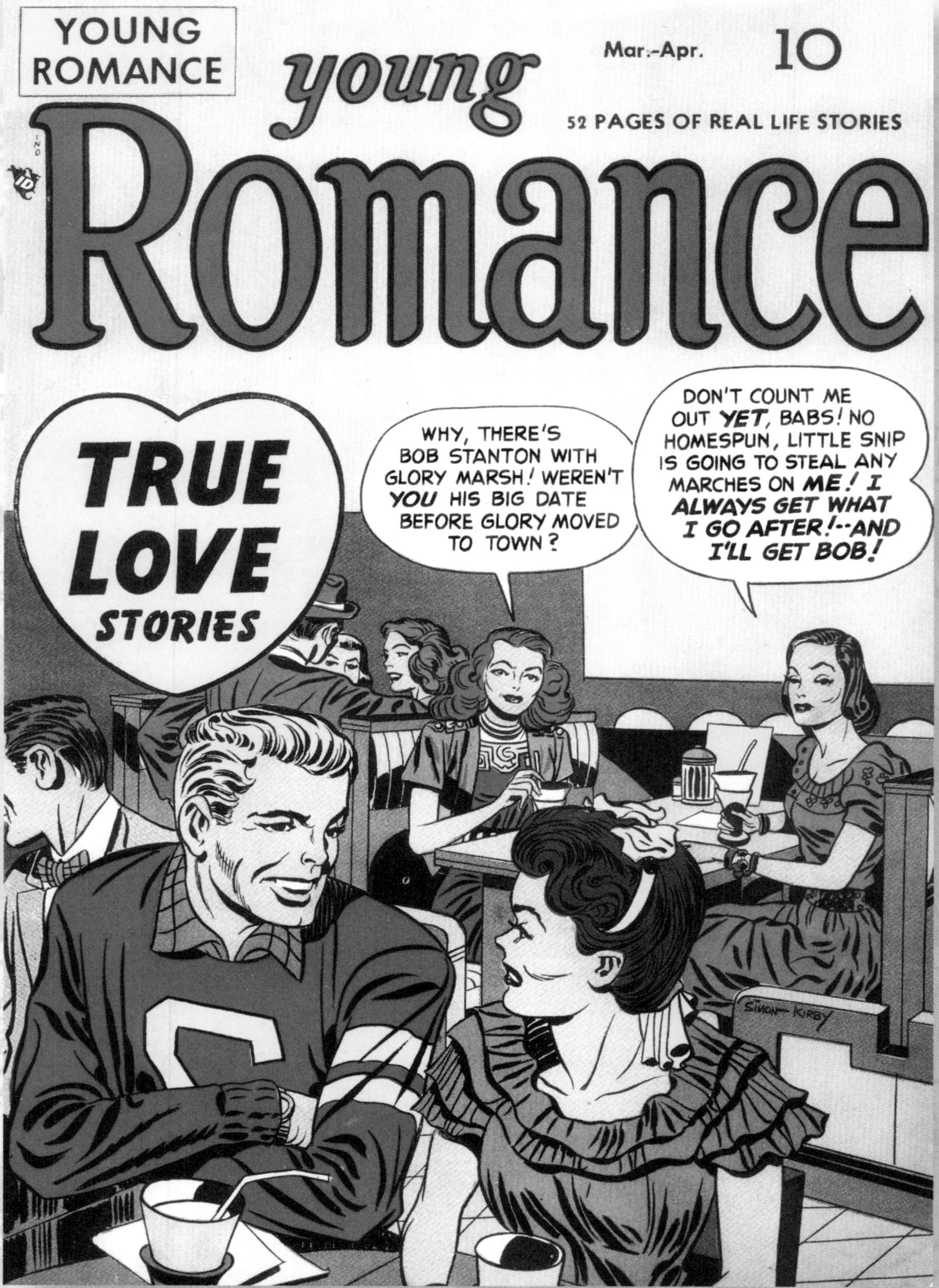
YOUNG ROMANCE
young Romance
Mar.-Apr.
10
52 PAGES OF REAL LIFE STORIES
TRUE LOVE STORIES
WHY, THERE'S BOB STANTON WITH GLORY MARSH! WEREN'T YOU HIS BIG DATE BEFORE GLORY MOVED TO TOWN?
DON'T COUNT ME OUT YET, BABS! NO HOMESPUN, LITTLE SNIP IS GOING TO STEAL ANY MARCHES ON ME! I ALWAYS GET WHAT I GO AFTER!--AND I'LL GET BOB!
SIMON—KIRBY

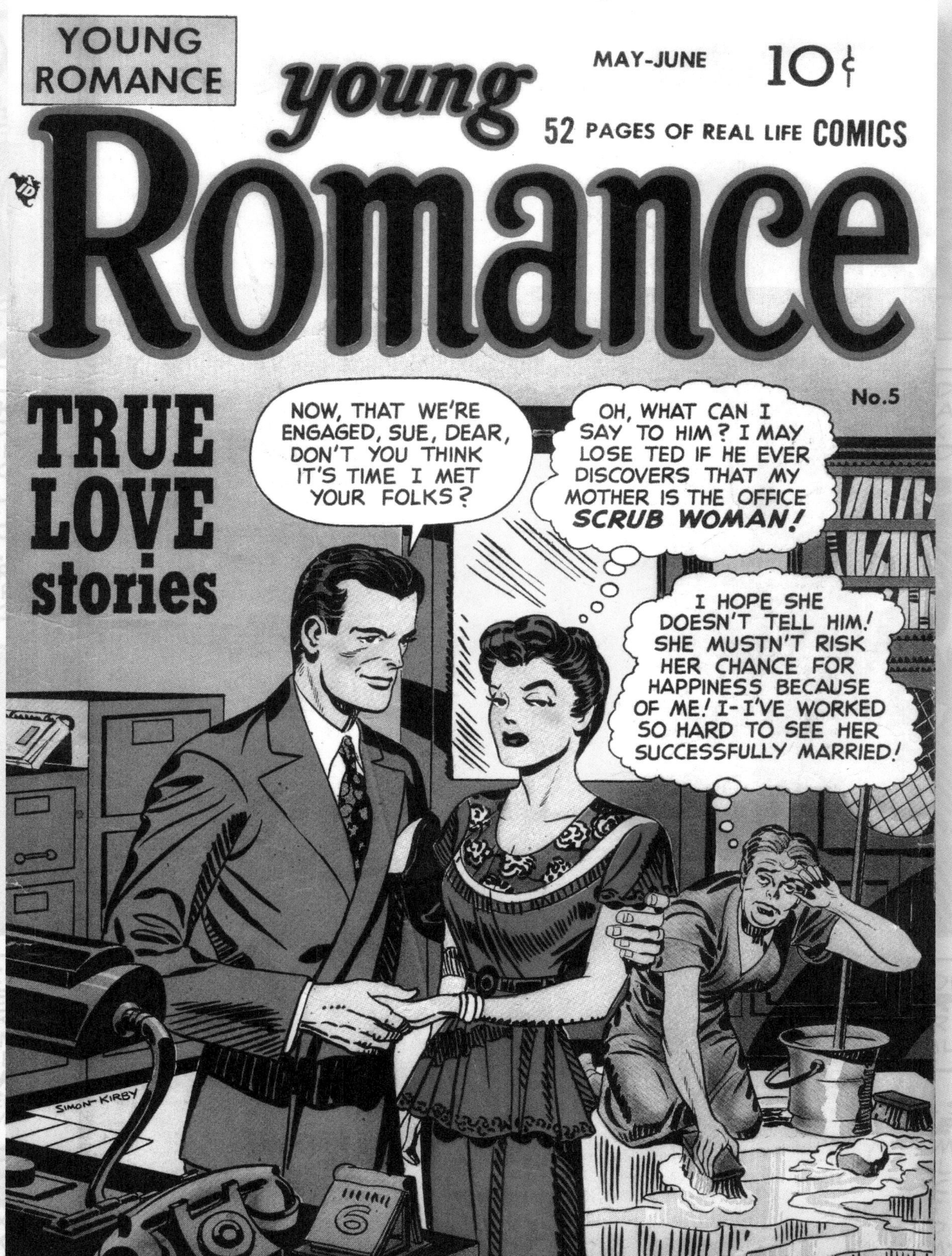
YOUNG ROMANCE
MAY-JUNE
10¢
young Romance
52 PAGES OF REAL LIFE COMICS
No.5
TRUE LOVE stories
NOW, THAT WE'RE ENGAGED, SUE, DEAR, DON'T YOU THINK IT'S TIME I MET YOUR FOLKS?
OH, WHAT CAN I SAY TO HIM? I MAY LOSE TED IF HE EVER DISCOVERS THAT MY MOTHER IS THE OFFICE SCRUB WOMAN!
I HOPE SHE DOESN'T TELL HIM! SHE MUSTN'T RISK HER CHANCE FOR HAPPINESS BECAUSE OF ME! I-I'VE WORKED SO HARD TO SEE HER SUCCESSFULLY MARRIED!
SIMON-KIRBY

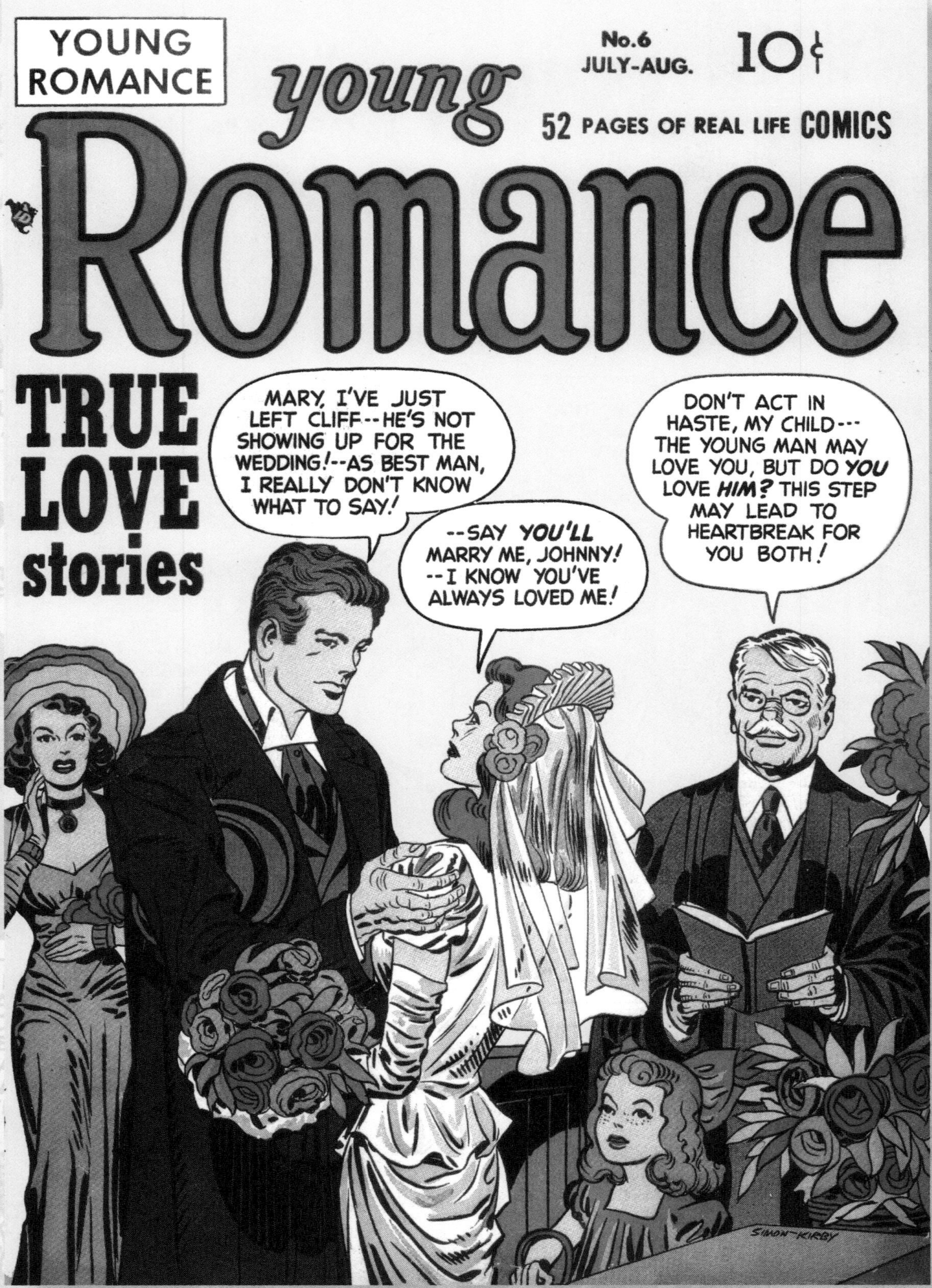
YOUNG ROMANCE
No.6
JULY-AUG.
10¢
young Romance
52 PAGES OF REAL LIFE COMICS
TRUE LOVE stories
MARY, I'VE JUST LEFT CLIFF--HE'S NOT SHOWING UP FOR THE WEDDING!--AS BEST MAN, I REALLY DON'T KNOW WHAT TO SAY!
--SAY YOU'LL MARRY ME, JOHNNY! --I KNOW YOU'VE ALWAYS LOVED ME!
DON'T ACT IN HASTE, MY CHILD--- THE YOUNG MAN MAY LOVE YOU, BUT DO YOU LOVE HIM? THIS STEP MAY LEAD TO HEARTBREAK FOR YOU BOTH!
SIMON-KIRBY

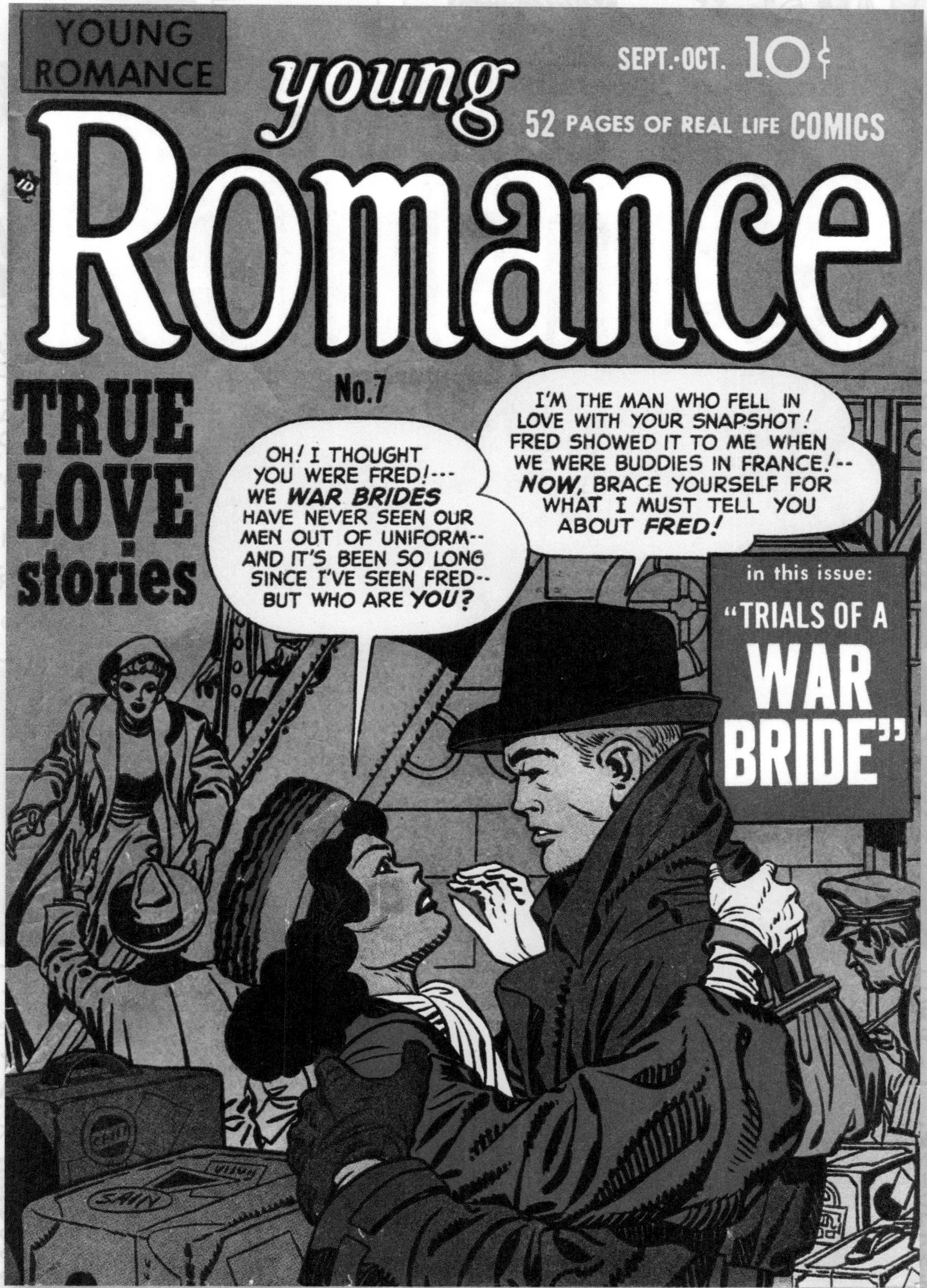
YOUNG ROMANCE
young Romance
SEPT.-OCT. 10¢
52 PAGES OF REAL LIFE COMICS
No.7
TRUE LOVE stories
OH! I THOUGHT YOU WERE FRED!--- WE WAR BRIDES HAVE NEVER SEEN OUR MEN OUT OF UNIFORM-- AND IT'S BEEN SO LONG SINCE I'VE SEEN FRED-- BUT WHO ARE YOU?
I'M THE MAN WHO FELL IN LOVE WITH YOUR SNAPSHOT! FRED SHOWED IT TO ME WHEN WE WERE BUDDIES IN FRANCE!-- NOW, BRACE YOURSELF FOR WHAT I MUST TELL YOU ABOUT FRED!
in this issue:
"TRIALS OF A WAR BRIDE"

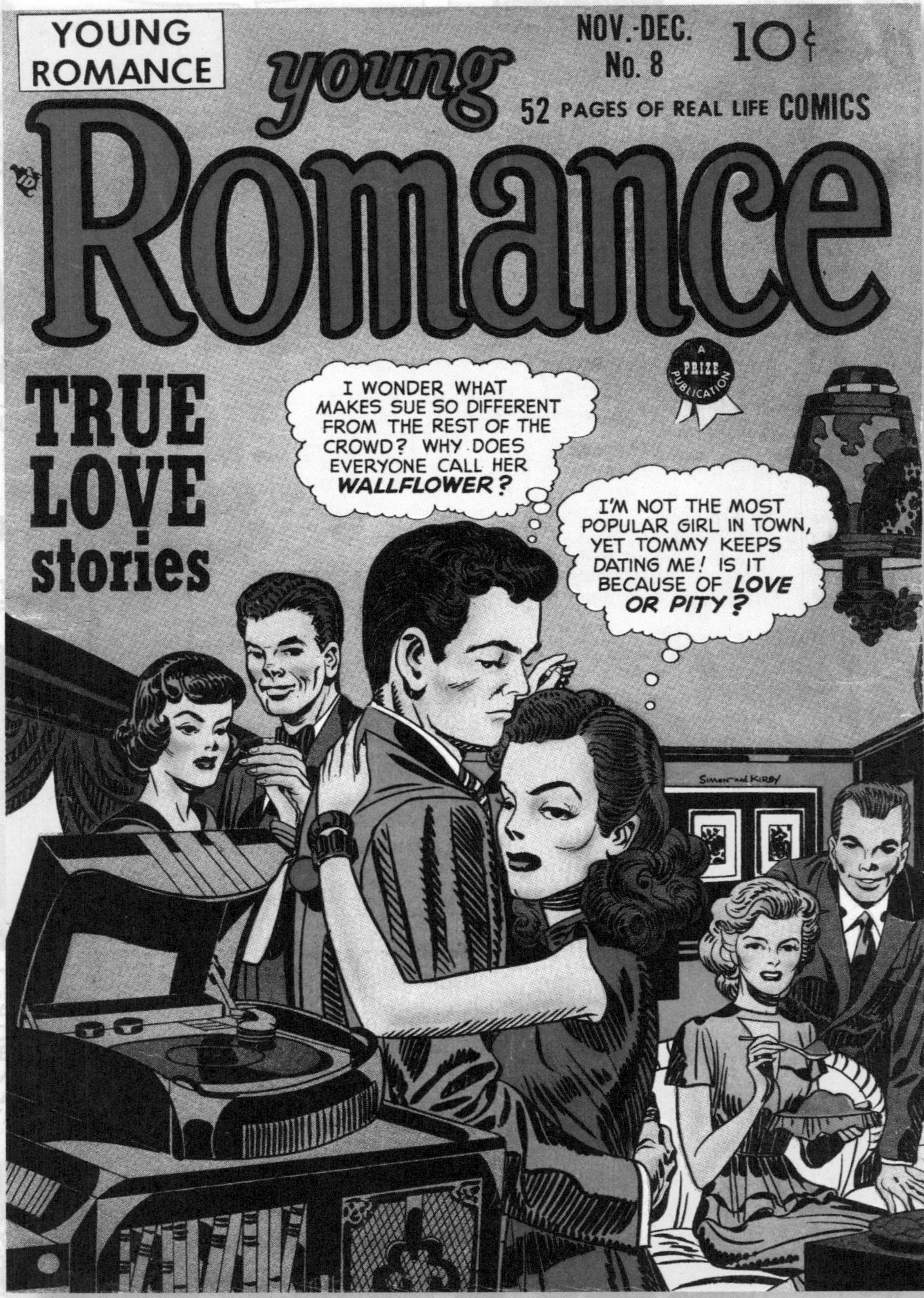
YOUNG ROMANCE
NOV.-DEC. No. 8
10¢
young Romance
52 PAGES OF REAL LIFE COMICS
A PRIZE PUBLICATION
TRUE LOVE stories
I WONDER WHAT MAKES SUE SO DIFFERENT FROM THE REST OF THE CROWD? WHY DOES EVERYONE CALL HER WALLFLOWER?
I'M NOT THE MOST POPULAR GIRL IN TOWN, YET TOMMY KEEPS DATING ME! IS IT BECAUSE OF LOVE OR PITY?
SIMON AND KIRBY

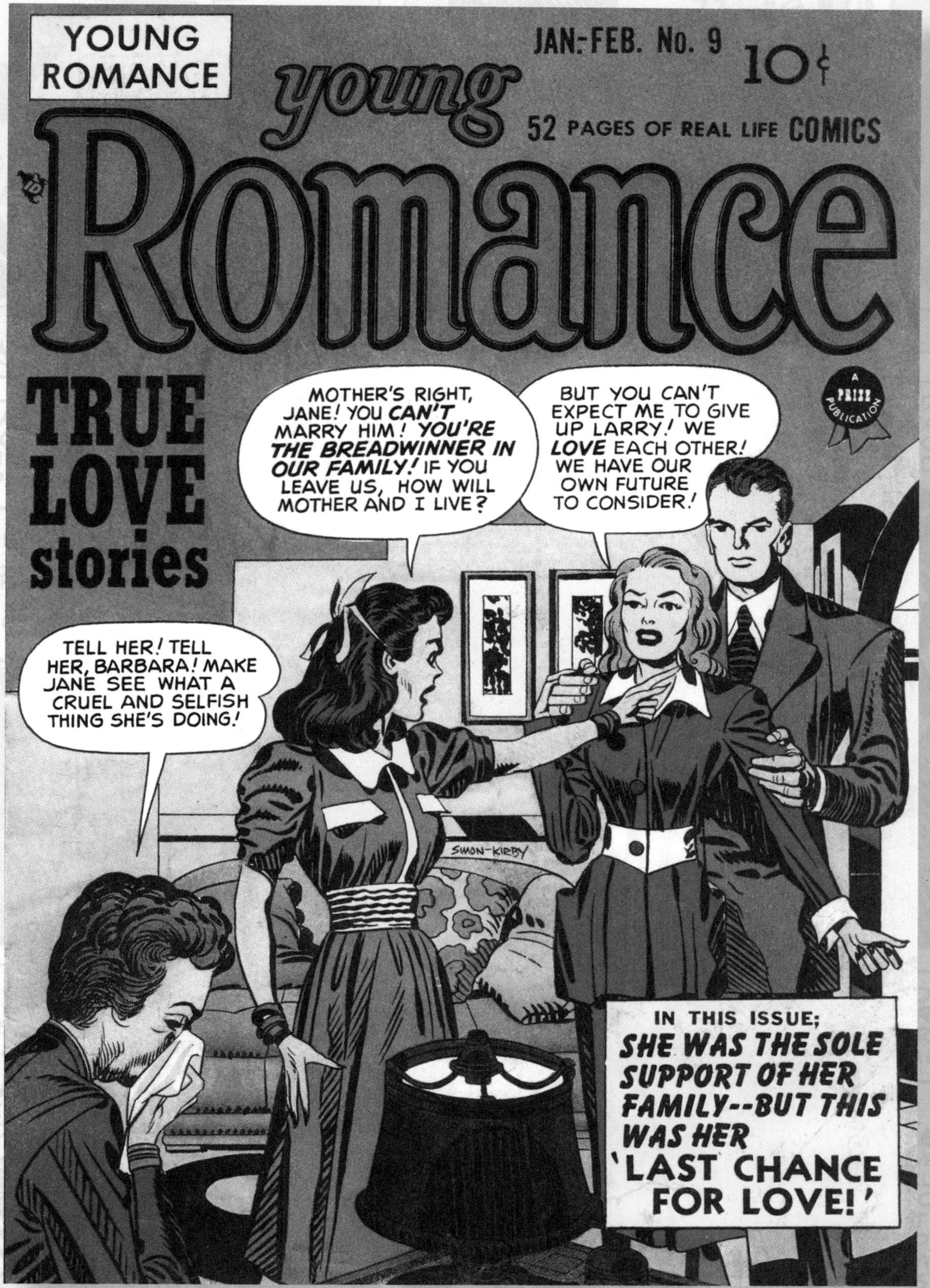
YOUNG ROMANCE
JAN.-FEB. No. 9
10¢
young Romance
52 PAGES OF REAL LIFE COMICS
TRUE LOVE stories
A PRIZE PUBLICATION
MOTHER'S RIGHT, JANE! YOU CAN'T MARRY HIM! YOU'RE THE BREADWINNER IN OUR FAMILY! IF YOU LEAVE US, HOW WILL MOTHER AND I LIVE?
BUT YOU CAN'T EXPECT ME TO GIVE UP LARRY! WE LOVE EACH OTHER! WE HAVE OUR OWN FUTURE TO CONSIDER!
TELL HER! TELL HER, BARBARA! MAKE JANE SEE WHAT A CRUEL AND SELFISH THING SHE'S DOING!
SIMON-KIRBY
IN THIS ISSUE; SHE WAS THE SOLE SUPPORT OF HER FAMILY--BUT THIS WAS HER 'LAST CHANCE FOR LOVE!'

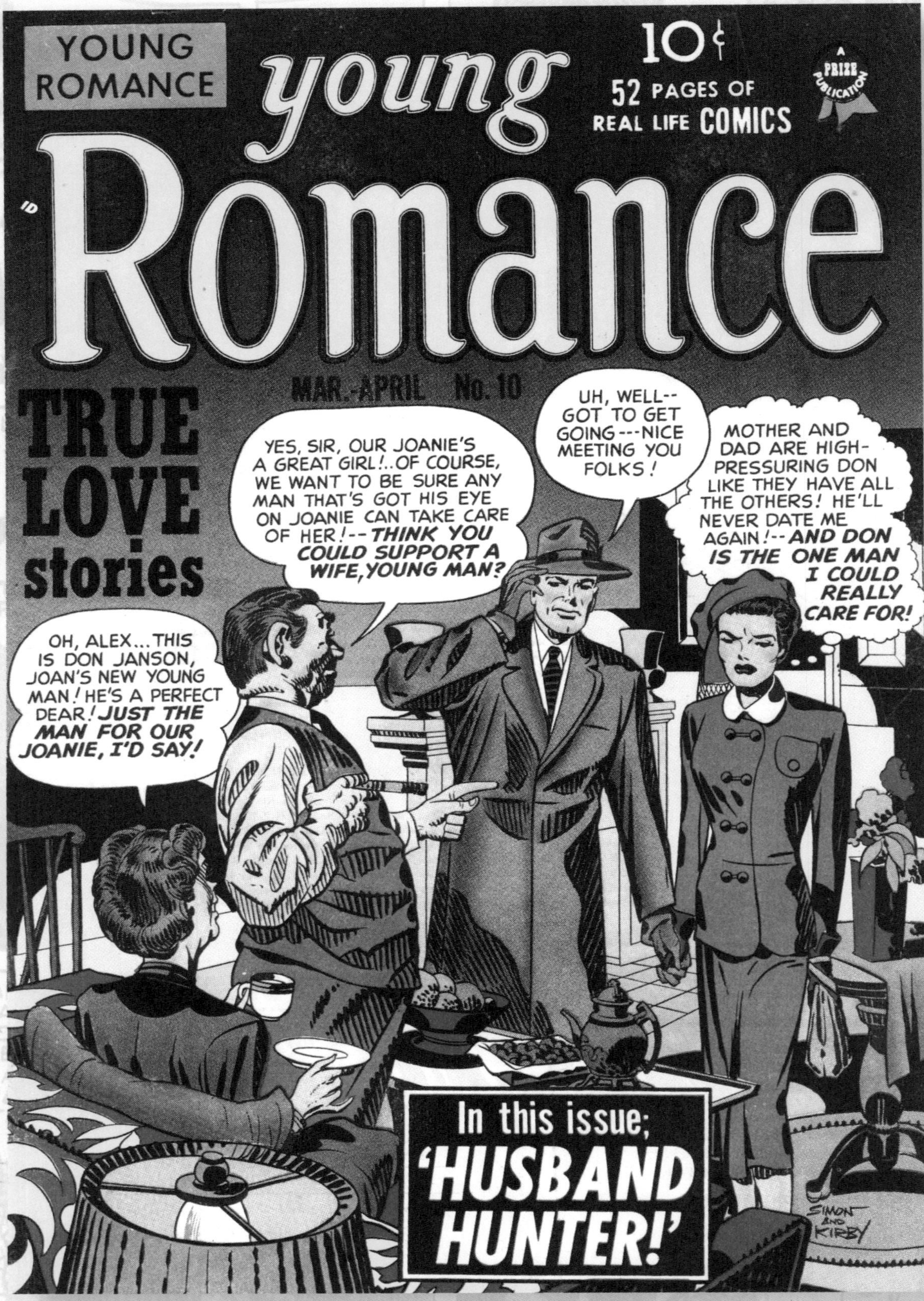
YOUNG ROMANCE
young Romance
10¢
52 PAGES OF REAL LIFE COMICS
A PRIZE PUBLICATION
MAR.-APRIL No. 10
TRUE LOVE stories
YES, SIR, OUR JOANIE'S A GREAT GIRL!..OF COURSE, WE WANT TO BE SURE ANY MAN THAT'S GOT HIS EYE ON JOANIE CAN TAKE CARE OF HER!--THINK YOU COULD SUPPORT A WIFE,YOUNG MAN?
UH, WELL-- GOT TO GET GOING---NICE MEETING YOU FOLKS!
MOTHER AND DAD ARE HIGH-PRESSURING DON LIKE THEY HAVE ALL THE OTHERS! HE'LL NEVER DATE ME AGAIN!--AND DON IS THE ONE MAN I COULD REALLY CARE FOR!
OH, ALEX...THIS IS DON JANSON, JOAN'S NEW YOUNG MAN! HE'S A PERFECT DEAR! JUST THE MAN FOR OUR JOANIE, I'D SAY!
In this issue; 'HUSBAND HUNTER!'
SIMON AND KIRBY

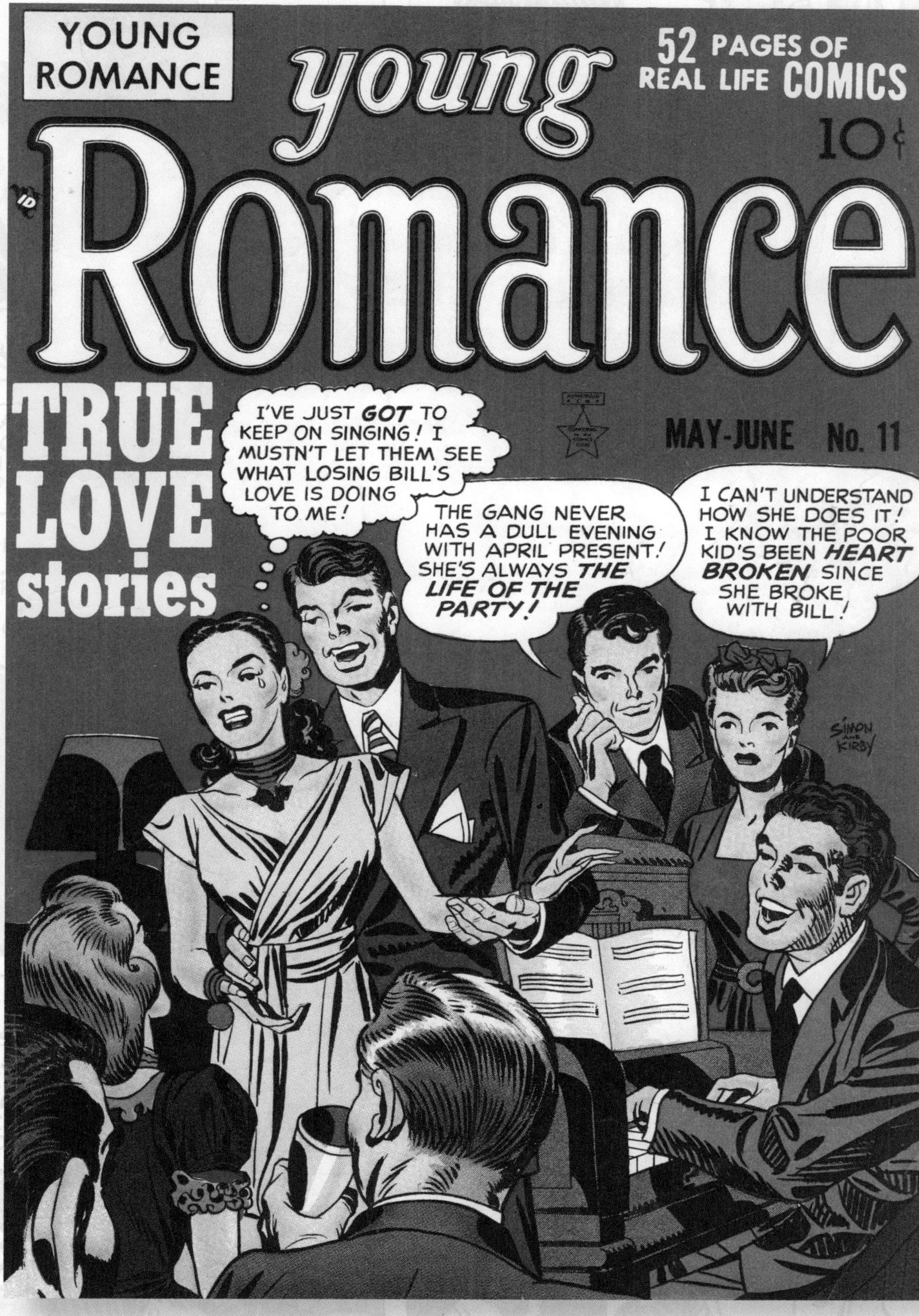
YOUNG ROMANCE
52 PAGES OF REAL LIFE COMICS
young Romance
10¢
TRUE LOVE stories
MAY-JUNE No. 11
I'VE JUST GOT TO KEEP ON SINGING! I MUSTN'T LET THEM SEE WHAT LOSING BILL'S LOVE IS DOING TO ME!
THE GANG NEVER HAS A DULL EVENING WITH APRIL PRESENT! SHE'S ALWAYS THE LIFE OF THE PARTY!
I CAN'T UNDERSTAND HOW SHE DOES IT! I KNOW THE POOR KID'S BEEN HEART BROKEN SINCE SHE BROKE WITH BILL!
SIMON AND KIRBY

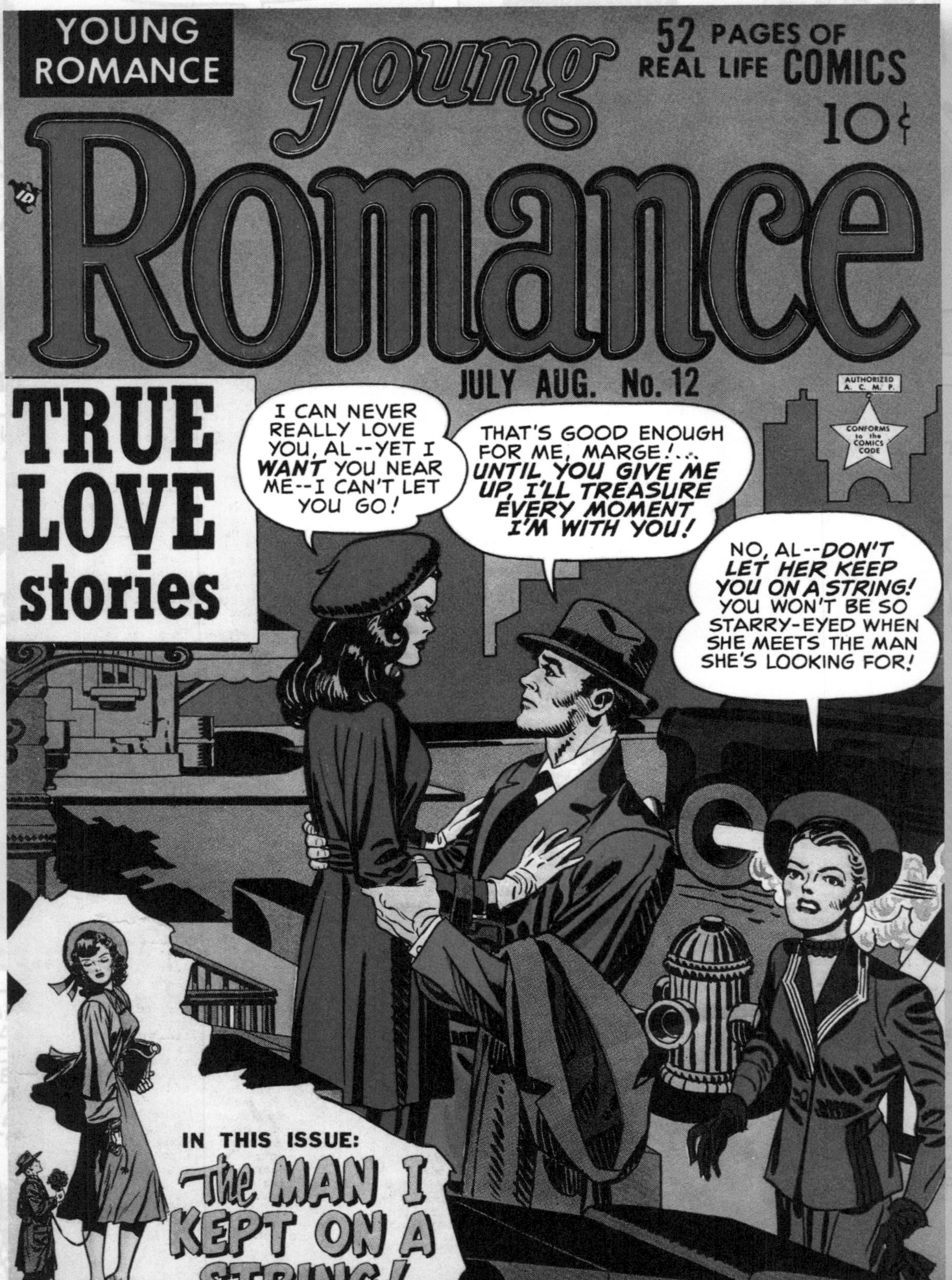
YOUNG ROMANCE
young Romance
52 PAGES OF REAL LIFE COMICS
10¢
JULY AUG. No. 12
AUTHORIZED A. C. M. P.
CONFORMS to the COMICS CODE
TRUE LOVE stories
I CAN NEVER REALLY LOVE YOU, AL--YET I WANT YOU NEAR ME--I CAN'T LET YOU GO!
THAT'S GOOD ENOUGH FOR ME, MARGE!... UNTIL YOU GIVE ME UP, I'LL TREASURE EVERY MOMENT I'M WITH YOU!
NO, AL--DON'T LET HER KEEP YOU ON A STRING! YOU WON'T BE SO STARRY-EYED WHEN SHE MEETS THE MAN SHE'S LOOKING FOR!
IN THIS ISSUE:
The MAN I KEPT ON A STRING!

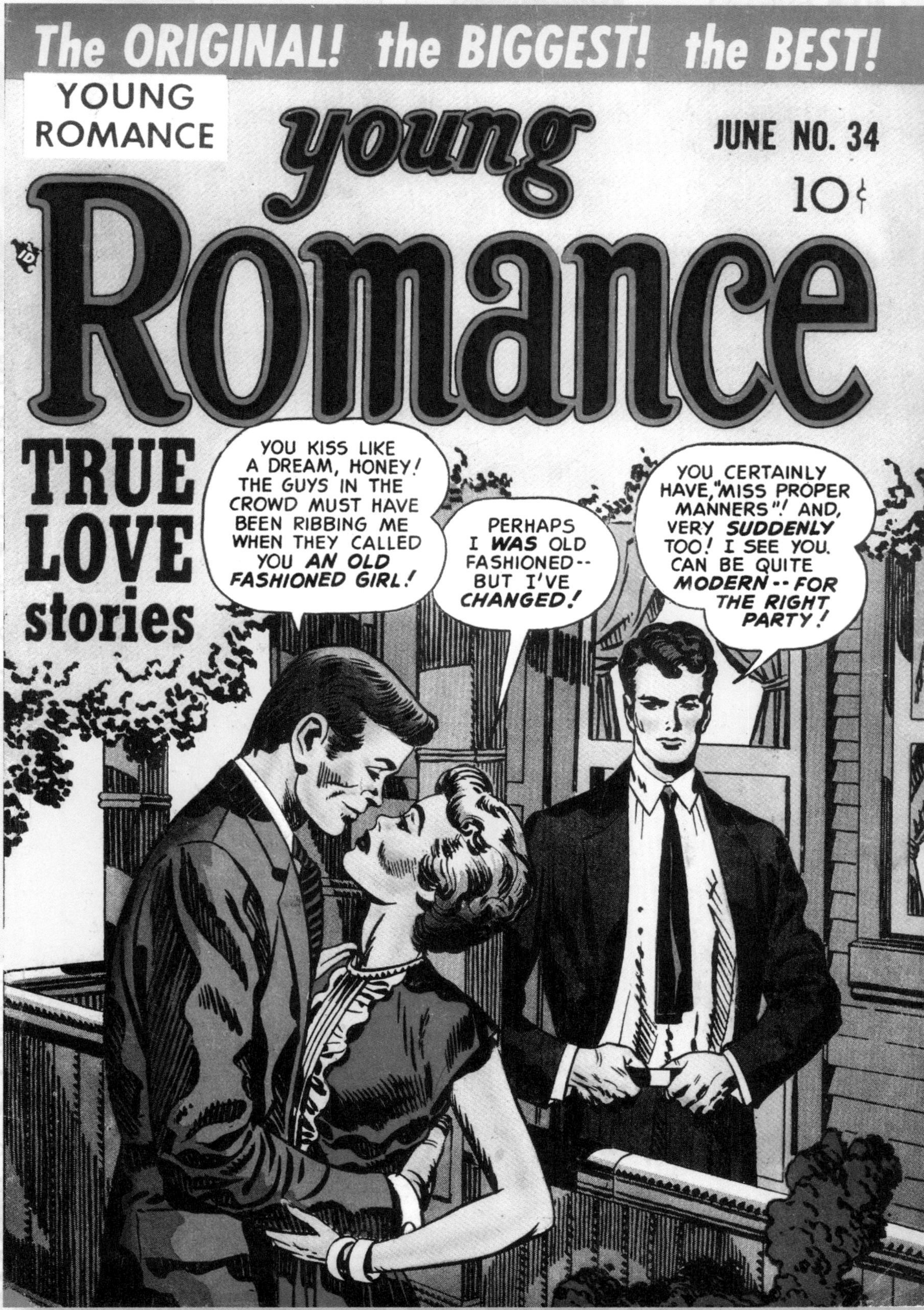
The ORIGINAL! the BIGGEST! the BEST!
YOUNG ROMANCE
young Romance
JUNE NO. 34
10¢
TRUE LOVE stories
YOU KISS LIKE A DREAM, HONEY! THE GUYS IN THE CROWD MUST HAVE BEEN RIBBING ME WHEN THEY CALLED YOU AN OLD FASHIONED GIRL!
PERHAPS I WAS OLD FASHIONED-- BUT I'VE CHANGED!
YOU CERTAINLY HAVE, "MISS PROPER MANNERS"! AND, VERY SUDDENLY TOO! I SEE YOU CAN BE QUITE MODERN-- FOR THE RIGHT PARTY!

THE POST-CODE ERA

The Code was established in 1954 as the industry's self-policing response to criticisms led by psychiatrist Fredric Wertham.

Wertham's 1953 book, *Seduction of the Innocent*, raised nationwide concerns about crime and horror comics, and the effect they might have on American children and teens.

The outcry grew so loud that the American Senate Judiciary formed a committee to investigate juvenile delinquency, with comic book content as its main focus.

Standards of the Comics Code Authority (excerpt)

Part C:

Marriage and Sex:

1) Divorce shall not be treated humorously nor shall be represented as desirable.

2) Illicit sex relations are neither to be hinted at or portrayed. Violent love scenes as well as sexual abnormalities are unacceptable.

3) Respect for parents, the moral code, and for honorable behavior shall be fostered. A sympathetic understanding of the problems of love is not a license for moral distortion.

4) The treatment of love-romance stories shall emphasize the value of the home and the sanctity of marriage.

5) Passion or romantic interest shall never be treated in such a way as to stimulate the lower and baser emotions.

6) Seduction and rape shall never be shown or suggested.

7) Sex perversion or any inference to same is strictly forbidden.

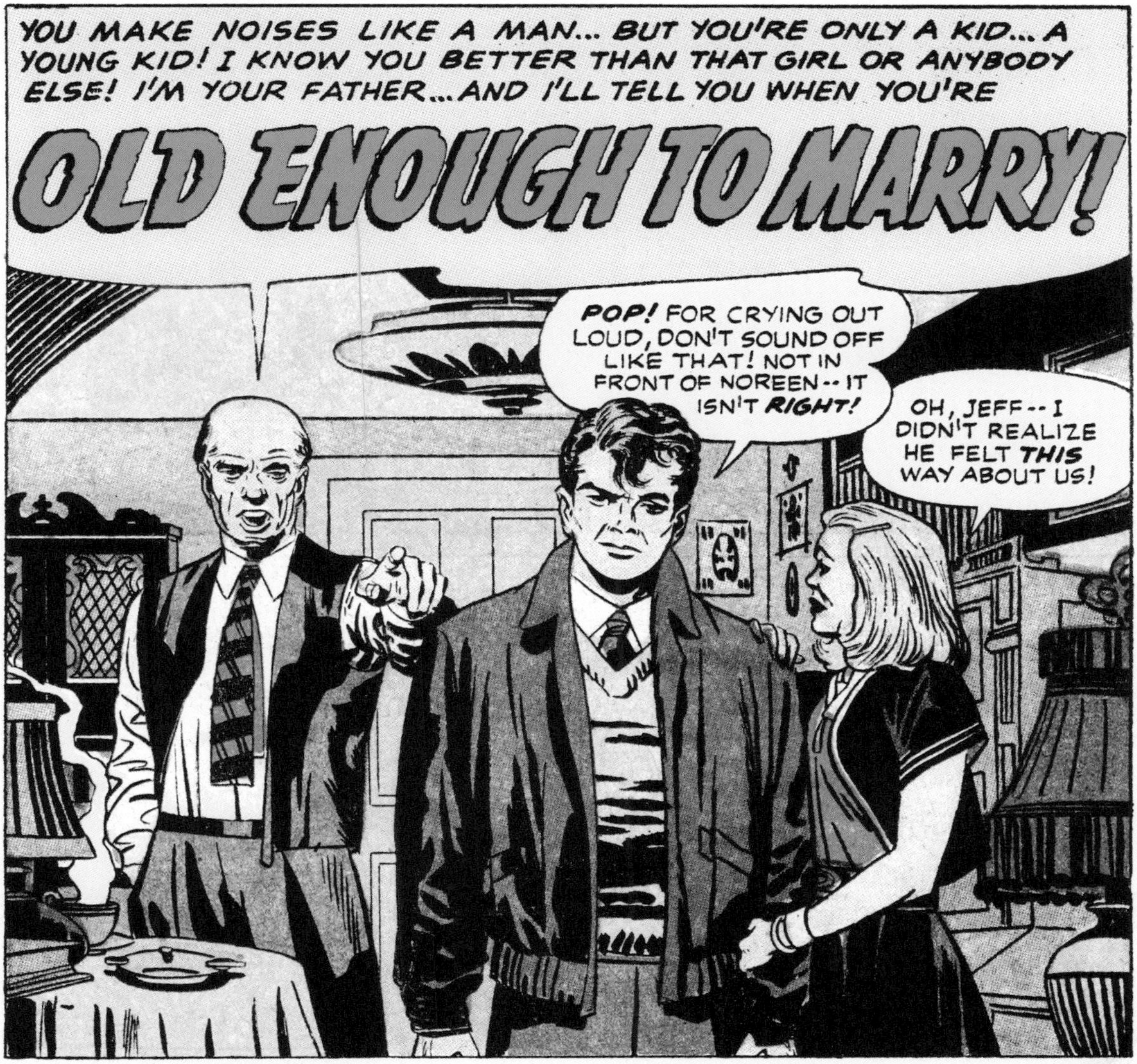
YOU MAKE NOISES LIKE A MAN... BUT YOU'RE ONLY A KID... A YOUNG KID! I KNOW YOU BETTER THAN THAT GIRL OR ANYBODY ELSE! I'M YOUR FATHER...AND I'LL TELL YOU WHEN YOU'RE
OLD ENOUGH TO MARRY!
POP! FOR CRYING OUT LOUD, DON'T SOUND OFF LIKE THAT! NOT IN FRONT OF NOREEN -- IT ISN'T RIGHT!
OH, JEFF -- I DIDN'T REALIZE HE FELT THIS WAY ABOUT US!

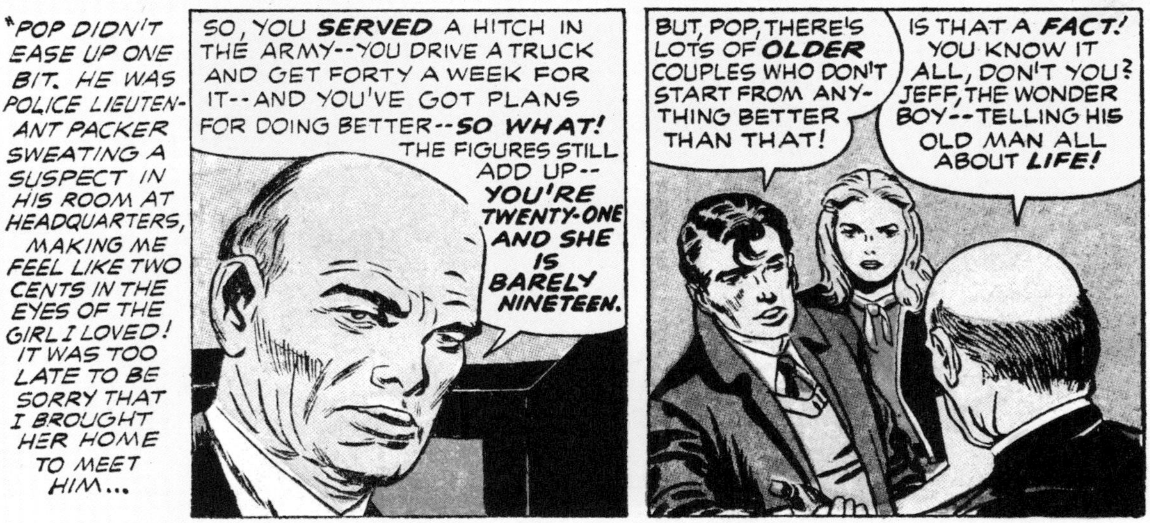
"POP DIDN'T EASE UP ONE BIT. HE WAS POLICE LIEUTENANT PACKER SWEATING A SUSPECT IN HIS ROOM AT HEADQUARTERS, MAKING ME FEEL LIKE TWO CENTS IN THE EYES OF THE GIRL I LOVED! IT WAS TOO LATE TO BE SORRY THAT I BROUGHT HER HOME TO MEET HIM...
SO, YOU SERVED A HITCH IN THE ARMY--YOU DRIVE A TRUCK AND GET FORTY A WEEK FOR IT--AND YOU'VE GOT PLANS FOR DOING BETTER--SO WHAT! THE FIGURES STILL ADD UP--YOU'RE TWENTY-ONE AND SHE IS BARELY NINETEEN.
BUT, POP, THERE'S LOTS OF OLDER COUPLES WHO DON'T START FROM ANYTHING BETTER THAN THAT!
IS THAT A FACT! YOU KNOW IT ALL, DON'T YOU? JEFF, THE WONDER BOY--TELLING HIS OLD MAN ALL ABOUT LIFE!

"DAD SCARED ME WHEN HE TALKED LIKE THAT. HE WAS TOUGH AND LOUD -- JUST LIKE HE WAS IN THE DAYS BEFORE I WAS DRAFTED...WHEN HE'D CATCH ME IN THE HALLWAY PLAYING CARDS WITH THE GUYS... AND WE'D TAKE OFF LIKE A FLOCK OF WILD-EYED BIRDS AT THE BLAST OF A GUN!

WELL, *I'M TELLING YOU TO WAIT*... OR I'LL MAKE YOU MIGHTY SORRY YOU DIDN'T!

I'LL SEE YOU LATER, POP!

I-I'M SORRY ABOUT ALL THIS, HONEY! BUT DON'T LET IT WORRY YOU... IT DOESN'T CHANGE THINGS! WE'RE GOING TO GET MARRIED, ANYWAY!

JEFF -- CAN YOUR FATHER MAKE TROUBLE FOR US? PERHAPS IT WAS A MISTAKE TO BREAK THE NEWS TO HIM SO SOON -- HE SEEMS TERRIBLY UPSET ABOUT IT!

HE'LL COME AROUND WHEN HE GETS USED TO THE IDEA! POP ISN'T TOUGH TWENTY-FOUR HOURS A DAY...FACT IS, HE'S A GOOD EGG! SAY, HE DIDN'T *SCARE* YOU, DID HE?

DON'T PRETEND *YOU'RE* NOT WORRIED TOO, JEFF! I CAN TELL YOU ARE! GOSH, I-I'D HATE FOR THINGS TO GO WRONG NOW... AFTER ALL THE PLANS WE'VE MADE!

"YES, I WAS WORRIED. I DIDN'T LIKE HAVING IT OUT WITH *POP*, BUT HE HAD TO KNOW IT WASN'T A KID GAME HE WAS TRYING TO *BREAK* UP WHEN HE CAME HOME. IT WAS LATE.

STILL AWAKE, JEFF? YOU OUGHT TO HIT THE HAY!

I WAS WAITING UP FOR YOU, POP. I WANT TO *TALK* TO YOU --

ALL YOU KIDS WANT TO TALK! YOU'VE ALL GOT A BEEF AGAINST YOUR ELDERS! THERE WAS A KID TONIGHT... *HIS* IDEA OF PROVING HIMSELF WAS CRACKING SAFES -- GETTING RICH -- HE'LL GET THE WHOLE BOOK!

YOU CAN'T COMPARE ME WITH A GUY LIKE THAT --

YOU'RE RIGHT, JEFF -- I SHOULDN'T HAVE PUT IT THAT WAY. YOU'RE A *GOOD* BOY! ACTUALLY, I'M PROUD OF THE WAY YOU THINK AND BEHAVE... BUT YOU'RE STILL --

I'M *NOT A BOY!* -- I'M *NOT A BOY!!* CAN'T YOU GET THAT THROUGH YOUR HEAD?

A GUY CAN LEARN *PLENTY* IN TWENTY-ONE YEARS! ABOUT THE WORLD... ABOUT PEOPLE... ABOUT HIMSELF! I THOUGHT I'D SHOWED YOU THAT! I THOUGHT YOU UNDERSTOOD--- BUT NO... NOT *YOU!* YOU'RE...

YOU'RE... *ASLEEP!* I'M CHEWING OUT MY HEART, AND YOU'RE ASLEEP! I GUESS I BORE YOU STIFF!

"I KNEW THAT WASN'T SO. DESPITE HIS HARD EXTERIOR, HE'D BEEN A DECENT OLD MAN TO ME. BUT I'D ALWAYS HAD TO BEAT MY BRAINS OUT TO GET THINGS MY OWN WAY. POP'S FACE WAS DRAWN AND TIRED. I PUT A BLANKET ON HIM AND WENT TO THE WINDOW... TO LOOK AT THE NIGHT AND MY OWN THOUGHTS."

"POP WAS STILL SLEEPING IN THE CHAIR EARLY THE NEXT MORNING, WHEN I PHONED NOREEN. I MADE A FAST CUP OF JAVA AND LEFT FOR CITY HALL. I WOULD HAVE A MORE SUBSTANTIAL BREAKFAST LATER... WITH MY WIFE!

IT LOOKS LIKE A BUSY DAY FOR CUPID! WE'LL HAVE TO WAIT OUR TURN, NOREEN!

JEFF... ARE YOU SURE YOU WANT TO GO THROUGH WITH IT?

MARRIAGE LICENSE BUREAU

YOU KNOW, LAST NIGHT, I KEPT THINKING ABOUT THIS MOMENT-- AND SUDDENLY, I FELT HAPPY-- HAPPIER THAN I'VE EVER BEEN! I WANT TO BE YOUR HUSBAND, NOREEN!

EVEN IF IT DISPLEASES YOUR FATHER?

ESPECIALLY WHEN IT DISPLEASES HIS FATHER!

POP!!

NOW, LISTEN, POP... IF YOU CAME HERE TO MAKE ANY TROUBLE FOR US-- *FORGET IT!*

FORGET MY OWN SON'S *MARRIAGE?*

3

YEAH--I SEE YOU BROUGHT ALONG AN USHER WITH YOU!

I'M JAKE FARLEY. I WORK WITH YOUR POP ON BURGLARY DETAIL!

YOU GUYS ARE OFF YOUR BEAT, AREN'T YOU?--I HEAR IT'S LEGIT TO GET A MARRIAGE LICENSE--

JEFF... PLEASE BE CAREFUL... *DON'T* SAY ANYTHING RASH!

NOREEN IS RIGHT, JEFF! THIS CAN ALL BE SETTLED QUIETLY. I WANT YOU BOTH TO COME WITH US!

ALL RIGHT--*ALL RIGHT!* WE'LL GO QUIETLY, OFFICER-- ONLY MAKE UP YOUR MIND TO ONE THING...

...NOREEN AND I ARE GETTING *MARRIED*, AND NO MATTER WHAT YOU'VE TRUMPED UP TO STOP US-- *IT WON'T WORK!* WE'RE YOUNG, BUT WE KNOW OUR RIGHTS!

WHY DON'T YOU DRY UP BEFORE YOU WEAR DOWN YOUR GUMS! I'VE HEARD ALL I CARE TO HEAR!

"WE WALKED SILENTLY, DOWN A LONG CORRIDOR. POP AND JAKE FARLEY FOLLOWED US LIKE ARMED KEEPERS. I WAS MAD AS A HORNET...

IN THERE... BOTH OF YOU!

"I OPENED THE DOOR AT MY FATHER'S ORDER. NOREEN AND I WALKED INTO AN OFFICE. THERE WERE SOME MEN WHO LOOKED US OVER RATHER SOLEMNLY...

4

SUDDENLY, EVERYONE BEGAN TO SMILE. THERE WERE EVEN A FEW WARM LAUGHS. IT WAS LIKE SOMEONE HAD TURNED ON THE LIGHTS AT A SURPRISE PARTY. THEN, NOREEN AND I FOUND OURSELVES IN MY POP'S EMBRACE...

COME ON, CALL IT OFF, YOU TWO! THIS IS NO WAY TO ACT AT YOUR **WEDDING!**

WHA--?

SURE, LAD! --YOU DIDN'T THINK WE WERE SENDING YOU UP THE RIVER, DID YOU?

OH, MISTER PACKER! YOU DON'T OBJECT AT ALL! THIS WAS ALL A--

IN **MY** BUSINESS, MY DEAR, IT'S HARD TO DEVELOP A PROPER SENSE OF HUMOR! FORGIVE ME IF I FRIGHTENED YOU. MY GOODNESS, BUT YOU'RE PRETTY! JEFF HAS ALWAYS DONE THINGS WELL... EVEN IN CHOOSING A BRIDE!

I'VE NEVER DOUBTED JEFF... OR HIS SENSE OF JUDGMENT! BUT HE'S SUCH A WHINEY KID WHEN IT COMES TO IMPORTANT DECISIONS -- DECISIONS WHICH CAN ONLY BE RESOLVED BY HIMSELF!

SO, I'VE ALWAYS TURNED THE PRESSURE ON -- TO MAKE HIM JUMP ONE WAY OR THE OTHER! A REAL MAN JUMPS ONLY THE WAY HE REALLY WANTS TO GO!

JEFF WOULD **NEVER** MARRY TO SPITE ME NOR ANYONE ELSE! HE'S MARRYING BECAUSE HE **WANTS** TO! HE'S FOUND THE RIGHT GIRL -- HE LOVES HER -- THAT'S WHAT YOU WERE THINKING LAST NIGHT -- WHEN YOU THOUGHT I WAS ASLEEP!

IN FACT, I WAS ALSO AWAKE WHEN YOU CALLED NOREEN THIS MORNING... ARRANGING FOR YOUR VISIT TO THE MARRIAGE LICENSE BUREAU! THEN I DID A LITTLE ARRANGING MYSELF! JEFF, I'M A VERY PROUD FATHER. WOULD YOU MIND IF THE CEREMONY TOOK PLACE HERE... AMONG MY FRIENDS?

OF COURSE NOT, POP!

"THEY WERE ALL MEN WHO WORKED WITH MY POP FOR YEARS. AND THE BIG MAN WAS A CHAPLAIN. WHEN THE ROOM BECAME SOLEMN ONCE MORE, NOREEN AND I WERE MARRIED.

AND I NOW PRONOUNCE YOU MAN AND WIFE!

The END

"ONCE DURING THE CEREMONY, I HAPPENED TO TAKE A FAST GLANCE AT POP AND I'LL BE DARNED IF THE TOUGH GUY DIDN'T HAVE TEARS IN HIS EYES! AND TO MAKE THINGS EVEN MORE SURPRISING, HE TOLD ME LATER, THAT WHEN HE'D MARRIED MY MOM, HE WAS ONLY NINETEEN, IT MADE ME FIT TO BUST!"

She wanted to see him strong and well again. But it was more than his affliction that kept him from walking. He was incurably...

LOVESICK!

I'd rather get my medicine from you than your father, Betty. If you keep on neglecting me... I may **never** get well!

Don't say **that**, I want so desperately for you to **walk** again! I'll spend more time with you--if it will help!

Let the doctor prescribe the cure, if you please! I suggest that he try to walk **without** the help of a nurse...

"I'll never forget that day when they carried Tim's limp form into the house. The plowing was almost finished for the day, and I had just finished helping Mother set the table for Daddy and the farmhands. But the usual routine of our little farm changed from that day on...

TIM! Daddy-- what happened to him?

Tractor turned over on him! Ground near the old stump gave way. It's his legs... can't seem to move them...

"Doctor Caldwell arrived in about an hour, which was fast time for him. He was old and slow-moving, but the only M.D. within a hundred miles. He looked Tim over methodically... applied splints and bandages and then called Daddy into the hall...

The boy's legs are paralyzed! I've seen cases like this before! Not much can be done for him--except rest and good care!

Doc, are you saying he'll never be able to **walk** again?

HE MIGHT AND HE MIGHT NOT! THAT'S A POINT THE SURGEONS IN THE CITY WILL HAVE TO DECIDE. I'VE DONE ALL I CAN DO. TOUGH ON THE BOY... GOT NO FOLKS--

DON'T WORRY ABOUT THAT! TIM HAS A HOME HERE WITH US... AS LONG AS HE WANTS TO STAY! WE'LL TAKE GOOD CARE OF HIM-- WON'T WE, BETTY?

"I NODDED. MY VOICE WAS TOO CHOKED UP WITH EMOTION TO SPEAK. TIM WAS MORE THAN A FARMHAND-- ESPECIALLY TO ME. WE'D PRAC- TICALLY GROWN UP TOGETHER. I FELT VERY DEEPLY ABOUT TIM... AND I KNEW HE WAS IN LOVE WITH ME...

GOOD GIRL, BETTY! YOU'LL BE BETTER FOR HIM THAN ANY NURSE! I'LL LEAVE SOME MEDICATION WITH YOU... GOT TO KEEP HIM ON A STRICT SCHEDULE!

THE SHOCK OF THOSE FIRST DAYS GRADUALLY FADED INTO THE PAST. THERE WAS NO MORE PAIN FOR TIM. IT WAS GOOD TO SEE HIM SMILE AGAIN! I OFTEN LOOKED FORWARD TO THE EVENINGS WHEN THE CHORES WERE DONE, AND WE WOULD SIT AND READ -- OR WATCH TELEVISION TOGETHER...

YOU'RE MISSING A LOT, BETTY. I SAW A PROGRAM THAT MADE ME HOWL! I WISH YOU COULD HAVE SEEN IT WITH ME...

I KNOW HOW IT IS. YOU JUST CAN'T SEEM TO REMEMBER THE JOKES WHEN YOU WANT TO TELL THEM TO SOME- ONE...

I'D RATHER HAVE YOU UP HERE IN THE EVENINGS -- WHEN THE DRAMAS ARE ON, SOME OF THEM MAKE ME RECALL THE GOOD TIMES WE HAD IN THE PAST. REMEMBER THE HARVEST PARTY LAST YEAR, BETTY?

YOU WERE MY PARTNER -- WE WON THE JITTER- BUG CONTEST... OH, TIM, I'M SORRY! I JUST DIDN'T THINK!

FORGET IT -- I LIKE TO REMEMBER THOSE DAYS! BESIDES, YOU DON'T THINK I EXPECT TO BE FLAT ON MY BACK FOR THE REST OF MY LIFE, DO YOU?

I'LL GET MY BREAK! YOUR DAD'S BEEN IN TOUCH WITH SOME PRETTY BIG SURGEONS IN THE CITY. THEY'VE GOT HOPE FOR ME...

I'VE NEVER LOST HOPE, DARLING! YOU HAVE FAITH -- AND LOVE ON YOUR SIDE!

LOVE? BETTY, SOME DAY, I'LL TELL YOU ABOUT LOVE... SOME DAY! BUT I WANT TO MAKE SURE IT'S NOT CONFUSED WITH PITY!

TIM -- IT -- IT'S LATE... I'LL GET YOUR MEDICINE...

2

"TIM HAD TOUCHED ON A SUBJECT THAT HAD BEEN CAUSING ME MANY SLEEPLESS NIGHTS LATELY. HAD I EVER LOVED HIM? DID I LOVE HIM NOW? WHAT DID I OWE HIM? HOW MUCH OF MY TIME...OF MY LIFE? I STOOD FOR A LONG MOMENT OUTSIDE HIS DOOR THAT EVENING, PONDERING THESE QUESTIONS.

HE CAN'T EXPECT ME TO LIVE IN THAT LITTLE SHELL HE'S BUILT AROUND HIMSELF. IT'S NOT FAIR! I WANT TO BE WITH OTHER YOUNG PEOPLE, TOO.. AND THAT WOULD BREAK TIM'S HEART!

"THERE SEEMED TO BE NO ANSWER--FOR THE PRESENT, AT LEAST. A YEAR PASSED BY. THE CHANCES TO HELP TIM SEEMED FAR AWAY. DADDY COULDN'T RAISE THE KIND OF MONEY SUCH AN OPERATION WOULD REQUIRE. AND THEN ONE DAY--

HELLO! I'M DAVID KENT. DOCTOR CALDWELL IS GOING TO TAKE A MUCH NEEDED REST... AND I'LL TAKE OVER HIS PRACTICE FOR A WHILE!

COME IN, DOCTOR...I'LL SHOW YOU TO TIM'S ROOM...

YOU MUST BE BETTY. HE'S A MOST INTERESTING CASE, YOUR TIM! DOCTOR CALDWELL THINKS HE CAN BE HELPED. WHAT ARE THE CHANCES FOR SURGERY?

PRETTY SLIM, RIGHT NOW... WE CAN'T AFFORD IT!

"DOCTOR KENT SPENT A FEW MINUTES EXAMINING TIM--AND ABOUT AN HOUR TALKING TO HIM. WHEN HE WAS THROUGH, HE TALKED TO DADDY AND ME...

I'VE DISCUSSED THE OPERATION WITH THE BOY. THERE'S A CHANCE OF SUCCESS, BUT THE RISKS WILL BE GREAT!

DOCTOR KENT, YOU MUST UNDERSTAND--

--WE'D DO **ANYTHING** TO HELP TIM! BUT IT WILL BE YEARS BEFORE WE'RE ABLE TO PAY FOR IT!

THAT'S NOT IMPORTANT, NOW! OUR PRIMARY OBJECTIVE RIGHT NOW IS TO SEE THAT TIM IS IN THE FRAME OF MIND TO GO THROUGH WITH IT. FROM MY TALK WITH HIM, I FEEL THAT BETTY CAN HELP US ON THAT SCORE!

I'M SURE THAT WON'T BE ANY PROBLEM!

GOOD! BETTY, YOU DROP AROUND TO MY OFFICE TOMORROW...WE'LL GO INTO A FEW DETAILS. WE'LL HAVE TO WORK TOGETHER DURING THE NEXT FEW WEEKS!

3

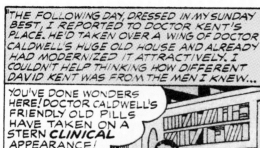

"THE FOLLOWING DAY, DRESSED IN MY SUNDAY BEST, I REPORTED TO DOCTOR KENT'S PLACE. HE'D TAKEN OVER A WING OF DOCTOR CALDWELL'S HUGE OLD HOUSE AND ALREADY HAD MODERNIZED IT ATTRACTIVELY. I COULDN'T HELP THINKING HOW DIFFERENT DAVID KENT WAS FROM THE MEN I KNEW..."

YOU'VE DONE WONDERS HERE! DOCTOR CALDWELL'S FRIENDLY OLD PILLS HAVE TAKEN ON A STERN *CLINICAL* APPEARANCE!

WE'VE GOT TO BE PROGRESSIVE, WHETHER WE'RE IN A FOXHOLE IN KOREA -- OR A SKYSCRAPER IN THE CITY! THERE'S NO EXCUSE FOR SECOND-RATE MEDICINE -- OR SECOND-RATE LIVING!

I THINK I KNOW WHAT YOU MEAN...

WE HERE...WE TALK ABOUT DOING THINGS UP RIGHT...TIM TALKS ABOUT GETTING WELL... DAD TALKS ABOUT ARRANGING THINGS...BUT NOBODY REALLY --I MEAN *REALLY* TRIES! IT WAS ALL TALK... UNTIL *YOU* CAME!

WHAT ABOUT YOURSELF, BETTY?

HOW DO YOU FEEL ABOUT--PROGRESS?

EXACTLY LIKE THE OTHERS! I TALK--ABOUT LIVING--ABOUT GOING OUT WITH YOUNG PEOPLE. I TALK ABOUT THE FUTURE AND EVERY EVENING I GO UPSTAIRS TO SIT WITH TIM--BECAUSE I DON'T WANT TO HURT HIS FEELINGS!

THAT'S A *PERFECT* EXAMPLE OF SECOND-RATE LIVING! YOU KNOW YOU CAN DO BETTER-- BUT YOU'RE TOO LAZY TO TRY. WHAT DO YOU THINK OF MY PSYCHOLOGY?

A VERY INTERESTING THEORY! I WONDER IF IT WORKS...

WELL, LET'S FIND OUT, LADY! WE CAN TALK JUST AS WELL IN MY CAR. AND LATER, YOU CAN SHOW ME WHERE THE MORGANS LIVE... I THINK IT'S MEASLES...

OH-OH... THAT DOESN'T SOUND LIKE PROGRESS TO ME!

"THAT WAS THE FIRST OF MY MANY VISITS WITH DAVID KENT. HE MADE EVERYTHING FEEL LIKE FUN. HE WAS FUN. AS IT TURNED OUT, I DIDN'T EVEN REALIZE THAT I WAS HIS PATIENT--ALONG WITH TIM..."

IT'S BEEN THREE MONTHS SINCE YOU FIRST CAME TO MY OFFICE, BETTY. YOU WERE WITHDRAWN, MELANCHOLY--A MOST UNHAPPY GIRL! I'M HAPPY TO SAY YOU HAVE EMERGED COMPLETELY FROM YOUR LITTLE SHELL!

CONTINUED AFTER NEXT PAGE

AND I DID IT ALL WITH MY LITTLE KNOWLEDGE OF PSYCHIATRY!

A LITTLE LEARNING CAN BE A DANGEROUS THING! WHERE DO I GO FROM HERE?

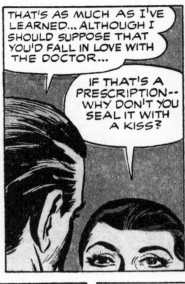

THAT'S AS MUCH AS I'VE LEARNED... ALTHOUGH I SHOULD SUPPOSE THAT YOU'D FALL IN LOVE WITH THE DOCTOR...

IF THAT'S A PRESCRIPTION-- WHY DON'T YOU SEAL IT WITH A KISS?

I HAVE TO GO NOW... WHAT ABOUT TIM?

ALL ARRANGEMENTS HAVE BEEN MADE. YOU CAN BREAK IT TO HIM... HE WON'T BE DISAPPOINTED!

"THAT EVENING, I WAS HAPPIER THAN ANY GIRL HAD A RIGHT TO BE. THE DREARY OUTLOOK OF THREE MONTHS AGO HAD CHANGED ABRUPTLY TO A ROSY FUTURE FOR ALL OF US. NOW, I HAD TO TELL TIM OF HIS GOOD LUCK...

TIM!

BETTY! GOSH, IT'S GOOD TO SEE YOU! DO YOU REALIZE HOW LONG IT'S BEEN SINCE WE'VE SPENT AN EVENING TOGETHER?

NO--NO, I HADN'T REALIZED! BUT TIM, I HAVE WONDERFUL NEWS FOR YOU... YOU'RE GOING TO HAVE YOUR OPERATION SOON--VERY SOON. DOCTOR KENT HAS ARRANGED EVERYTHING!

HAS HE?

WHY, TIM... I THOUGHT YOU'D BE THRILLED! JUST THINK-- YOU HAVE A CHANCE--A CHANCE TO WALK AGAIN!

THERE'S ALSO A CHANCE THAT I MAY NOT LIVE THROUGH IT... HAVE YOU CONSIDERED THAT, BETTY?

5

TELL YOU WHAT--I'LL LEAVE IT UP TO YOU. THE DECISION IS IN YOUR HANDS, COMPLETELY! YOU'VE GOT A MAN'S LIFE TO PLAY AROUND WITH NOW, BETTY. A MAN WHO LOVES YOU--WHO WOULDN'T WANT TO LIVE WITHOUT YOU AT ANY COST! I'LL DO JUST AS YOU SAY...

TIM--THAT'S NOT FAIR! I COULDN'T MAKE A DECISION LIKE THAT!

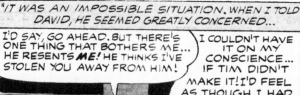

"IT WAS AN IMPOSSIBLE SITUATION. WHEN I TOLD DAVID, HE SEEMED GREATLY CONCERNED...

I'D SAY, GO AHEAD. BUT THERE'S ONE THING THAT BOTHERS ME... HE RESENTS **ME!** HE THINKS I'VE STOLEN YOU AWAY FROM HIM!

I COULDN'T HAVE IT ON MY CONSCIENCE... IF TIM DIDN'T MAKE IT! I'D FEEL AS THOUGH I HAD SENT HIM TO HIS DEATH--BECAUSE HE WAS A PROBLEM I COULDN'T SOLVE!

SO HE'S IN **LOVE** WITH YOU! THAT PUTS ME IN A TOUGH SPOT, DOESN'T IT?

HE KNOWS I'VE BEEN SEEING YOU OFTEN!

THE BOY'S **A FOOL!** WHAT CHANCE DOES HE HAVE TO WIN YOU--THE WAY HE IS. HE'S GOT TO TAKE THE RISK. YOU MUST CONVINCE HIM OF THAT!

DAVID, I CAN'T PROMISE HIM **ANYTHING!**

"FINALLY I WENT BACK TO TIM, TO IMPLORE HIM TO GO THROUGH WITH THE OPERATION. HE AGREED PASSIVELY. AND BEFORE LONG DAVID TOOK HIM TO THE MAKE-SHIFT OPERATING ROOM HE HAD PREPARED FOR SURGERY.

YOU'LL BE HERE, WON'T YOU, BETTY? YOU'LL BE NEAR ME WHEN IT'S HAPPENING?

I'LL BE HERE, TIM. BE BRAVE, AND--GOOD LUCK!

"IN THOSE NEXT HOURS I SUFFERED TORMENT I NEVER DREAMED POSSIBLE. WHAT IF HE DIED, I KEPT ASKING MYSELF...WHAT TORTURES WILL HAUNT MY CONSCIENCE FOR THE REST OF MY DAYS?

"THE DAY DRAGGED ON-- AND THEN IT WAS OVER. DAVID CAME OUT FIRST, PALE AND TIRED...BUT SMILING!

IT WENT OFF FINE! NOW WE'LL JUST HAVE TO WAIT--SEE HOW HE PROGRESSES...

"A FEW DAYS LATER, TIM WAS BROUGHT BACK TO OUR HOUSE AND TO HIS OLD ROOM. THEN BEGAN THE TRYING PERIOD OF WAITING, HOPING FOR THE SIGNS OF RECOVERY--

TIM, WON'T YOU TRY? IF YOU ONLY MADE AN ATTEMPT TO WALK--PERHAPS IT WOULD GIVE DOCTOR KENT SOMETHING TO WORK ON!

DOCTOR KENT-- DOCTOR KENT! I'VE HAD ENOUGH OF HIM--EVEN IF YOU HAVEN'T, BETTY!

HE'S HAD HIS CHANCE! ALL RIGHT, I RISKED MY LIFE. IT DIDN'T WORK. IT'S OVER AND DONE WITH-- LET'S FORGET IT!

TIM--- I'M SORRY--- FOR THE PAIN-- FOR LETTING YOU TAKE THE RISK-- IT WAS MY FAULT!

"DAVID CAME TO VISIT OFTEN AT FIRST. AND WHEN HIS BEDSIDE MANNER WAS SMOOTH AND COMFORTING AT THE BEGINNING, IT DEGENERATED INTO A SCOLDING, IMPATIENT HARANGUE THAT BROUGHT ONLY FRUSTRATION TO POOR TIM.

DAVID, HOW CAN YOU SPEAK TO TIM THAT WAY! IT'S NOT HIS FAULT THAT HE CAN'T WALK!

WHY DON'T YOU SAY WHAT YOU MEAN? THAT THE OPERATION WAS A FAILURE... THAT I'M A QUACK WHO TALKED YOU INTO A BILL OF GOODS!

IT'S NOT YOUR FAULT--AND IT'S NOT TIM'S EITHER! THE OPERATION WAS-- UNFORTUNATE, BUT I WON'T HAVE YOU BERATING TIM IN THAT POMPOUS MANNER OF YOURS!

I CAN'T UNDERSTAND IT!--I DON'T SEE WHERE I COULD HAVE FAILED. MAYBE, SOME DAY WE'LL HAVE THE ANSWER!

"AFTER THAT, DAVID AND I WENT OUT TOGETHER A FEW TIMES, BUT IT WASN'T THE SAME ANYMORE. TOO MANY HARSH WORDS HAD BEEN SPOKEN...TOO MANY THOUGHTS REMAINED UNSAID. FINALLY, WHEN HE TOLD ME HE WAS LEAVING, IT WAS ALMOST A RELIEF!

"SO DAVID WAS GONE! AND IF I THOUGHT I DIDN'T CARE...THAT I WOULDN'T MISS HIM... I WAS TERRIBLY WRONG! NONETHELESS, I HID MY TEARS FROM TIM. POOR TIM HAD HIS OWN PROBLEMS...

TIM-- I WENT SHOPPING TODAY. I PICKED UP A NOVEL YOU'RE BOUND TO ENJOY!

GOSH! IT'S LIKE OLD TIMES, HONEY!--NICE SEEING YOU AROUND SO OFTEN!

HONEY... I'VE GOT A REAL SURPRISE FOR YOU! TURN AROUND--AND DON'T PEEK!

WHY? WHAT IS IT, TIM?

LOOK!

TIM...

TIM... H-HOW LONG HAVE YOU BEEN ABLE TO GET AROUND LIKE THIS?

WH-WHY, I-I JUST STARTED... UH... *YESTERDAY!*

YOU *COULDN'T* JUST GET UP AND WALK! YOU MUST HAVE BEEN ABLE TO MOVE AROUND SINCE JUST AFTER THE OPERATION! TIM, YOU'VE BEEN FAKING... *LYING!* BUT WHY?

YOU KNOW WHY-- *DOCTOR KENT!*

HE'D BE THE BIG HERO! HE'D TAKE YOU AWAY FROM ME, BETTY! I COULDN'T LET YOU GO! I COULDN'T LET YOU MAKE THAT MISTAKE! DAVID KENT *ISN'T* LIKE US! HE'S AMBITIOUS... BIG CITY-- YOU'RE WORLDS APART!

YOU THOUGHT YOU WERE IN LOVE WITH HIM-- I KNEW IT ALL ALONG... BUT YOU KNOW *BETTER* NOW-- YOU FOUND OUT WHAT HE'S LIKE, DIDN'T YOU? SO, YOU SEE WHAT I DID WAS *RIGHT!*

TIM WAS *STILL* TALKING WHEN I WALKED OUT. WHY BOTHER TO ANSWER, IF HE DIDN'T KNOW WRONG FROM RIGHT AT HIS AGE, HE'D NEVER LEARN. BESIDES, I HAD A LONG JOURNEY AHEAD OF ME, AND THERE WAS PACKING TO DO...

THE TRAIN WAS SPEEDING ME TOWARD THE CITY-- DAVID'S CITY-- AND I WAS LIGHT AND FREE-- AS IF A GREAT WEIGHT HAD BEEN LIFTED FROM MY SHOULDERS...

THE END

"TIM WAS NO LONGER MY RESPONSIBILITY. FROM NOW ON THERE WAS ONLY DAVID KENT. I WASN'T AFRAID. I KNEW THAT WHATEVER I HAD TO SAY TO HIM-- HE WOULD MAKE IT EASY!"

GET READY... GET SET... YOU ELIGIBLE BACHELORS! THE BONDS OF MATRIMONY MAY NEVER LOOK SO GOOD TO YOU AGAIN...

LIZZIE'S BACK IN TOWN!

LIZZIE! IT'S GREAT TO SEE YOU AGAIN! I'VE BEEN THINKING ABOUT YOU ALL THIS TIME!

YOU HAVEN'T CHANGED ANY, HORTON! WHEN ARE YOU GOING TO LEARN GOOD MANNERS?

IT WAS JUST AS I'D LEFT IT--THE TOWN, THE PEOPLE AND *HORTON MILES*. HE HAD THE SAME BRASH SMILE AND UNKEMPT LOOK--

GOSH, YOU LOOK SWEET, LIZZIE! CUTE AS A DAISY IN SACKER'S MEADOW!

YOU SURE WOULD WOW THE GIRLS AT FINISHING SCHOOL, HORTON!

YOUR DAD SHOULD NEVER HAVE SENT YOU TO THAT SNOOTY SCHOOL! I CAN'T SEE WHAT YOU GAINED FROM IT!

PERSPECTIVE FOR ONE THING--OR DON'T YOU KNOW THE MEANING OF THE WORD?

NO--*TEACH ME!* LEARNING BIG WORDS MAY BE MORE FUN THAN BUYING HORSES!

HORTON, YOU STOP THIS-- YOU'RE EMBARRASSING ME!

THE BIG STOOP WOULDN'T KNOW THAT! HI, LIZZIE--I HEARD YOU WERE BACK--

YEAH? AND I'D HATE TO SPOIL HER WELCOME BY PUNCHING YOU IN THE NOSE, STONEY!

PLEASE, BOYS-- NOT *AGAIN!*

NO, THINGS HADN'T CHANGED. THEY WERE STILL AT IT-- HORTON AND STONEY--FACING EACH OTHER LIKE TWO ANGRY BULLS--

THEN DAD ARRIVED TO SEPARATE THEM AS HE'D ALWAYS DONE BEFORE--

DAD WAS A BIG MAN--BIGGER THAN ANYBODY, IT SEEMED EVEN HORTON AND STONEY DIDN'T RELISH TANGLING WITH HIM--

DOGGONE, IF YOU AREN'T THE SCRAPPIEST PAIR I EVER DID SEE!

I WAS AFRAID *THIS* WOULD HAPPEN WHEN LIZZIE GOT BACK--SO I'VE GOT NEWS FOR YOU BOYS!

I WANT BOTH OF YOU TO STAY CLEAR OF LIZZIE FROM NOW ON! YOU'RE GOOD BOYS, BUT I'VE GOT *OTHER* PLANS FOR HER!

ONE WOULD NEVER KNOW THOSE TWO WERE BROTHERS WHEN THEY SET EYES ON YOU, LIZ!

DAD-- WHAT DID YOU MEAN BY-- *OTHER* PLANS?

2

DAD SAID NOTHING ABOUT HIS PLANS UNTIL LATER THAT EVENING. WHEN DINNER WAS OVER, HE FINALLY GOT AROUND TO THE SUBJECT--

YOU KNOW, LIZ--I'VE ALWAYS HAD ONE SORE SPOT-- THAT YOU WEREN'T A *BOY!*

WELL, IT'S NEVER BEEN *MY* SORE SPOT! I THINK I'VE DONE YOU PROUD ---EVEN AS A *DAUGHTER!*

CONFOUND IT-- I KNOW THAT! BUT-- WELL, YOU SEE-- IT'S STILL NOT LIKE-- WHY DON'T YOU GIVE ME A CHANCE TO FINISH? *YOU'RE JUST LIKE YOUR MOTHER!*

LIKE MOTHER, I'M AWAY AHEAD OF YOU! YOU'RE PROBABLY NOW IN STAGE THREE!

AND WHAT IN THUNDERATION IS STAGE *THREE?*

YOU'RE READY TO BECOME A GRAND-FATHER! THAT MEANS I'M TO BE MARRIED OFF--MOST LIKELY TO SOMEONE YOU'VE *ALREADY* CHOSEN!

I DON'T RECALL EVER DOING ANYTHING THAT WASN'T BEST FOR YOU!

I'VE FOLLOWED THE PATTERN YOU CUT FOR ME, DAD. IT WAS GOOD FOR ME--UNTIL *NOW!*

BUT YOU'RE A GROWN WOMAN, NOW, LIZ, AND--

YES, AND THE NEXT LOGICAL STEP IS MARRIAGE, IT'S STRANGE, DAD-- BUT I FEEL THE SAME WAY ABOUT IT!

OH, I'VE THOUGHT OF GADDING ABOUT, SEEING NEW PLACES, DOING NEW THINGS-- BEING CAREFREE--

BUT YOU DID TOO GOOD A JOB ON MY LIFE, DAD! I'M REALLY A VERY *ORDERLY* PERSON!

THEN WHY THE FUSS? WHY FIGHT ME?

YOU MAY PICK THE CLOTHES FOR A LITTLE GIRL, OR THE RIGHT SCHOOL FOR A TEEN-AGER, BUT--

ALL RIGHT! CHOOSE YOUR OWN HUSBAND! WHO WILL IT BE-- STONY? HORTON? OR SOME OTHER WILD OAF?

WHY NOT? STONEY AND HORTON MAY LACK POLISH, BUT THEY'RE MEN-- *REAL MEN!*

SO'S MY FOREMAN, HANK SMITH! WHAT'S MORE, HE LIKES THE LUMBER BUSINESS AS MUCH AS I DO!

I SHOULD HAVE KNOWN. DAD HAD IT ALL NEATLY PACKAGED. WELL, I WOULD SHOW HIM-- I'D SHOW HANK SMITH, TOO! THIS TIME, I WOULD BREAK THE PATTERN--

GOOD MORNING, MISS REED-- NICE TO SEE YOU AGAIN! IS YOUR DAD HERE?

I WOULDN'T KNOW-- I HAVEN'T LOOKED FOR HIM!

WELL, HE CALLED THE OFFICE AND ASKED ME TO DROP IN HERE FOR A CONFAB!

FOR A CONFAB WITH ME, I'LL WAGER! ONLY I'M NOT STAYING LONG ENOUGH FOR *THAT!* I WAS JUST GOING OUT!

THAT'S TOO BAD! YOUR DAD'S IDEA WAS QUITE INTERESTING-- EVEN IF I CAN'T FIGURE IT OUT!

YOU'LL PARDON ME IF I DON'T WASTE ANY TIME GOING INTO IT FURTHER!

I LEFT HIM STANDING THERE AND WENT OFF TO PLAY TENNIS. HE HAD A NERVE, TRYING TO MAKE ME BELIEVE THAT HE AND DAD DIDN'T COOK UP THAT LITTLE INCIDENT TOGETHER! I WENT RIDING WITH STONEY LATER--

CAN'T BEAT THESE LITTLE OLD FOREIGN JOBS FOR TEARING ABOUT!

IF YOU'RE OUT TO TAKE MY BREATH AWAY-- YOU'RE SUCCEEDING!

I GUESS WE CAN STOP HERE FOR A SPELL-- THE VIEW'S MIGHTY NICE!

I DON'T SUPPOSE YOU'D PICK OUT ONE THAT WASN'T ROMANTIC!

4

YOU KNOW HOW I FEEL ABOUT YOU, LIZ--I'VE NEVER TRIED TO HIDE IT!

I KNOW, STONEY--

I'VE *LOVED* YOU SINCE WE WERE KIDS! NOW THAT YOU'RE BACK--

YES, STONEY?

THERE'S NOTHING MORE TO SAY-- I WANT TO *MARRY* YOU!

ALL RIGHT, YOU'VE HAD YOUR SAY WITH LIZ! *NOW, GET!* I'VE GOT MY HEART SET ON HER, TOO!

HOW DID *YOU* GET HERE?

NEVER MIND! LIZ IS IN TROUBLE, ESPECIALLY IF SHE'S CONSIDERING A NO-ACCOUNT LIKE YOU!

WHY DON'T YOU GIVE UP, HORTON? LIZ WOULDN'T HAVE YOU ON A BET!

STONEY! THAT ISN'T FAIR! I THINK HORTON IS A FINE BOY! YOU'RE BOTH A BIT WILD, BUT YOU'D MAKE GOOD HUSBANDS!

THEN JUST CHOOSE THE HANDSOMEST ONE--ME!

I TOLD THEM I WOULD MAKE A CHOICE BETWEEN THEM. THAT SEEMED AGREEABLE TO STONEY AND HORTON. EACH WAS CONFIDENT HE WAS THE BETTER MAN. THAT NIGHT, I WAS GIVING SERIOUS THOUGHT TO IT ALL, WHEN--

GOOD EVENING, MISS REED.

ARE YOU STILL LOOKING FOR DAD, HANK SMITH?

CONTINUED AFTER NEXT PAGE

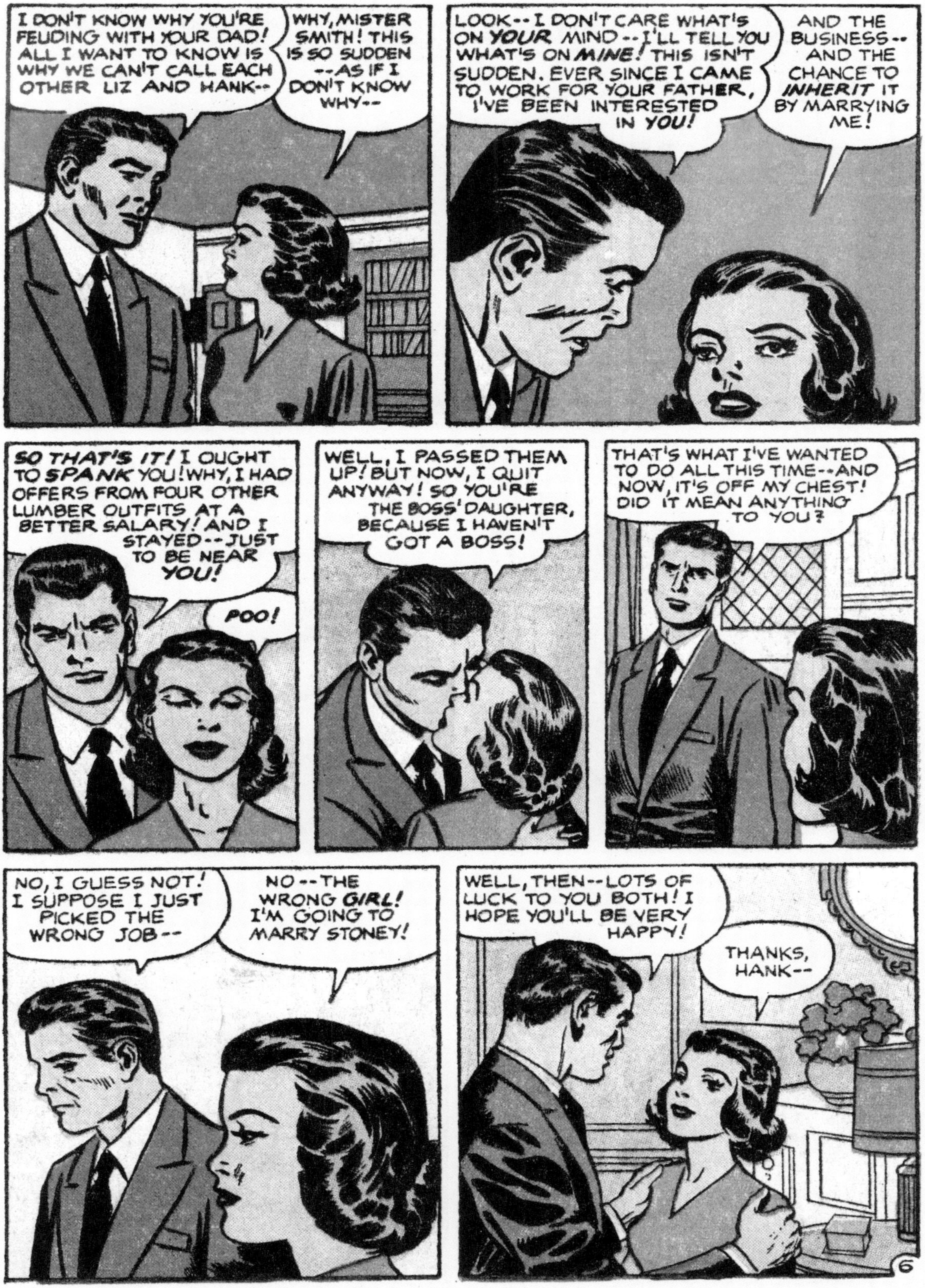
I DON'T KNOW WHY YOU'RE FEUDING WITH YOUR DAD! ALL I WANT TO KNOW IS WHY WE CAN'T CALL EACH OTHER LIZ AND HANK--
WHY, MISTER SMITH! THIS IS SO SUDDEN --AS IF I DON'T KNOW WHY--
LOOK--I DON'T CARE WHAT'S ON YOUR MIND--I'LL TELL YOU WHAT'S ON MINE! THIS ISN'T SUDDEN. EVER SINCE I CAME TO WORK FOR YOUR FATHER, I'VE BEEN INTERESTED IN YOU!
AND THE BUSINESS-- AND THE CHANCE TO INHERIT IT BY MARRYING ME!
SO THAT'S IT! I OUGHT TO SPANK YOU! WHY, I HAD OFFERS FROM FOUR OTHER LUMBER OUTFITS AT A BETTER SALARY! AND I STAYED--JUST TO BE NEAR YOU!
POO!
WELL, I PASSED THEM UP! BUT NOW, I QUIT ANYWAY! SO YOU'RE THE BOSS' DAUGHTER, BECAUSE I HAVEN'T GOT A BOSS!
THAT'S WHAT I'VE WANTED TO DO ALL THIS TIME--AND NOW, IT'S OFF MY CHEST! DID IT MEAN ANYTHING TO YOU?
NO, I GUESS NOT! I SUPPOSE I JUST PICKED THE WRONG JOB--
NO--THE WRONG GIRL! I'M GOING TO MARRY STONEY!
WELL, THEN--LOTS OF LUCK TO YOU BOTH! I HOPE YOU'LL BE VERY HAPPY!
THANKS, HANK--
6

THE NEXT DAY WHEN I MET STONEY, I WALLOPED HIM. WITH THE SAME STATEMENT--

I-I'M SORRY, STONEY! IT'S HORTON I LOVE--I'M GOING TO MARRY HIM!

HORTON! BUT, LIZ-- HOW COULD YOU BE SO STUPID--

HOW DARE YOU! YOU'RE A FINE SPORT TO TAKE IT THIS WAY!

HOW YOU COULD CHOOSE HIM TO ME--IT'S RIDIC-ULOUS! I'VE LOST ALL RESPECT FOR YOU, LIZ!

HORTON FUMED WHEN I TOLD HIM--

WELL, THERE'S A LOT OF GIRLS WHO THINK I'M A GREAT CATCH! I CAN SEE I WASTED MY TIME ON YOU!

YOU'RE VERY VAIN, HORTON! BUT WON'T YOU WISH STONEY AND ME ANY HAPPINESS?

HORTON ONLY WISHED ME TO LEAVE HIM AND HIS TRAMPLED EGO ALONE. THAT NIGHT I HAD A CONFERENCE WITH DAD--

I SUPPOSE YOU'RE PRETTY SMUG--KNOWING IT WOULD BE HANK SMITH ALL ALONG!

I KNEW HANK WAS REALLY IN LOVE WITH YOU! I KNEW YOU WOULD FIND THAT OUT--SENSIBLY...ORDERLY... LIKE ME!

IT WASN'T EXACTLY PLAYING FAIR--BUT HOW IS A GIRL TO FIND OUT WHEN SHE ISN'T SURE! HAS HANK QUIT THE FIRM?

YEAH--HE'S CLEAR OUT OF THE TERRI-TORY BY NOW!

BUT I COULD CHANGE MY MIND--AND RE-ENLIST FOR THE DURATION!

HANK!

WON'T I EVER GET OUT OF YOUR WEB? I SUPPOSE YOU HAVE THE NAME PICKED OUT FOR YOUR GRAND-CHILD!

IT'LL BE A BOY! I'M GOING TO CALL HIM BRAD!

THAT'S HOW I FINALLY TRIPPED UP THE OLD PIRATE! TWO YEARS AFTER HANK AND I WERE MARRIED, WE HAD A LITTLE GIRL AND CALLED HER CLARISSA. I NEVER SAW DAD SO DUMB-FOUNDED!

THE END.

ONE OF THE BOYS WOULDN'T BE A GENTLEMAN. THE OTHER COULD HARDLY REMAIN A GENTLEMAN. THE REASON WAS... THAT THEY EACH WANTED TO BE THE...

LADY'S CHOICE!

POUR ME A CUP OF HOT JAVA, BEAUTIFUL!

COMING RIGHT UP--

TOMMY ROPER CAME TO OUR DINER SEEMINGLY FROM NOWHERE. HE DIDN'T LOOK OLDER THAN MYSELF--AND I WAS JUST SEVENTEEN. MY DAD HAD OWNED THE DINER AS LONG AS I COULD REMEMBER. AFTER MOTHER DIED, I HELPED HIM RUN IT. WHEN TOMMY CAME INTO THE DINER, HE LOOKED LIKE HE WAS JUST RUNNING--

IS COFFEE ALL YOU'RE GOING TO HAVE?

THAT'S WHAT I SAID!

YOU SOUND LIKE YOU'RE FROM THE EAST--THE BIG CITY!

YEAH--FROM THE BIG CITY ALLEYS! HOW ABOUT THE JAVA?

CONTINUED AFTER NEXT PAGE

I—I WAS ONLY TRYING TO BE FRIENDLY--

SO THE WHOLE WORLD IS FRIENDLY! SO WHAT'S IT TO ME?

DAD WAS WATCHING HIM SUSPICIOUSLY. IT WAS LATE-- AND TOMMY WAS OUR LAST CUSTOMER FOR THE DAY. TO BE FRANK, HE DID LOOK LIKE HE MIGHT BE UP TO MISCHIEF.

YOU GETTING READY TO LOCK UP FOR THE NIGHT?

YES-- AS SOON AS YOU'RE THROUGH WITH YOUR COFFEE!

THEN I SAW HIS HAND PLUNGE INTO THE POCKET OF HIS WORN LEATHER JACKET. I MOVED QUICKLY AND CLUTCHED HIS ARM--

DON'T DO IT! YOU'LL ONLY GET INTO TROUBLE! THE MONEY IN OUR CASH REGISTER WON'T GET YOU FAR ENOUGH FROM TROUBLE!

I—I NEED THE MONEY! A GUY CAN HITCH A RIDE--BUT HE'S GOT TO EAT, TOO! ALL I'VE GOT IS A DIME FOR COFFEE AND A GUN!

YOU DON'T NEED THAT-- NOT ANYWHERE... IF YOU GIVE PEOPLE A CHANCE TO HELP YOU!

SURE! EVERY- ONE'S JUST GOING TO FALL OVER ME!

MEET US HALFWAY-- THERE'S AT LEAST A GOOD MEAL IN IT FOR YOU!

HE LISTENED--THAT WAS GOOD. I DIDN'T KNOW WHAT HE WAS DOING WITH A GUN. BUT IF HE WAS A CRIMINAL, HE WOULDN'T HAVE LISTENED--

AFTER YOU FINISH THAT STEW, I'LL GET YOU A BOWL OF NICE, HOT VEGETABLE SOUP!

I'VE GOT ROOM FOR IT. YOU SURE SERVE GOOD FOOD HERE!

2

I STILL DON'T KNOW WHAT MADE ME DO IT, BUT WHEN DAD CAME OVER, THE WORDS JUST SPILLED OUT--SPONTANEOUSLY!

DAD, I STILL DON'T KNOW THIS YOUNG MAN'S NAME. BUT I DO KNOW HE'S DOWN ON HIS LUCK--WE CAN USE SOME HELP--

HEY, NOW-- WAIT A MINUTE!

WHAT'S THE MATTER-- DON'T YOU LIKE THE IDEA OF WORKING?

WELL, I WAS PLANNING TO GO ON TO THE COAST--BUT I GUESS A JOB HERE IS AS GOOD AS ANYPLACE ELSE!

THANKS! WHAT'S YOUR NAME, YOUNG FELLER?

TOMMY-- TOMMY ROPER!

WE GOT TOMMY A ROOM IN TOWN, AND HE REPAID OUR TRUST IN HIM BY HIS EFFICIENCY. POP WASN'T YOUNG ANY MORE--AND TOMMY MADE HIS WORK A LOT EASIER--

WELL, I'VE BEEN HERE TWO WEEKS NOW--AM I DOING OKAY?

TOMMY-- I--I'M REALLY PROUD OF YOU!

NO ONE'S EVER TOLD ME THAT BEFORE. SEEMS KINDA FUNNY-- HEARING THAT!

TOMMY, I--I KNOW I SHOULDN'T ASK-- BUT HAVE YOU STILL GOT--THE GUN?

NO. I GOT RID OF IT,-- FOR GOOD! I NEVER WANTED TO USE IT ANYWAY! I WAS KIDDING MYSELF ALONG-- I'M NOT TOUGH!

BUT YOU'VE GOT COURAGE, TOMMY! NOT EVERYONE CAN CHANGE HIS WAYS LIKE YOU HAVE!

TOMMY FINALLY TOLD ME ABOUT HIS TENEMENT NEIGHBORHOOD, THE ROUGH COMPANY--HOW HE BROKE HIS TIES WITH IT ALL WHEN HIS FATHER DIED. HOW HE BEGAN HITCHHIKING WEST TO GET A NEW START--

THAT'S ABOUT ALL OF IT, MARY! IT ISN'T PRETTY--

IT CERTAINLY ISN'T HOPELESS! YOU'VE PROVEN THAT!

3

TOMMY WAS GETTING ALONG FINE. HOW-EVER, MY STEADY DATE, ANDY CURTIS, DIDN'T SEEM TO THINK MUCH OF HIM--

HE LOOKS LIKE A HOODLUM TO ME! LIKE A MEMBER OF ONE OF THOSE BIG CITY STREET GANGS!

AS A MATTER OF FACT, HE WAS! BUT HE'S OUT OF THAT SORT OF THING, NOW!

AFTER ALL, ANDY, HE WASN'T RAISED IN YOUR TYPE OF EN-VIRONMENT! TOMMY'S FATHER WASN'T EXACTLY A MEMBER OF THE CHAMBER OF COMMERCE!

TOMMY--TOMMY--TOMMY! WHO WANTS TO TALK ABOUT *HIM* ALL EVENING?

WELL, HE'S MY PET PROJECT-- I THINK HE'S A FINE BOY!

YOU'RE *MY* PET PROJECT-- AND I THINK YOU'RE A PEACH OF A GAL!

ANDY TOOK ME DANCING. ALL OUR FRIENDS WERE THERE AND WE WERE HAVING A WON-DERFUL TIME. THEN, I WAS STARTLED BY THE APPEARANCE OF TOMMY IN THE CROWD--

WHY, TOMMY! WHAT ARE YOU DOING HERE?

GETTING ACQUAINTED WITH THE KIDS IN TOWN--I LIKE TO DANCE!

COME TO THINK OF IT--I'VE NEVER DANCED WITH YOU! MAY I?

ANDY DIDN'T SEEM TO CARE MUCH FOR THE IDEA. BUT I COULDN'T SEE WHY I SHOULD REFUSE TOMMY--

YOUR BOY FRIEND LOOKED A LITTLE PEEVED. MAYBE I SHOULDN'T HAVE--

OH, ANDY DOESN'T MIND. HE'S NOT LIKE THAT!

YOU TWO GOING STEADY?

YES--I SUPPOSE YOU MIGHT SAY THAT!

4

THAT ANY SORT OF RIVALRY WOULD DEVELOP BETWEEN ANDY AND TOMMY SEEMED LIKE A FAR-FETCHED POSSIBILITY TO ME, UNTIL ONE DAY--

ANDY, WHAT'S THIS I HEAR ABOUT YOUR KEEPING TOMMY OUT OF THE BICYCLE CLUB--

HE HASN'T GOT A BICYCLE! BESIDES, I DON'T LIKE HIM!

ANDY, I'M SURPRISED AT YOU! WHAT POSSIBLE EXCUSE CAN YOU HAVE FOR FEELING LIKE THAT?

I DON'T LIKE THE WAY HE LOOKS AT *YOU*... MY GIRL!

WHY, ANDY-- I-I NEVER HEARD YOU TALK *THAT* WAY!

DON'T YOU THINK I'M CAPABLE OF BEING JEALOUS?

WELL, YOU'VE ALWAYS BEEN SO STAID AND PROPER--LIKE YOUR DAD! I-I JUST NEVER PICTURED YOU BEING LIKE THIS--

THIS IS *DIFFERENT!* I DON'T WANT YOU TO ENCOURAGE TOMMY IN ANY WAY!

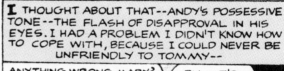

I THOUGHT ABOUT THAT--ANDY'S POSSESSIVE TONE--THE FLASH OF DISAPPROVAL IN HIS EYES. I HAD A PROBLEM I DIDN'T KNOW HOW TO COPE WITH, BECAUSE I COULD NEVER BE UNFRIENDLY TO TOMMY--

ANYTHING WRONG, MARY? YOU LOOK LIKE A GAL WITH SOMETHING ON HER MIND--

OH -- IT'S NOTHING, TOMMY!

DON'T GIVE ME *THAT!* YOU'RE UNHAPPY--IT ISN'T ANYTHING I'VE DONE, IS IT?

OF COURSE NOT, TOMMY! I COULDN'T THINK MORE HIGHLY OF ANY BOY!

TOMMY...

I CAN'T PUT INTO WORDS WHAT I FEEL ABOUT YOU, MARY! IF ANYBODY'S MADE YOU SAD, I'LL--

5

177

When a man makes it known in no uncertain terms that he loves you, and if he's as handsome as my Andy, there was only one thing to do—I married him as soon as possible!

THE END.

RESORT ROMEO

They flock around every pretty girl who's on vacation. In fact, they're not bad looking themselves. But no smart girl would rely on the word of a...

CAN'T YOU TAKE INDIFFERENCE FOR AN ANSWER?

COME NOW-- I CAN'T BE *THAT* MUCH OF A BORE!

I SUPPOSE THERE'S ONE AT EVERY RESORT. THE ONE THAT DOESN'T CHASE THE OTHER GIRLS -- BUT PICKS YOU AS HIS TARGET! THIS ONE'S NAME WAS MATT BROWN.

AND YOUR NAME--? IT'S REAL PRETTY, I'LL BET!

IT'S PRUNELLA-- *PRUNELLA POTTS!*

IT *COULDN'T* BE---

NO-- IT ISN'T BUT THEN, IT'S NONE OF YOUR BUSINESS WHAT IT IS!

YOU MUST BE A VERY LUCKY GIRL!

PLEASE DON'T GO ON! I'LL JUST TAKE IT FOR GRANTED WHAT YOU HAD TO SAY WAS WITTY AND CLEVER!

YOU'RE MUCH TOO KIND!

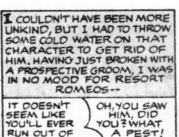

I COULDN'T HAVE BEEN MORE UNKIND, BUT I HAD TO THROW SOME COLD WATER ON THAT CHARACTER TO GET RID OF HIM. HAVING JUST BROKEN WITH A PROSPECTIVE GROOM, I WAS IN NO MOOD FOR RESORT ROMEOS--

IT DOESN'T SEEM LIKE YOU'LL EVER RUN OUT OF MALE ADMIRERS, RITA!

OH, YOU SAW HIM, DID YOU? WHAT A PEST!

THAT KIND CAN PESTER ME ALL DAY--HE'S REAL HANDSOME!

THEY USUALLY ARE! THEY STRUT ABOUT LIKE BRONZE APOLLOS--JUST OOZING WITH CHARM. ONLY THIS GIRL IS NOT IMPRESSED!

PAM CARTER STUDIED ME WITH THAT BIG SISTER LOOK OF HERS--SO FULL OF SYMPATHY AND CONCERN. I SUPPOSE THAT'S WHY SHE CAME WITH ME TO THE RESORT HOTEL--TO LOOK AFTER ME WHILE I GOT OVER JERRY BLAINE--

DON'T SAY THAT, RITA! WHY DON'T YOU GIVE HIM A CHANCE? IT MIGHT--

TAKE MY MIND OFF JERRY?--I DON'T EVEN REMEMBER HIM!

DON'T KID ME!--A GAL DOESN'T FORGET A BROKEN ENGAGEMENT OVERNIGHT! BUT THAT DOESN'T MEAN THAT JERRY CAN'T BE REPLACED! MAYBE NOT BY THIS BOY, BUT---

OH, PAM--ALL I WANT IS TO BE LEFT ALONE! BELIEVE ME, SELF RECRIMINATION HAS NOTHING TO DO WITH IT!

NOR DO I BLAME JERRY! IT WAS JUST A STAR-CROSSED ROMANCE THAT FORTUNATELY DIDN'T DEVELOP INTO AN UNHAPPY MARRIAGE! BUT IT'S NOTHING TO CELEBRATE ABOUT! I'M IN NO MOOD FOR GAYETY OR FLIRTATIONS!

THERE WAS A DANCE IN THE CASINO THAT NIGHT. BUT I DIDN'T DRESS FOR IT BECAUSE I DIDN'T ATTEND IT. I JUST SAT AND RELAXED IN THE COOL NIGHT, LISTENING TO THE MUSIC--

2

MAY I HELP?

OH, NO! IT CAN'T BE YOU!

ALL RIGHT--WHAT'S ON YOUR SCHEMING LITTLE MIND NOW? WHAT MAKES YOU THINK I'M IN NEED OF HELP?

I'M NOT UNFAMILIAR WITH THE SYMPTOMS OF BROODING-- SELF-PITY! YOU SHOULD BE AT THAT DANCE--WITH ME--WITH ANYBODY!

SO THAT'S YOUR NEW APPROACH, IS IT? WELL, I MUST SAY I'VE HEARD EVERYTHING NOW!

WELL, LET ME TELL YOU...

W-WHY, HE'S GONE!

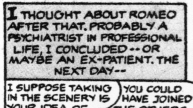

I THOUGHT ABOUT ROMEO AFTER THAT. PROBABLY A PSYCHIATRIST IN PROFESSIONAL LIFE, I CONCLUDED--OR MAYBE AN EX-PATIENT. THE NEXT DAY--

I SUPPOSE TAKING IN THE SCENERY IS YOUR IDEA OF SPENDING A PERFECT DAY!

YOU COULD HAVE JOINED THE OTHERS ON THE TENNIS COURT, PAM--

NOW, REALLY, RITA! WHEN ARE YOU--

LOOK! UP THERE!!

ACROSS THE FACE OF A HIGH CLIFF OPPOSITE OUR LEDGE, THE FIGURE OF A MAN MADE ITS WAY SLOWLY TOWARD THE SUMMIT!

I WOULDN'T EVEN TRY THAT IN AN AIRPLANE! I WONDER WHO HE IS?

3

SOMEHOW, EVEN AT THAT DISTANCE, THE CLIMBER SEEMED FAMILIAR TO ME. HOWEVER, PAM AND I WATCHED IN FASCINATION--IN APPREHENSION--

GOODNESS! I-I THINK HE SLIPPED!

NO--NO! HE'S FOUND HIS FOOTING AGAIN!

WELL, HE MADE IT TO THE SUMMIT, BUT I'M NOT GOING TO WAIT AROUND FOR THE DESCENT--IT'LL MAKE A WRECK OF ME!

NOW, THERE'S A SILLY WAY OF SPENDING A VACATION ---

WHEN WE GOT BACK TO THE HOTEL, PAM, ALREADY BORED TO TEARS, RAN OFF TO JOIN THE CROWD, AND A RATHER HANDSOME BOY NAMED FARLEY DIX SEEMED INCLINED TO JOIN ME--

SO YOUR WATCH-DOG HAS LEFT YOU ALONE! GOOD DEAL FOR ME, I'D SAY!

MY COMPANY DROVE HER AWAY--IT MIGHT DO THE SAME FOR YOU!

I'LL TAKE MY CHANCES THERE! YOU'RE SMILING! YOU RARELY DO THAT-- I KNOW--I'VE BEEN WATCHING YOU!

MY, WHAT BIG EYES YOU HAVE! I GUESS I'VE BEEN SOMEWHAT OF A GLOOMY GUSSIE AT THAT!

THEN THE ANSWER IS LAUGHS! A YARD FULL OF YOKS, HONEY, I'M AN EXPERT IN THAT DEPARTMENT!

THERE'S A FELLOW WHO MUST GET HIS THRILLS FROM DANGEROUS LIVING-- I SAW HIM CLIMBING LOOKOUT CLIFF!

WHO? MATT BROWN? HE'S AN AMAZING GUY, ALL RIGHT-- BUT I DOUBT IF HE'D TRY CLIMBING CLIFFS!

I'M SURE IT WAS HE I SAW-- HE'S EVEN DRESSED FOR IT!

BUT IT COULDN'T HAVE BEEN MATT, HONEY! HE GETS AROUND FINE FOR A BLIND MAN--BUT HE'D BE FOOLHARDY TO TRY ANY CLIMBING!

BLIND... MAN?

4

YOU CAN IMAGINE HOW SHOCKED I WAS TO LEARN THIS ABOUT ROMEO! IT LEFT ME OFF BALANCE -- IN A MAZE OF NEW EMOTIONS. I FOUND MYSELF THINKING LESS OF MY OWN PROBLEMS -- AND MORE OF ROMEO --

HEY! ARE YOU ACTUALLY GOING TO THE CASINO TONIGHT?

A GAL CAN'T WASTE HER YOUNG LIFE JUST FRETTING, NOW CAN SHE?

LISTEN TO YOU! SAY -- WHAT GOT YOU OUT OF THE DOLDRUMS? DON'T TELL ME -- I'LL BET IT'S A MAN!

MUST IT ALWAYS BE A **MAN?** I'M JUST TIRED OF READING MAGAZINES, THAT'S ALL!

I DID HAVE FUN AT THE DANCE. IT SEEMED THAT LIFE HAD BEGUN MOVING AGAIN. I TRIED TO FIND THE ONE WHO WAS RESPONSIBLE FOR IT--

YOU DANCE LIKE A DREAM, RITA!

THANK YOU. I THOUGHT I'D FORGOTTEN HOW!

BELIEVE IT OR NOT, THERE'S A PHONE CALL FOR YOU, DIX!

I SUPPOSE YOU ARRANGED IT!

MY HEART SKIPPED A BEAT-- IT WAS ROMEO! HOW HE COULD PICK US OUT FROM THE CROWD SEEMED UNCANNY TO ME!

AND DID **YOU** ARRANGE THIS LITTLE COUP?

I PROBABLY WOULD HAVE IF THE CALL HADN'T COME IN. I'VE WANTED TO DANCE WITH YOU!

HOW DO **YOU** KNOW WHO I AM?

SO YOU KNOW ABOUT ME! THAT COULD MEAN THAT YOU INQUIRED -- DID YOU?

IN A WAY -- YES! YOU'VE BEEN SUCH A PEST -- A GIRL HAS TO KNOW SOMETHING ABOUT THE MAN SHE MIGHT HAVE TO HAUL INTO COURT!

THE PATIO WILL DO -- IT'S VERY LOVELY OUT THERE NOW!

CONTINUED AFTER NEXT PAGE

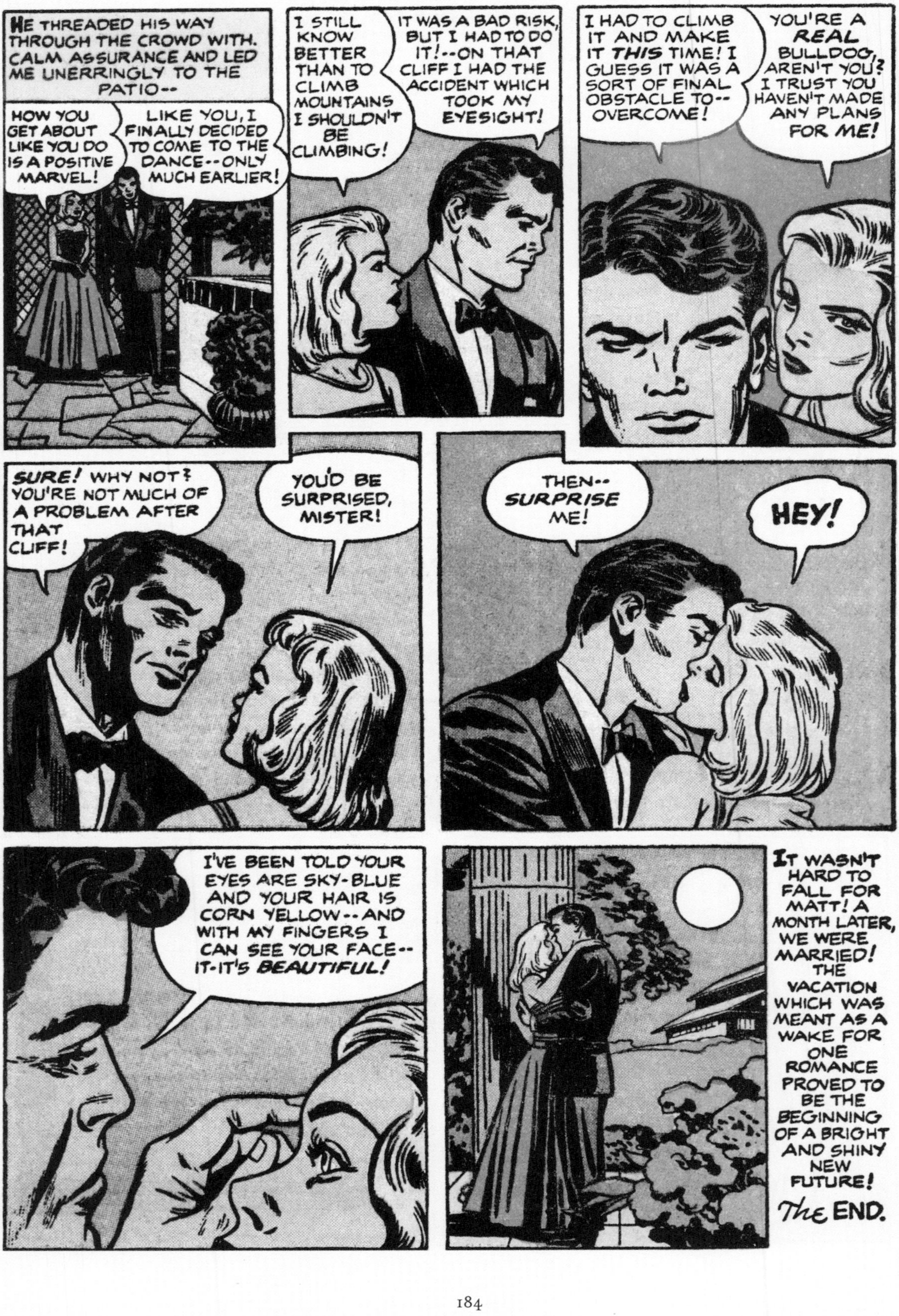

HE THREADED HIS WAY THROUGH THE CROWD WITH. CALM ASSURANCE AND LED ME UNERRINGLY TO THE PATIO--
HOW YOU GET ABOUT LIKE YOU DO IS A POSITIVE MARVEL!
LIKE YOU, I FINALLY DECIDED TO COME TO THE DANCE--ONLY MUCH EARLIER!
I STILL KNOW BETTER THAN TO CLIMB MOUNTAINS I SHOULDN'T BE CLIMBING!
IT WAS A BAD RISK, BUT I HAD TO DO IT!--ON THAT CLIFF I HAD THE ACCIDENT WHICH TOOK MY EYESIGHT!
I HAD TO CLIMB IT AND MAKE IT THIS TIME! I GUESS IT WAS A SORT OF FINAL OBSTACLE TO--OVERCOME!
YOU'RE A REAL BULLDOG, AREN'T YOU? I TRUST YOU HAVEN'T MADE ANY PLANS FOR ME!
SURE! WHY NOT? YOU'RE NOT MUCH OF A PROBLEM AFTER THAT CLIFF!
YOU'D BE SURPRISED, MISTER!
THEN--SURPRISE ME!
HEY!
I'VE BEEN TOLD YOUR EYES ARE SKY-BLUE AND YOUR HAIR IS CORN YELLOW--AND WITH MY FINGERS I CAN SEE YOUR FACE--IT-IT'S BEAUTIFUL!
IT WASN'T HARD TO FALL FOR MATT! A MONTH LATER, WE WERE MARRIED! THE VACATION WHICH WAS MEANT AS A WAKE FOR ONE ROMANCE PROVED TO BE THE BEGINNING OF A BRIGHT AND SHINY NEW FUTURE!
The END.

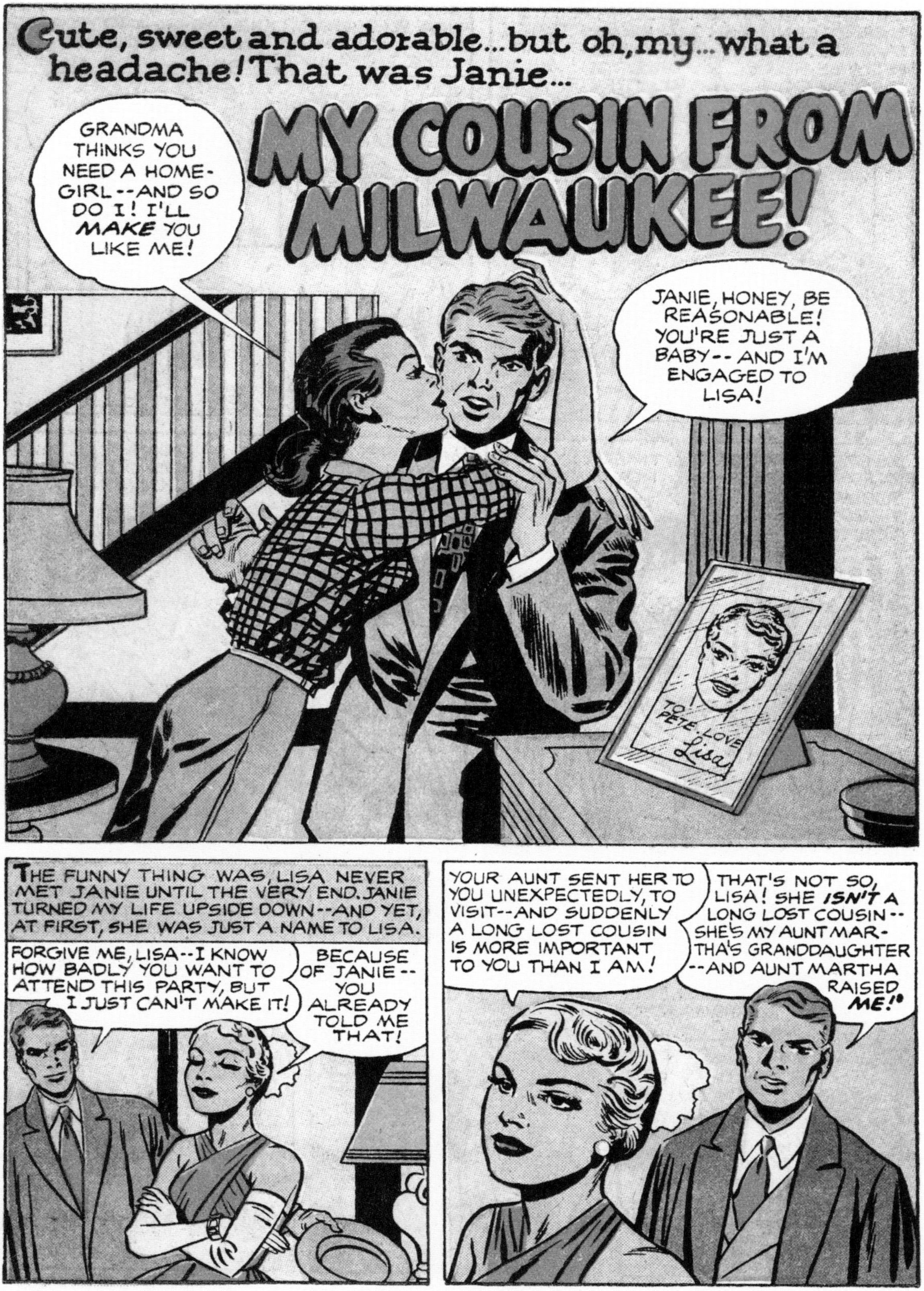

Cute, sweet and adorable...but oh, my...what a headache! That was Janie...
MY COUSIN FROM MILWAUKEE!
GRANDMA THINKS YOU NEED A HOME-GIRL--AND SO DO I! I'LL MAKE YOU LIKE ME!
JANIE, HONEY, BE REASONABLE! YOU'RE JUST A BABY--AND I'M ENGAGED TO LISA!
TO PETE LOVE Lisa
THE FUNNY THING WAS, LISA NEVER MET JANIE UNTIL THE VERY END. JANIE TURNED MY LIFE UPSIDE DOWN--AND YET, AT FIRST, SHE WAS JUST A NAME TO LISA.
FORGIVE ME, LISA--I KNOW HOW BADLY YOU WANT TO ATTEND THIS PARTY, BUT I JUST CAN'T MAKE IT!
BECAUSE OF JANIE--YOU ALREADY TOLD ME THAT!
YOUR AUNT SENT HER TO YOU UNEXPECTEDLY, TO VISIT--AND SUDDENLY A LONG LOST COUSIN IS MORE IMPORTANT TO YOU THAN I AM!
THAT'S NOT SO, LISA! SHE ISN'T A LONG LOST COUSIN--SHE'S MY AUNT MARTHA'S GRANDDAUGHTER--AND AUNT MARTHA RAISED ME!

JANIE'S JUST A *KID!* I CAN'T SEND HER PACKING. SHE'LL ONLY BE HERE TWO WEEKS!

SO FOR TWO WEEKS I SIT HERE AND WAIT FOR YOU! ALL RIGHT, PETER, I'LL SHARE YOU-- BUT ONLY FOR *TWO WEEKS*, REMEMBER!

THE WAY IT BEGAN-- LISA WASN'T HAPPY. LISA WAS STRICTLY NEW YORK AND I CAME FROM MILWAUKEE. SO SHE COULDN'T FEEL LIKE I DID. LATER--

HOW IS SHE, MRS. WALSH? IT'S A GOOD THING I'VE GOT A HOUSEKEEPER-- AT LEAST JANIE'LL HAVE A CHAPERONE!

BUT MRS. WALSH CAN'T SHOW ME THE TOWN, COUSIN PETER!

JANIE! I THOUGHT YOU'D BE ASLEEP! YOU MUST BE TIRED AFTER YOUR TRIP--

TIRED? I'M NOT *TIRED!*

I-I COME ALL THIS WAY, AND YOU *IGNORE* ME! YOU DON'T WANT TO SHOW ME THE SIGHTS-- YOU DON'T WANT ME HERE!

OKAY-- I'LL TAKE YOU OUT-- ONLY DON'T *CRY!*

AND SO, OFF WE WENT. LISA SAT HOME ALONE, WHILE I WAS ON THE TOWN WITH JANIE.

I'LL BE RIGHT BACK, JANIE-- GOTTA MAKE A PHONE CALL!

TO YOUR GIRL-- LISA CHASE? THE ONE YOU WROTE GRANDMA ABOUT?

THAT'S RIGHT-- I WON'T BE A MINUTE!

NO, COUSIN PETER! PLEASE DON'T LEAVE ME ALONE! THIS IS ALL SO-- NEW TO ME--

SO I DIDN'T CALL LISA-- SHE CALLED ME A FEW DAYS LATER. I WAS SITTING BY THE PHONE, NOT FEELING GOOD, WHEN JANIE CAME DOWN.

WRONG? NO-- I JUST HAD A PHONE CALL, BUT THERE'S NOTHING WRONG!

GOOD! THEN WE CAN GO, CAN'T WE? YOU PROMISED TO TAKE ME TO CONEY ISLAND TODAY, DIDN'T YOU?

CONTINUED AFTER NEXT PAGE

I MADE A DOZEN DATES WITH LISA AND BROKE THEM ALL! NO WONDER SHE WAS ANGRY. BUT DESPITE MY QUALMS, I WAS HAVING A GOOD TIME--

YOU GOT A BRASS RING--*ATTA GIRL!*

GOLLY! THIS IS FUN!

IT *WAS* FUN, RUNNING ABOUT WITH JANIE, BUT IT COULDN'T LAST. EVENTUALLY, I BROKE AWAY AND SAW LISA. AND WHEN I GOT HOME, THE COMPLICATIONS STARTED--

JANIE! WHAT ON EARTH ARE YOU CRYING ABOUT?

BECAUSE OF *HER!* YOU'VE SEEN HER, HAVEN'T YOU? YOU'RE IN *LOVE* WITH HER!

OF COURSE I AM! WHY, JANIE, YOU AREN'T *JEALOUS*, ARE YOU? --W-WHY, THAT'S RIDICULOUS!

I HATE HER! SHE'LL *NEVER* MAKE A GOOD WIFE FOR SOMEONE FROM MILWAUKEE!

SO AUNT MARTHA TOLD YOU THAT! BUT JANIE, I'M DIFFERENT, NOW-- LISA IS GOOD FOR ME--SHE KNOWS ALL THE RIGHT PEOPLE--

I DON'T CARE! GRANDMA SAYS YOU NEED A DIFFERENT KIND OF GIRL, SOMEONE LIKE *ME!*

YOU? JANIE, HONEY, YOU DON'T KNOW WHAT YOU'RE SAYING! Y-YOU'RE JUST A BABY--W-WHY NOT JUST RELAX--AND ENJOY YOUR STAY!

OH, YOU--YOU *MIXED-UP MALE!* YOU DON'T UNDERSTAND!

Y-YOU DON'T WANT TO UNDERSTAND! YOU'RE *HATEFUL!*

MISTER HARRIS! WHAT HAVE YOU BEEN SAYING TO THIS POOR CHILD?

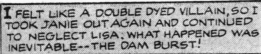

I FELT LIKE A DOUBLE DYED VILLAIN, SO I TOOK JANIE OUT AGAIN AND CONTINUED TO NEGLECT LISA. WHAT HAPPENED WAS INEVITABLE--THE DAM BURST!

LISA! YOU'RE JOKING! Y-YOU WOULDN'T BREAK OUR ENGAGEMENT!

WOULDN'T I? I'VE SEEN YOU TWICE IN ALMOST TWO WEEKS! I'M BEGINNING TO WONDER ABOUT THIS COUNTRY COUSIN OF YOURS!

TELL ME, PETER--JUST HOW OLD IS SHE? YOU HAVE NEVER BEEN VERY EXPLICIT ABOUT THAT!

I-I DON'T REALLY KNOW--BUT SHE'S ONLY A BABY! LISA--WHAT ON EARTH ARE YOU HINTING AT--

LISA--YOU DON'T MEAN TO SAY I'M IN LOVE WITH--

I DON'T KNOW, PETER--BUT I INTEND TO FIND OUT!--I WANT TO MEET THIS JANIE, SO I'LL BE AT YOUR PLACE AT EIGHT TONIGHT!

WELL, OKAY--

YOU CAN KEEP THE RING UNTIL THEN! AFTERWARD, WE'LL SEE--

LISA WAS JEALOUS--JANIE WAS JEALOUS--AND I WAS IN THE MIDDLE! BUT WHEN I TOLD JANIE, SHE DIDN'T SEEM SURPRISED--

ALL RIGHT, COUSIN PETER--I'LL BE NICE TO HER, I PROMISE!

YOU'RE A SWEET KID! NOW RUN ALONG AND GET READY!

I'LL BE EXTRA SPECIAL NICE-- JUST FOR YOU!

4

188

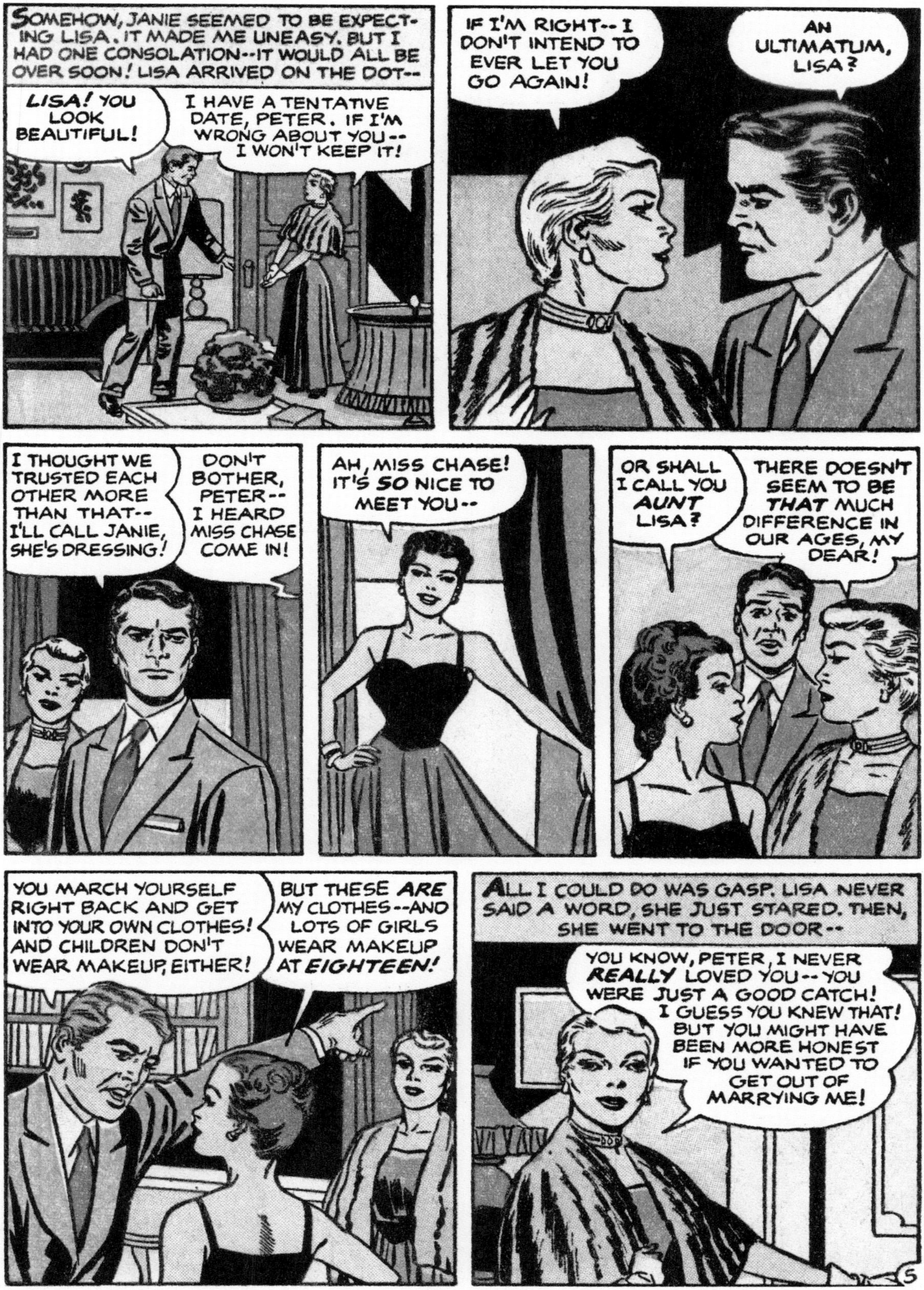
SOMEHOW, JANIE SEEMED TO BE EXPECTING LISA. IT MADE ME UNEASY. BUT I HAD ONE CONSOLATION--IT WOULD ALL BE OVER SOON! LISA ARRIVED ON THE DOT--
LISA! YOU LOOK BEAUTIFUL!
I HAVE A TENTATIVE DATE, PETER. IF I'M WRONG ABOUT YOU -- I WON'T KEEP IT!
IF I'M RIGHT-- I DON'T INTEND TO EVER LET YOU GO AGAIN!
AN ULTIMATUM, LISA?
I THOUGHT WE TRUSTED EACH OTHER MORE THAN THAT-- I'LL CALL JANIE, SHE'S DRESSING!
DON'T BOTHER, PETER-- I HEARD MISS CHASE COME IN!
AH, MISS CHASE! IT'S SO NICE TO MEET YOU--
OR SHALL I CALL YOU AUNT LISA?
THERE DOESN'T SEEM TO BE THAT MUCH DIFFERENCE IN OUR AGES, MY DEAR!
YOU MARCH YOURSELF RIGHT BACK AND GET INTO YOUR OWN CLOTHES! AND CHILDREN DON'T WEAR MAKEUP, EITHER!
BUT THESE ARE MY CLOTHES--AND LOTS OF GIRLS WEAR MAKEUP AT EIGHTEEN!
ALL I COULD DO WAS GASP. LISA NEVER SAID A WORD, SHE JUST STARED. THEN, SHE WENT TO THE DOOR--
YOU KNOW, PETER, I NEVER REALLY LOVED YOU-- YOU WERE JUST A GOOD CATCH! I GUESS YOU KNEW THAT! BUT YOU MIGHT HAVE BEEN MORE HONEST IF YOU WANTED TO GET OUT OF MARRYING ME!
5

After she slammed the door behind her, I dropped into a chair as if someone had clubbed me--

Peter, oh, Peter--I never dremed you'd take it like this! we--i only wanted to help you--

I know I had no right to do what I did! I can see that now! I'll go after Lisa--I'll explain--

You'll do no such thing! You heard her-- she never loved me! you and aunt martha were right!

Cousin Peter--

And now we'll see if you were right about the kind of girl I really need!

I shouldn't have let you kiss me--not until you said the words, first!

Okay, I'll say then

I love you, Janie! I realize now how easy it is to say those words to you! I want you to marry me!

Oh, cousin Peter--

Well--!

THE END.

ONE BY ONE MY FRIENDS MARRIED, WHILE I WAITED FOR TED TO GET HIS LAW DEGREE! I DIDN'T MIND, FOR I WAS TED'S GIRL--HEART AND SOUL! HOW COULD I GIVE HIM UP TO ANOTHER WOMAN WHEN I HAD A WEAPON-- MY WHEEL CHAIR -- WITH WHICH TO FIGHT FOR--

The LOVE I LOST!

JOAN, DARLING, THIS IS DOCTOR PETER HARMON, THE MAN WHO IS GOING TO MAKE YOU WELL AGAIN, MEND YOUR LEGS!

AND THEN TED WILL BE FREE OF ME! YES, YOU'LL MEND MY LEGS AND BREAK MY HEART-- MISTER HARMON!

TED AND I WERE ON A SKI DATE, WHEN HE FIRST MET LORNA LEWIS. MY FRIENDS WERE SHOCKED AS I, BY THE SPELL SHE SEEMED TO CAST OVER HIM...

JOAN! LET'S GO! HOW CAN YOU STAND HERE WATCHING TED FLIRTING WITH HER LIKE THAT!

STOP TALKING THAT WAY, EVE! TED LOVES ME! THIS IS JUST A--A SILLY INTERLUDE!

BUT ALONE IN MY ROOM AT THE SKI-LODGE I FOUGHT A TREMBLING FEAR!

HE HASN'T SPENT A MOMENT WITH ME SINCE THAT GIRL ARRIVED! OH, TED, TED! I--I COULDN'T LIVE WITHOUT YOU! OH, TED, DON'T HURT ME THIS WAY!

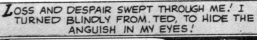

MY PRAYER SEEMED ANSWERED! THAT AFTER-NOON TED ASKED ME TO GO UP TO CHRISTIANA HILL WITH HIM! THEN...

JOAN, I WON'T AVOID THIS BY DRAGGING IT OUT! I'VE FALLEN IN LOVE WITH LORNA LEWIS! I-I'M SORRY, JOAN!

TED! NO!

LOSS AND DESPAIR SWEPT THROUGH ME! I TURNED BLINDLY FROM TED, TO HIDE THE ANGUISH IN MY EYES!

HE--HE MEANS IT! HE NEVER SOUNDED SO SURE OF ANYTHING! I CAN'T STAY HERE! I CAN'T FACE IT!

JOAN, WAIT! YOU LITTLE FOOL! YOU DON'T KNOW THIS SLOPE! YOU'LL INJURE YOURSELF!

HIS WORDS ECHOED, I SPUN, ENDING IN A SCREAMING CRASH! THEN THE SENSE OF LYING IN A BED OF ICE, OF PAIN...

HOURS LATER, THE PAIN WAS STILL THERE, BUT THE BED WAS WARM AND SMOOTH BENEATH MY INJURED BODY! MY EYES OPENED...

EASY, DARLING! YOU'RE IN THE HOSPITAL! DON'T BE FRIGHTENED!

TED...

IT'S YOU I LOVE! I SWEAR TO YOU, DARLING! WHEN I SAW YOU LYING THERE I KNEW HOW MUCH I LOVED YOU! THE OTHER WAS JUST INFATUATION, JOAN!

M-MY DARLING TED! I-I HAVE YOU BACK!

ONLY TED'S RENEWED LOVE COULD HAVE HELPED ME BEAR THE DOCTOR'S VERDICT!

PARALYSIS OF BOTH LEGS? IS IT PERMANENT, DOCTOR SAMSON?

TIME WILL TELL! AND CHEERFUL SPIRITS WILL HELP, JOAN! NO TEARS NOW... SOME FRIENDS ARE OUTSIDE WAITING TO HELP YOU!

JOAN, YOU POOR BABY! THEY WOULDN'T LET US VISIT UNTIL NOW!

GUESS I'LL GO SWEET! LOOKS LIKE A HEN PARTY! SEE YOU TONIGHT AFTER LAW CLASS!

I POURED OUT MY HEART TO EVE AND SALLY! DID TED LOVE ME -- OR PITY ME?

HE SAYS NOW THAT IT WAS JUST INFATUATION WITH LORNA, BUT--

LORNA LEWIS IS A LITTLE FLIRT, JOAN, AND SHE'D HAVE RUINED TED'S CAREER! YOU AND TED BELONG TOGETHER!

WHY THE LITTLE SNIP WAS WAITING FOR HIM JUST NOW OUT IN THE CORRIDOR -- TRYING TO TAKE HIM AWAY WHILE YOU LIE HELPLESS!

WE MADE SURE SHE DIDN'T GET TO TED! TOLD HER WHAT WE THOUGHT OF HER, TILL SHE TURNED AND RAN!

TED'S BETTER OFF WITHOUT HER KIND! ANYWAY, WHEN YOU LOVE A MAN, YOU HOLD ON TO HIM ANY WAY YOU CAN!

"ANY WAY YOU CAN"! YOU'RE RIGHT! I- I'LL REMEMBER!

THAT NIGHT I SAW TED'S QUIET EYES AND SOMETHING WRENCHED THROUGH ME! SHOULD I TELL HIM OF LORNA'S VISIT? NO -- NO I COULDN'T!

SOMETHING BOTHERING YOU, DARLING?

IT'S JUST THAT-- THAT I COULDN'T BEAR IT IF YOU FELT TIED DOWN TO ME, TED!

CONTINUED AFTER NEXT PAGE

IT WAS TED WHO FOUND AND CONTACTED A DOCTOR PETER HARMON IN NEW YORK WHO FELT CONFIDENT HE COULD HELP ME! WEEKS LATER, I WAS IN DOCTOR HARMON'S CARE...

OH, DOCTOR HARMON DID YOU SEE MY CHARTS TODAY?

INDEED I DID! AND THE THERAPIST TELLS ME YOU TOOK THE DAYS OF TREATMENT LIKE A TROOPER! ROUGH WAS IT?

I DIDN'T HAVE TO WORRY ABOUT TED'S LETTERS, THOSE FIRST WEEKS IN THE NEW YORK HOSPITAL!

I'M SO HAPPY OVER THIS LETTER FROM TED-- I-I DON'T EVEN MIND THE PAIN!

THE PAIN MEANS YOU'RE GETTING WELL, JOAN! I SUPPOSE YOU'RE ANXIOUS TO LEAVE...

AND THEN, CAME THE DAY WHEN PETER HARMON SAID...

THIS IS YOUR DEBUT, JOAN! YOU'RE GOING TO **WALK** THIS MORNING!

WALK! BUT I-I CAN'T! PETER **DON'T** MAKE ME!

I MADE IT! I DID IT! STRAIGHT INTO PETER'S WAITING ARMS, WHERE I WEPT WITH JOY! I WAS CURED!

OH, PETER-- PETER--I--

CRY IT OUT, JOAN! IN A FEW DAYS I'LL SEND YOU HOME AND YOU WON'T HAVE TO CRY ANYMORE!

A WEEK LATER...

LET ME KNOW HOW YOU PROGRESS, JOAN! I-I'LL BE CONCERNED ABOUT YOU!

GOODBYE, PETER... YOU'VE BEEN WONDERFUL TO ME!

YES PETER HAD BEEN WONDERFUL-- AND I KNEW QUITE WELL HIS INTEREST WAS MORE THAN CLINICAL... BUT THE TRAIN SURGED ON TOWARD THE FUTURE--AND TED!

HOME--TO TED! I'M SURE I'LL FEEL RIGHT WHEN HE TAKES ME IN HIS ARMS AGAIN! OH, WHY DO I FEEL SO SAD-- SO SAD TO LEAVE PETER--

4

WHEN I ARRIVED AT TED'S HOUSE I HEARD LORNA READING A LOVE LETTER MEANT FOR ME!

THANKS, LORNA SWEET! IT'S HARD TO WRITE LOVE LETTERS TO ONE GIRL WHEN MY HEART BELONGS TO ANOTHER!

IT'S THE GAMBLE OF OUR LIVES, TED! IF THESE LETTERS MAKE JOAN WELL, WE'RE FREE TO LOVE AGAIN! IF NOT-- WE'LL SEE TO IT THAT SHE NEVER KNOWS!

SHAME FILLED ME, THESE TWO PEOPLE WOULD SACRIFICE THEIR LOVE FOR MY SAKE! I RUSHED INTO THE ROOM-- INTO TED'S ARMS...

OH, TED! TED, HOW SELFISH I'VE BEEN!

JOAN! YOU'RE WALKING AGAIN! OH, THANK HEAVEN!

OH!--YOU--YOU HEARD US, JOAN?

YES! AND I WISH YOU BOTH HAPPINESS! I THINK YOU'RE THE MOST WONDERFUL PEOPLE IN THE WORLD AND I JUST WANT ONE MORE FAVOR! TO USE YOUR PHONE-- LONG DISTANCE!

5

YES, OPERATOR! HELLO! PETER? I-I'M HOME! OH, PETER, CAN YOU COME AND GET ME AGAIN-- FOR KEEPS?

THE SELFISH DREAM OF A BITTER YOUNG GIRL WHO'D THOUGHT OF USING HER ILLNESS AS WEAPON TO HOLD A MAN, VANISHED IN THE LIGHT OF A NEWBORN MATURITY...

The End

WHY I MADE THIS BOOK
by Michel Gagné

I've been an avid fan of Jack Kirby since I discovered his work at the age of 7. Kirby took me to the stars, introduced me to powerful beings, and ignited my young imagination.

A few years ago, while reading a book on the history of comics, I realized that there was an entire facet of Kirby's work that I hadn't even seen: romance. Indeed, Kirby and his partner at the time, Joe Simon, had set the comics world on fire in the late 1940s with the creation of a new genre that resulted in some of the best-selling comics of all time.

I became curious and wanted to read some of these stories. I started searching on the Internet, and at comic stores and bookstores, in the hope of finding a book compiling some of this obscure work. To my surprise, there was very little available. The only book

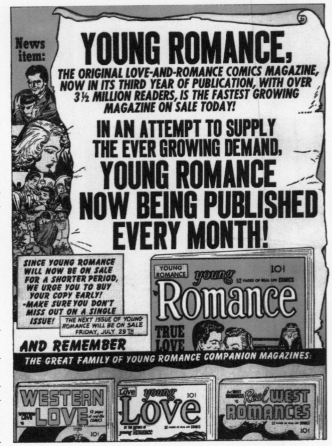

I found was the long-out-of-print *Real Love: The Best of the Simon and Kirby Romance Comics* by Richard Howell: a volume featuring black-and-white reprints of thirteen stories, including nine by Simon and Kirby. The featured Simon and Kirby stories were excellent, but they only spanned a three-year period (1949-1951), while the team's romance output lasted 12. Granted, 1949 to 1951 was a potent period in terms of mature storytelling and lavish artwork, but my inquisitive mind wanted a general overview of the entire output, not a mere snippet. My search to find sample reprints from the post-Code era (1954-1959) turned up nothing. That's when I started looking for the original comic: certainly not an easy task.

Romance comics were bought predominantly by girls and women who, contrary to their male counterparts, did not have a tendency to collect them. The comics were read and discarded. Even though the print runs were some of the highest in the history of American comics, very few copies survived and most of the ones that did are in pitiful shape. I quickly realized that if someone didn't make an effort to preserve this material, most of it would vanish into oblivion. That's

when it hit me! Perhaps I should be the one to start the ball rolling. I had been itching to do a comic book preservation project for a while and this would be the perfect opportunity. Thus, I made the decision to restore, compile, and edit a book featuring an overview of the entire span (1947-1959) of Simon and Kirby's romance comics.

In my effort to put this volume together, I hunted for the original comics on the Internet, at conventions, and reached out to collectors. After two years of treasure hunting, I managed to gather a wealth of material.

My next task was to decide how to present the work, which stories to include and how much restoration I should do (see "About the Restoration"). In selecting the 21 stories featured in this book, I purposely avoided any which had already been presented in Howell's book. I also didn't include any of the stories from *Young Romance* #1, as DC Comics reprinted that particular comic in its entirety in 2000. I narrowed my

choice to the stories that I found most appealing and exciting. I believe the chosen material is a good representation of the three major periods:

1947-48: The Birth of a Genre
1949-53: The Big Boom
1954-59: The Post-Code Era

To complete the overview, I included two examples of the Western sub-genre, a selection of covers, and never-before-reprinted post-Code stories, including one of the last stories created by the team.

Putting this book together has been a labor of love. I hope you enjoy it!

SIMON AND KIRBY'S ROMANCE COMICS:
A HISTORICAL OVERVIEW

by Michel Gagné

In the 1940s, Joe Simon and Jack Kirby were the most established creative team in the comic book industry, with an unparalleled résumé that included notable hits such as *Captain America*, *Boy Commandos*, and *Newsboy Legion*. The team's artistic ability and commercial success earned them great respect within the profession.

By the late 1940s, the superhero genre was in decline. The time was ripe for Simon and Kirby to try out new concepts. In 1947, they produced *My Date* #1. The bi-monthly series, which ran four issues, featured humorous teen love stories, a genre originally popularized by Archie Comics. *My Date* not only managed to gather a strong following, it also helped steer the creative team in a new direction. Simon and Kirby quickly followed *My Date* with a more "grown-up" variation of the idea. They brought their concept to Mike Epstein and Ted Blier, owners of Crestwood Publications, and *Young Romance* was given the go ahead.

Young Romance #1, using the Prize Comics imprint, hit the stands in the summer of 1947, with a September cover date. A large orange banner across the cover notified potential customers that *Young Romance* was "designed for the more adult readers of comics." In a bold move, Simon and Kirby had successfully stretched the medium's appeal by creating mature stories with adult concerns. It was unlike anything comic book readers had seen before.

Free of competition, *Young Romance* #1 tapped into a huge audience, including a sizable chunk that were not typical comic book buyers. Over 92 percent of the first printing sold (when 60 percent was considered good), and print runs were set to a million copies. With a newly negotiated contract that earned them a 50 percent share of the profits, Simon and Kirby were generously compensated. In trademark style, Simon and Kirby had produced another comic book hit and introduced America to the most popular genre of post-World War II comic books: romance.

Young Romance proved once again that Simon and Kirby were masters at marketing comic books. The covers often displayed characters in awkward situations that made readers eager to find out more about the outcome. Behind those tantalizing covers were carefully crafted stories told with

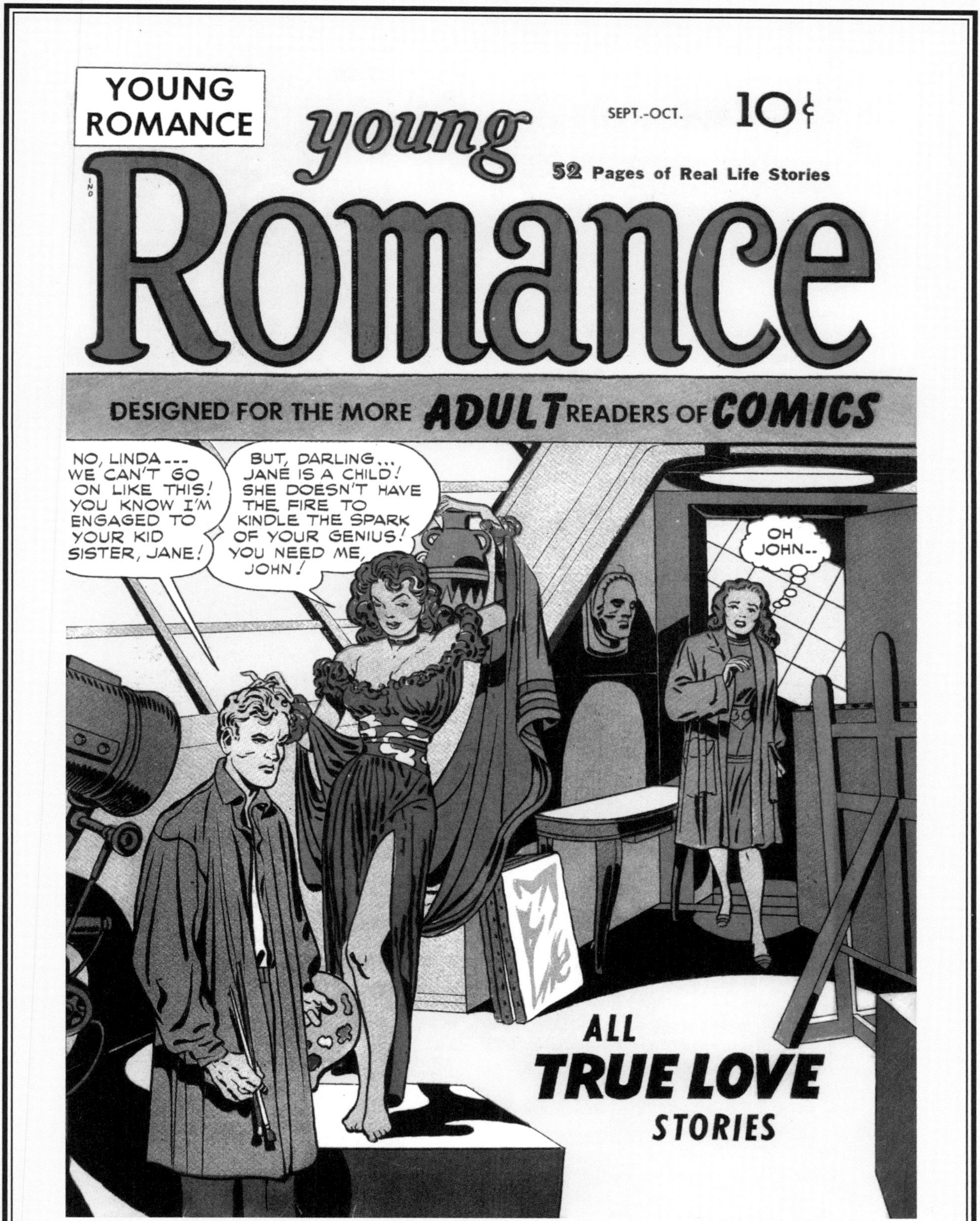
YOUNG ROMANCE
young Romance
SEPT.-OCT.
10¢
52 Pages of Real Life Stories
DESIGNED FOR THE MORE ADULT READERS OF COMICS
NO, LINDA--- WE CAN'T GO ON LIKE THIS! YOU KNOW I'M ENGAGED TO YOUR KID SISTER, JANE!
BUT, DARLING... JANE IS A CHILD! SHE DOESN'T HAVE THE FIRE TO KINDLE THE SPARK OF YOUR GENIUS! YOU NEED ME, JOHN!
OH JOHN--
ALL TRUE LOVE STORIES

personal aplomb and melodramatic panache. All of this was grounded in a level of realism that was seldom seen in comics at the time. The 1947 audience was spellbound.

Part of the team's appeal, up to that point, had been their ability to convey high-octane action through dynamic posing, exciting compositions, and larger-than-life characters. For Simon and Kirby, the romance comics were quite a change of pace.

"Occasionally we might show a car chase, or somebody getting slapped. Occasionally, we might have a couple of guys get into a scrap over a girl," Kirby commented, "but, basically there was no action — most of the story was in the acting."

While *Young Romance* was creating a buzz within the industry, Simon and Kirby's crime comics, *Headline Comics* and *Justice Traps the Guilty*, were also selling like hot cakes. The combined profit from these and other successful Crestwood books gave Simon and Kirby the best years they ever enjoyed as a team. 1947 was also one of Kirby's most prolific years of publication. In September alone, Kirby saw 142 pages and five covers published, a record he would not match until the 1960s. In response to this, Crestwood conceded to nearly every request Simon and Kirby made. Epstein and Bleier even freed up floor space so that the team could set up their own shop with their own artists. By 1948, Crestwood Publications was busier than ever, and the Prize Comics logo had virtually become a Simon and Kirby trademark.

Spurred on by the success of *Young Romance*, Simon and Kirby introduced new titles: *Young Love* (February 1949), *Real Western Romances* (April 1949), and *Western Love* (July 1949), and combined sales exceeded two million copies per month. By the end of 1949, the Simon and Kirby signature appeared exclusively on Crestwood's Prize titles.

As Richard Howell noted in his 1998 introduction to *Real Love: The Best of Simon and Kirby's Romance Comics*, "Simon and Kirby approached their romance comics with the same attitude they brought to superhero, adventure, humor and crime comics: Make them exciting! Electric compositions, active posing, and raw expressive inking were at a high point. Those qualities, coupled with the team's command of comics storytelling and the touching and incisive stories they had to tell, enabled them to create some of the most dramatic, affecting comic stories ever produced."

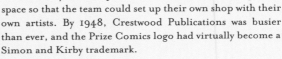

By 1949, dozens of publishers had entered the newly created genre with romances of their own. As many as 148 different romance books, published by 26 different imprints, were filling up the racks during the first half of 1950.

From 1948 to 1954, comic readership had reached unprecedented levels, and for the first time, thanks to the advent of romance comics, adult women were a big part of the equation. This period saw comic book sales approaching an impressive 60 million issues per month. In 1952, over 500 original romance comic books were published in America, accounting for more than a quarter of the entire market. Despite the heavy competition, *Young Romance* remained at the top of the charts, thanks to Simon and Kirby's vision and to their expert team of writers and artists. Up until the crippling Comics Code of 1954, Simon and Kirby produced romance stories that were adult in content, erotically charged, sometimes violent, and somewhat ambivalent about human nature and social conventions.

After 1954, the newly established Comics Code Authority forbade any sexual allusion in comics, and topics such as divorce, pre-marital sex, or abortion could not even be hinted at. A part of the original code decreed that "the treatment of love-romance stories shall emphasize the value of the home and the sanctity of marriage." From that point on, many of the romance stories ended with the couple in question happily walking down the aisle. While these restrictions might have hindered lesser artists, Simon and Kirby met the challenge by creating wholesome stories that still managed to bring forth delicate topics such as racism and social disparity.

By the late '50s, the romance genre had lost most of its steam, and the creators were focusing their energies in new directions. Although romance comics continued to appear throughout the 1960s and '70s, 1959 certainly marked the end of an era, as the last two romance stories penciled by Jack Kirby for Prize Comics appeared in *Young Romance* #103 (December 1959). Prize continued to publish *Young Romance* until #124 (June-July 1963) under Joe Simon's supervision, but by that time, the Simon and Kirby team was no more.

In the 1960s, Simon sporadically continued to work in comics, before shifting his focus to the lucrative advertising field. Kirby continued to dabble in the romance genre (most notably in *Love Romances* and *Teen-age Romance* for Marvel Comics), but his attention was on something else. He was busy teaming up with Stan Lee to create the Marvel Universe...

SOURCES:

The Art of Jack Kirby (Blue Rose) ©1992 Ray Wyman, Jr.
Master of Imagination: The Comic Book Artists Hall of Fame (Taylor Publishing Company) ©1994 Mike Benton
"The King" (*Wizard* #36) ©1994 William A. Christensen and Mark Seifert
Comics: Between the Panels (Dark Horse) ©1998 Steve Duin and Mike Richardson
The Jack Kirby Checklist (Tommorows) ©1998 Blue Rose Press and the Jack Kirby Estate

Real Love: The Best of the Simon and Kirby Romance Comics (Eclipse Books) ©1998 Richard Howell
"A Very Brief History of Romance Comics" jennymiller.com/romancecomics/thegenre.html ©2001 Jenny Miller
"My Affair With Romance Comics - A Love Story, Born Out of Pain and Joy" (*LA Weekly* Jan. 2003) ©2003 Doug Harvey
The Comic Book Makers (Vanguard) ©2004 Joe and Jim Simon
"The 100 Greatest Comics of the 20th Century" centralcitycomicsdb.com ©2004 Mitchell Brown

PHOTO COVERS

By 1949, Prize Group started featuring photo-covers, reminiscent of magazines, in an effort to separate their romance titles from juvenile comics and attract a more adult readership.

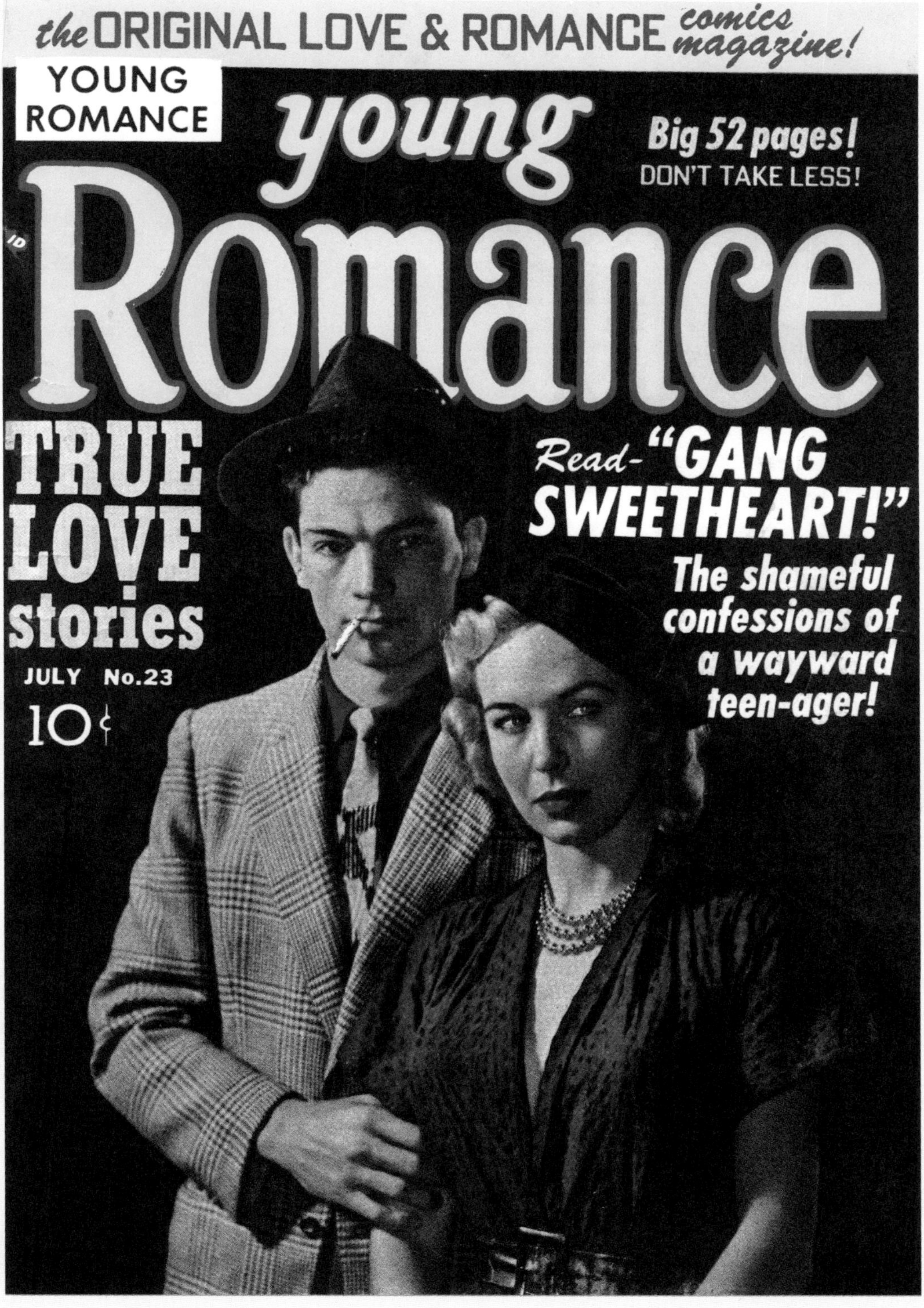
the ORIGINAL LOVE & ROMANCE comics magazine!
YOUNG ROMANCE
young Romance
Big 52 pages!
DON'T TAKE LESS!
TRUE LOVE stories
JULY No.23
10¢
Read- "GANG SWEETHEART!"
The shameful confessions of a wayward teen-ager!

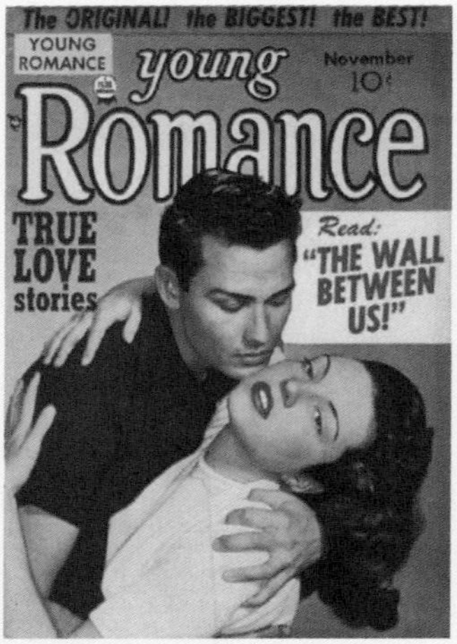

The ORIGINAL! the BIGGEST! the BEST!
YOUNG ROMANCE
young Romance
November 10¢
TRUE LOVE stories
Read: "THE WALL BETWEEN US!"

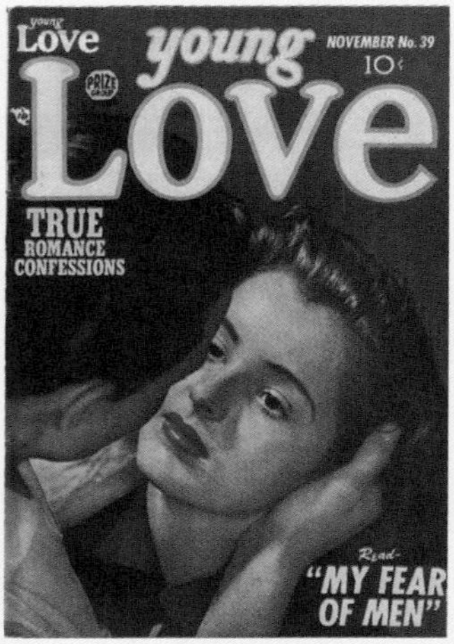

young Love
young Love
NOVEMBER No. 39
10¢
TRUE ROMANCE CONFESSIONS
Read- "MY FEAR OF MEN"

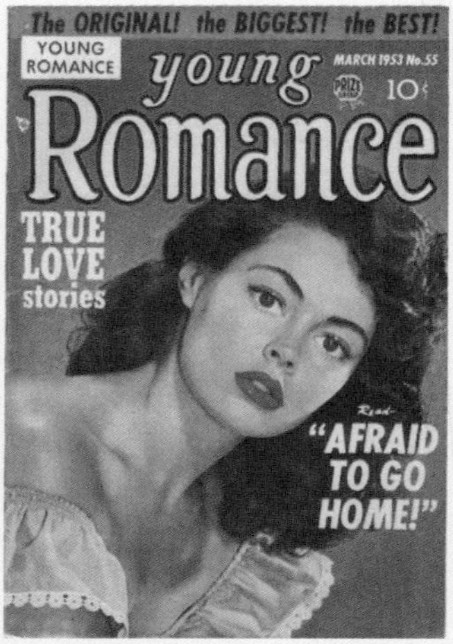

The ORIGINAL! the BIGGEST! the BEST!
YOUNG ROMANCE
young Romance
MARCH 1953 No. 55
10¢
TRUE LOVE stories
Read- "AFRAID TO GO HOME!"

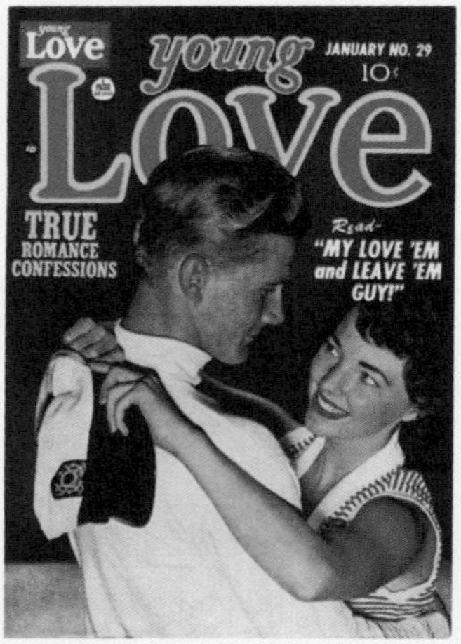

young Love
young Love
JANUARY NO. 29
10¢
TRUE ROMANCE CONFESSIONS
Read- "MY LOVE 'EM and LEAVE 'EM GUY!"

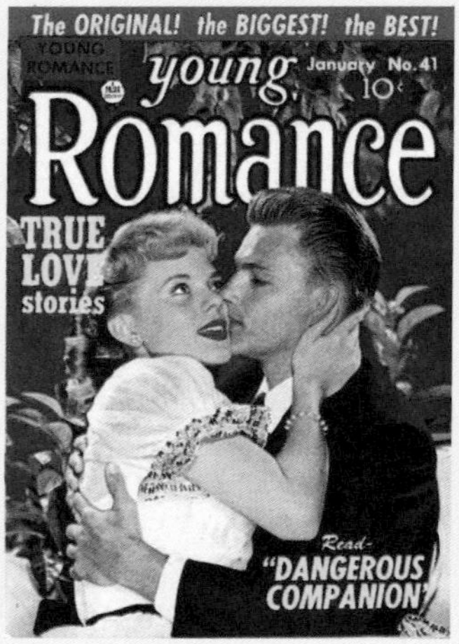

The ORIGINAL! the BIGGEST! the BEST!
YOUNG ROMANCE
young Romance
January No. 41
10¢
TRUE LOVE stories
Read- "DANGEROUS COMPANION"

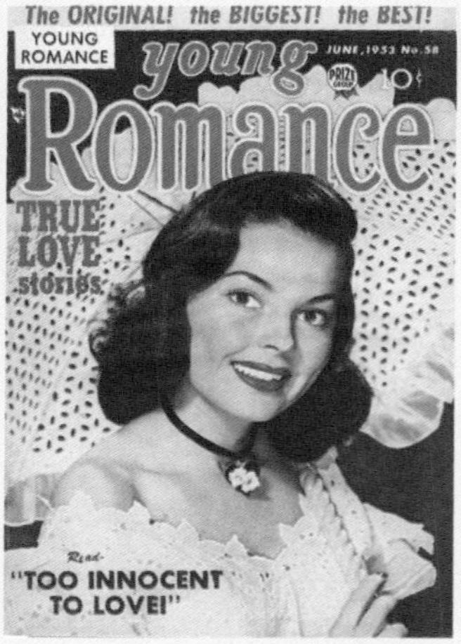

The ORIGINAL! the BIGGEST! the BEST!
YOUNG ROMANCE
young Romance
JUNE, 1953 No. 58
10¢
TRUE LOVE stories
Read- "TOO INNOCENT TO LOVE!"

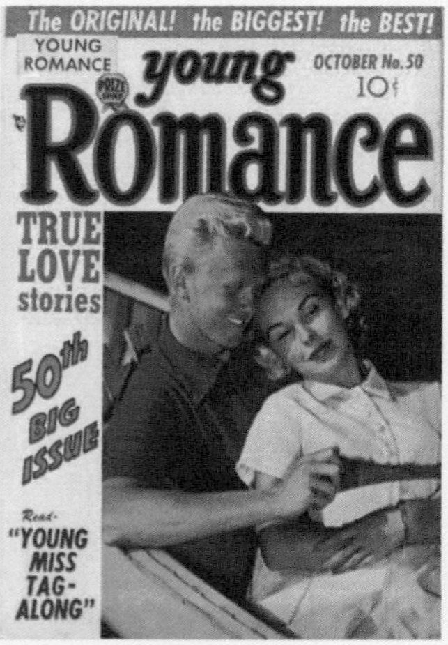

The ORIGINAL! the BIGGEST! the BEST!
YOUNG ROMANCE
young Romance
OCTOBER No. 50
10¢
TRUE LOVE stories
50th BIG ISSUE
Read- "YOUNG MISS TAG-ALONG"

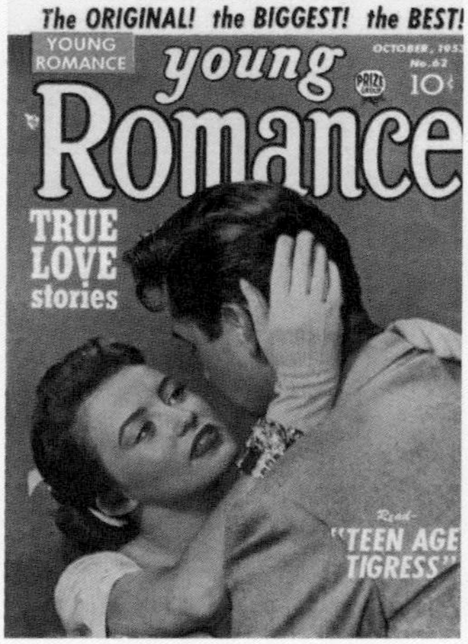

The ORIGINAL! the BIGGEST! the BEST!
YOUNG ROMANCE
young Romance
No. 62
10¢
TRUE LOVE stories
Read- "TEEN AGE TIGRESS"

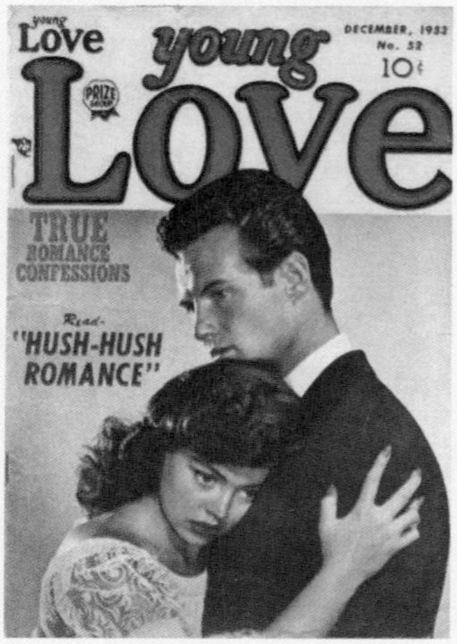

young Love
young Love
DECEMBER, 1952 No. 52
10¢
TRUE ROMANCE CONFESSIONS
Read- "HUSH-HUSH ROMANCE"

A NOTE ABOUT THE RESTORATION

The most time-consuming aspect of putting this book together was the restoration process, which was done on and off, on weekends and evenings, over a period of several years.

From high-resolution scans, I performed a myriad of delicate tasks: I cleaned the gutters and the text; I processed the colors and darkened the black ink; I realigned excessive off-register color when I felt it was too distracting; I repaired or recreated the color dot matrix when it was too messy; I removed aging paper artifacts (brown spots), water stains, rips, pencil and crayon markings.

Being an artist myself, the restoration of the comics was a true exercise in restraint. My goal was to make my work as unobtrusive as possible. Preserving the original line-work with complete accuracy, while respectfully keeping the feel of the original comics, was my primary concern.

"THE LANGUOR OF SLEEP WAS STILL WEARING OFF WHEN I LIFTED THE PHONE RECEIVER TO MY EAR... DAD'S VOICE SOUNDED MUFFLED AND INDISTINCT -- UNTIL HE MENTIONED RED'S NAME... THEN I SAT BOLT UPRIGHT!

DAD! YOU **SAW** JONAS PIKE? DID YOU INVITE HIM TO DINNER?

YES, I DID, GIRL... HE WASN'T INTERESTED. HAD OTHER PLANS... PERHAPS IT'S JUST AS WELL THAT HE DECLINED... RED'S NOT YOUR TYPE! HE'S NOT **ANYBODY'S** TYPE! YOU'D PROBABLY FIND HIM A BORE! NOW, COME DOWN TO EARTH AND WE'LL DISCUSS THAT TRIP TO BOSTON THIS EVENING!

"I KNEW WHAT DAD WAS REALLY SAYING! ONLY HE COULDN'T RISK BEING DIRECT WITHOUT MAKING ME FEEL LIKE A NAÏVE ADOLESCENT. WAS IT JUST AN ILLUSION I WAS PURSUING? PERHAPS IT WAS. BUT THE TEARS IT BROUGHT TO MY EYES WERE VERY, VERY REAL... THAT AFTERNOON I STRUCK OUT FOR THE SEASHORE. I DECIDED IF I HAD TO SULK, I WOULD CHOOSE AN APPROPRIATE ATMOSPHERE...

THAT AROMA -- SMELLS LIKE TOBACCO SMO -- SMO-- AAACHOOOO!

BLESS YOU!

" THE LANGUOR OF SLEEP WAS STILL WEARING OFF WHEN I LIFTED THE PHONE RECEIVER TO MY EAR... DAD'S VOICE SOUNDED MUFFLED AND INDISTINCT -- UNTIL HE MENTIONED RED'S NAME... THEN I SAT BOLT UPRIGHT!

DAD! YOU **SAW** JONAS PIKE? DID YOU INVITE HIM TO DINNER?

YES, I DID, GIRL... HE WASN'T INTERESTED.. HAD OTHER PLANS... PERHAPS IT'S JUST AS WELL THAT HE DECLINED... RED'S NOT YOUR TYPE! HE'S NOT **ANYBODY'S** TYPE! YOU'D PROBABLY FIND HIM A BORE! NOW, COME DOWN TO EARTH AND WE'LL DISCUSS THAT TRIP TO BOSTON THIS EVENING!

"I KNEW WHAT DAD WAS REALLY SAYING! ONLY HE COULDN'T RISK BEING DIRECT WITHOUT MAKING ME FEEL LIKE A NAIVE ADOLESCENT. WAS IT JUST AN ILLUSION I WAS PURSUING? PERHAPS IT WAS. BUT THE TEARS IT BROUGHT TO MY EYES WERE VERY, VERY REAL... THAT AFTERNOON I STRUCK OUT FOR THE SEASHORE. I DECIDED IF I HAD TO SULK, I WOULD CHOOSE AN APPROPRIATE ATMOSPHERE..

THAT AROMA -- SMELLS LIKE TOBACCO SMO - - SMO.. AAACHOOOO!

BLESS YOU!

BIOGRAPHIES

Joe Simon

BORN ON OCTOBER 11, 1913.

Joe Simon started his art career in the newspaper field. In the mid-1930s, he came to New York and stumbled into the then-new publishing venture called comic books.

With his longtime partner, Jack Kirby, he helped define the golden age of comic books and created many comics of historical significance. Their collaboration extended to several genres, which they helped pioneer: Western (*Boys' Ranch*), science fiction (*Blue Bolt*), crime (*Justice Traps the Guilty*), horror (*Black Magic*), superhero (*Captain America*), kidss gang (*Newsboy Legion*), and romance (*Young Romance*).

Jack Kirby

BORN ON AUGUST 28, 1917.

Jack Kirby was one of the most influential, recognizable, and prolific artists in American comic books, and the co-creator of such enduring characters and pop culture icons as the Fantastic Four, X-Men, The Incredible Hulk, Captain America, Iron Man, Silver Surfer, and hundreds of others, stretching back to the earliest days of the medium.

His output was legendary, with one count estimating that he produced over 25,000 pages of comic art.

He died on February 6, 1994.

Michel Gagné

Michel Gagné was born in Quebec, Canada. As a young man, he studied animation at Sheridan College School of Visual Arts in Ontario, Canada.

In 1985, he began a successful career drawing characters, special effects, and conceptual designs for movie studios, as well as doing books, comics, animated short films, and videogames. He lives with his family in the Pacific Northwest.

You can visit his website at www.gagneint.com.